# BORN
# OF WAR

# BORN
# OF WAR

## Protecting Children of
## Sexual Violence Survivors
## in Conflict Zones

---

Edited by

**R. Charli Carpenter**

Kumarian
**Press, Inc.**

*Born of War*
Published in 2007 in the United States of America by Kumarian Press, Inc.,
1294 Blue Hills Avenue, Bloomfield, CT 06002 USA

The text of this book is set in 10/12 Janson Text.

Production and design by Joan Weber Laflamme, jml ediset.
Proofread by Beth Richards.
Index by Robert Swanson.

Printed in the United States of America by United Graphics, Inc. Text printed
with vegetable oil-based ink.

∞The paper used in this publication meets the minimum requirements of the
   American National Standard for Information Sciences—Permanence of Paper for printed Library Materials, ANSI Z39.48–1984

---

### Library of Congress Cataloging-in-Publication Data

Born of war : protecting children of sexual violence survivors in conflict zones /
edited by R. Charli Carpenter.
   p. cm.
   Includes bibliographical references and index.
   ISBN-13: 978–1–56549–237–0 (pbk. : alk. paper)
1.  Illegitimate children. 2.  Rape as a weapon of war. 3.  Children and war.
4. Women and war. 5.  Children's rights. 6.  War crimes. I. Carpenter, R. Charli.
   HQ998.B57 2007
   362.87—dc22

                                                                  2007005868

---

16 15 14 13 12 11 10 09 08 07      10 9 8 7 6 5 4 3 2 1     First Printing 2007

# Contents

# Acknowledgments

This collection of essays began as two interdisciplinary workshops, which would not have been possible without the generous support of the International Studies Association, the National Science Foundation, and the John D. and Catherine T. MacArthur Foundation. University of Pittsburgh's Graduate School of Public and International Affairs, Department of Women's Studies, and Ford Institute of Human Security provided additional support during the course of the research initiative. Special thanks to Betcy Jose-Thota, Robyn Wheeler, Robert Filar, Sandy Monteverde, Angela Gasparetti, and Emily Huisman for administrative and research assistance.

As editor, I received invaluable feedback and comments from scholars and practitioners in a variety of settings as this project took shape. Thanks to those who took the time to engage with the ideas in this book at the International Studies Association 2005 Conference, UNICEF's Innocenti Institute and New York Headquarters, and the Peace Research Institute of Oslo. Two anonymous reviewers also assisted greatly in helping improve the essays before publication with extremely thoughtful and reflective comments on the manuscripts.

I am also grateful to the entire faculty at University of Pittsburgh's Graduate School for Public and International Affairs, as well as to its students, for providing such an encouraging environment in which to write and think about these issues; to Jim Lance at Kumarian Press for his patience and encouragement; and to all those who participated in the working group for creating a sense of community in which to think about one of the great understudied problems of our time.

—R. Charli Carpenter

# BORN
# OF WAR

# 1

# Gender, Ethnicity, and Children's Human Rights

*Theorizing Babies Born of Wartime Rape and Sexual Exploitation*

## R. Charli Carpenter

"We Want to Make a Light Baby," screamed the *Washington Post* headline in late June 2004 (Wax 2004). The story: mass rape and forced impregnation of black African women and girls in Darfur by Arab militiamen associated with the Khartoum government (Human Rights Watch 2004). Since 2003, "janjaweed" forces on horseback have swept through villages in the Darfur region of Western Sudan, burning, killing, looting, and gang-raping women and girls with the stated intent of causing them to bear Arab-looking babies (Raghavan 2004). The military logic of this mass rape campaign is in part to encourage the cleansing of Darfur by terrorizing civilians into fleeing (Amnesty International 2004). But forced pregnancy is also expected by the perpetrators and the news media that report on their crimes to exert long-term effects on Darfur's non-Arab population as well by visibly marking the rape victims with the ongoing humiliation of enemy-induced pregnancy. It will inflict a generation of unwanted children on the victimized civilian population. And it will have devastating effects on the children themselves, as they grow up in a community that associates them with their janjaweed fathers (Matheson 2004).

When stories about babies born of systematic rape hit the newsstands, the media often present this crime against humanity as unprecedented in horror and scope (Stanley 1999). But the creation of children as a result of wartime sexual violence is not a phenomenon isolated to the contemporary world's particularly brutal hotspots. The intentional

1

production of babies by enemy rape is an ancient tool of war (Brownmiller 1976), with recent examples in conflicts as diverse as Bangladesh (d'Costa 2003), Bosnia-Herzegovina (Stiglmayer 1994), and Darfur (Wax 2004). Moreover, sexual violence and exploitation of other, less-trumpeted varieties are endemic in war-affected regions, and babies are often born as a result of these acts, whether or not their conception was systematically planned by the perpetrators (Rehn and Sirleaf 2002). Overall, it has been estimated that tens of thousands of children have resulted from mass rape campaigns or sexual exploitation and abuse during times of war in the last decade alone (Grieg 2001).

Anecdotal reports such as those now pouring out of Darfur suggest that these children born of war often face stigma, discrimination, and even infanticide. Conceived in conflicts around the globe—East Timor, Bosnia, Rwanda, Kosovo, Liberia, to name a few—children born of wartime rape and sexual exploitation are often viewed as children "of the enemy" (Powell 2001; Rozario 1997; Smith 2000; Weitsman 2003; Gaylor 2001). Local and international actors contest their ethnic identities and citizenship rights (Carpenter 2000a); their rights to education, family, identity, physical security, and even survival may be severely curtailed.[1]

This is the picture that emerges from the press, from conversations within the aid community, and from the literature on war rape. But beyond such anecdotes, very little scholarship exists to date that systematically tracks these children's status and fate from a human rights perspective, assesses the efficacy of attempts to protect them, or evaluates the global and local politics surrounding their births. We know, for example, that the rejection of these children by their communities is not uniform, but we do not fully understand the conditions under which rape survivors and their families are empowered to accept them (Rehn and Sirleaf 2002). Despite the burgeoning interest of the international humanitarian community, both in sexual violence as a problem in conflict situations and to the protection of war-affected children, to date there have been no systematic fact-finding missions at the global level to assess the needs and interests of children born of war in different contexts and to establish best practices with respect to advocating for and securing their human rights. This lack of research and legal attention to the fate and well-being of these children is problematic. Without a better understanding of the scope and nature of the problem, best practices regarding their care cannot be established, promoted, or evaluated. This requires theorizing children born of war as subjects of human rights law and beneficiaries of the protection that the humanitarian community claims to afford war-affected civilian populations.

Doing so is the goal of this book. The chapters that follow are the result of a two-year collaborative project that brought together twenty-five scholars from fourteen disciplines and ten countries to consider how to better protect the human rights of children born of wartime rape and exploitation. For the purposes of this book, we use the term *children born of war* to refer to persons of any age conceived as a result of violent, coercive, or exploitative sexual relations in conflict zones.[2] Although this definition is broad enough to include births resulting from various forms of gender-based violence, we are particularly concerned in this volume with births resulting from rape and sexual slavery deployed by soldiers as a practice of organized warfare (Enloe 2000), and (to a lesser extent) from sexual exploitation by occupation forces, peacekeepers, and humanitarian workers (UN 2003).[3] This is because we are interested in the specific social stigma that attaches to children whose fathers are perceived to come from outside a conflict-affected community, a stigma that is of particular importance to understanding the obstacles to securing the human rights of children born of war.

This book aims to highlight the distinctive vulnerability of this population relative to other children born during or affected by armed conflict. We present case studies amalgamating what is known about these children's whereabouts, status, and needs in different country contexts and theoretical essays considering the human security dimensions of this issue for the first time. Important and difficult questions must be asked in order to begin crafting an appropriate policy response to these children and their mothers in line with international standards on child rights. How can the stigma against children of rape or sexual exploitation—often by the very communities who are understood as the victims of massive human rights violations—be best understood, and how can it be alleviated? How does it manifest differently in different contexts, regions, and cultures? Humanitarian practitioners and human rights activists need to know why some rape survivors kill their children, and what enables others to embrace them; why some postwar governments prefer to sequester children born of war in orphanages rather than allow them to be adopted abroad; why there is such a silence on this issue in major humanitarian organizations; and how to integrate a respect for the needs and rights of rape survivors with those of their children in the aftermath of armed conflict.

These important questions must be taken seriously by local and global actors claiming an interest in the "protection of war-affected civilians" or "human security" as we move into the twenty-first century (McRae and Hubert 2001). Indeed, other questions must also be asked about the role of actors and discourses throughout global civil society in producing and mitigating these outcomes. Are the legal norms and political practices surrounding children's rights and wartime sexual violence and exploitation sufficient to protect this category of child, or are they fundamentally complicated by issues such as these? In what ways are states, international organizations, and well-intentioned transnational actors implicated in the mistreatment or misrepresentation of these children? Why have children born of war by and large remained invisible on the international agenda, and how can this be changed?

The chapters in this book develop preliminary answers to some of these questions. Each is informed by two fundamental underlying questions: (1) what are the obstacles to securing human rights for this category of children, and (2) in what ways can these obstacles be overcome? Chapters 2 through 6 consist of region-specific case analyses on these children's human rights and efforts to respond to them; chapters 7 through 9 critically reexamine conceptual and legal frameworks for addressing their rights, with an eye to the role of local and global political actors in promoting or, indeed, blocking positive change. We conclude the volume with a discussion of ethical dilemmas attending research on vulnerable populations in conflict-affected areas, and a critical analysis of the entire project of "constructing" *children born of war* as a category of concern.

Contributors to the volume take different positions on all these questions and come at the subject from diverse disciplinary orientations. Each chapter in this volume, however, aims to theorize children born of war as subjects of human rights law and beneficiaries of the protection that the humanitarian community claims to afford war-affected civilian populations.

## Children Born of War in Multi-Country Context

Though systematic data on this issue is generally lacking, there exists a fair amount of anecdotal evidence pointing to a general pattern of severe discrimination against children born of wartime rape and sexual exploitation. The case studies in this volume attempt to evaluate these patterns in depth, as well as to determine the extent to which children of somewhat different origins experience these outcomes differently and how their situation overlaps with that of all small children growing up in a conflict situation. These chapters describe children born along a continuum of violence—from genocidal rape in Rwanda and Bosnia-Herzegovina, to "incidental" rape during post-referendum violence in East Timor, to sexual exploitation and slavery in the case of abducted girls in Uganda and Sierra Leone, to women in forced "marriages" during the Indonesian occupation of East Timor. The case studies also span continents and cultural/religious contexts, and each yields new insights regarding the contextual specificity of this crime against children and women.

The situation of children in some contexts (between and within country cases) is less acute than in others. For example, it seems that children are most at risk where their origins are visibly marked on their features, as with the "Vietnamerican" children born of exploitation by US troops, or the visibly half-Arab children born of janjaweed gang-rapes in Darfur; in conflict situations where ethnicity is less racialized or where rape lacked an ethnic basis, children of rape are easier to hide within the general population, a strategy adopted, for example, in Bosnia-Herzegovina. Other factors mitigating the various harms to which these children may be subject in specific country cases include the availability of psychosocial and economic support to the mothers, the extent to which extended families honor the children's existence and extend a safety net to support rape survivors, and the availability of alternative means of care for those mothers wishing to give up their children.

Yet the examination of this population across very different cases also allows us to see general patterns with respect to the way in which these children's biological origins affect the likelihood that their human rights will be secured. One of the clearest human rights issues faced by children born of war, upon which all the cases touch, is infanticide, a violation of infants' survival rights under Article 6(2) of the 1989 Convention on the Rights of the Child. As Daniel's chapter details in more depth, babies born of systematic rape campaigns during the war in the former Yugoslavia were neglected, abandoned, and sometimes killed (Niarchos 1995; Stiglmayer 1994, 137; Salzman 1998). Reports of infanticide infuse testimonies about births by rape in war zones, beyond the case studies described here; in Kosovo, one woman snapped her baby's neck in the presence of the WHO nurses who attended his birth (Smith 2000). According to a report by Human Rights Watch, some of the two thousand to five thousand children born as a result of the sexual violence during the 1994 Rwandan genocide have been killed (Nowrojee 1996). Death by neglect may also result if rape survivors are psychologically unable to care for their infants and community or humanitarian resources are unavailable to fill the gap (Aaldrich and Baarda 1994). The evidence from the cases suggests that it is crucial to begin establishing the scope of this fundamental child protection problem in conflict zones and then to identify effective strategies for prevention.

Children of rape who survive infancy may face severe stigma within their communities. In Rwanda, some have been maligned as "devil's children" (Nowrojee 1996); in Kosovo, "children of shame" (Smith 2000); in East Timor, "children of the enemy" (Powell 2001); in Nicaragua, "monster babies" (Weitsman 2003, 11). Some reports suggest that male babies are particularly at risk of being viewed not merely as illegitimate or as reminders of sexual torture and national humiliation, but in fact as fifth-column enemy combatants growing up within the community (Toomey 2003). The sources of this stigma are varied. In her chapter on identity, Patricia Weitsman notes the role of the global media as well as local postwar discourses in constructing these children as "other." Eunice Apio's discussion of naming practices in Uganda demonstrates that mothers themselves may be complicit in marking their children with the stigma of birth by rape. Michael Goodhart points out that all groups define themselves by reference to excluded members, rendering such stigma perhaps inevitable in times during which groups are asserting and redefining their identities. Yet as an unpublished report by UNICEF in the former Yugoslavia has found, such social exclusion exerts a psychosocial toll on these children, both when they are young, and when, as older children, they begin to search for meaningful social identities and to ask questions about their roots (see Balorda 2004).

Children born of sexual exploitation or sexual slavery during armed conflict face problems similar to those conceived in genocidal rape campaigns. Babies born to girl soldiers held as "wives" in slavery-like conditions are reported to be rejected by extended families when they escape the armed forces with their mothers, as chapters by Eunice Apio and by Giulia Baldi and Megan MacKenzie demonstrate (see also Bennett 2002, 74; Mazurana and McKay 2003, 21). Those children born to mothers who have been sexually exploited by peacekeepers, occupation forces, or humanitarian workers may grow up without claims to paternal rights, child support or a name (Naik 2002; Grieg 2001, 11; UN 2005). Deprived of extended family and other social networks, it has been suggested that these children are particularly vulnerable to being trafficked or becoming street children (Carpenter et al. 2005). They may also be maligned as mixed or different, particularly in contexts where their biological origins are evident in their physical features.

In political contexts where nationality and citizenship rights are determined according to ethnicity or patrilineal descent, children of sexual violence or exploitation are at risk of statelessness. According to Rehn and Sirleaf, Liberia is one of the very few countries whose constitution recognizes children born of war as citizens (2002, 18). Some children of Bosnian refugee mothers in neighboring Croatia were originally denied citizenship (Jordan 1995, 20A; Pine and Mertus 1994). Because international law on children's human rights is based on the assumption of state responsibility, this problematizes the possibilities of securing fundamental social benefits such as an education. Yet as Michael Goodhart notes in his concluding chapter, even where states satisfy children's rights to name and nationality under international law, the problem of social exclusion and the right to be a meaningful member of a social or ethnic group are more ambiguous and difficult to legislate or control. Indeed, as children born of wartime rape or exploitation grow older, the question of how to construct a meaningful social identity in this "deep" sense seems to be paramount (Balorda 2004). If Donnelly and Howard are right that "to exist as a human being, one must exist as a part of a community" (1998,

223), then practitioners thinking about the psychosocial dimension of child protection in conflict zones need to take stock of this ambivalence in law and practice on international children's rights.

## Rethinking Human Security
## and Human Rights Law and Discourse

The later chapters in this volume consider the question of these children's human rights in the context of existing knowledge and practice with respect to war-affected civilians and children in particular. As human beings, children born of war possess in theory all the rights articulated in the Universal Declaration of Human Rights and other major instruments, including notably the right to life and the right to be free of adverse discrimination. Additionally, a number of legal instruments regulate the treatment of children under international law, both in peacetime and in times of war, and all of these incorporate, in principle, the assumption of impartiality; that is, that children's human rights codified in law apply to all children, regardless of sex, nationality, religion, social, or biological origin.

The most important of these is the 1989 Convention on the Rights of the Child, which provides for all children's rights to know their parents (Article 7); to an adequate standard of living, social security, and health care (Article 6); to a nationality (Article 7); and to protection against abuse, maltreatment, or neglect (Article 19) (LeBlanc 1995). The Fourth Geneva Convention and its Additional Protocols also provide specific treatment for war-affected children, preventing forced recruitment of children, requiring families torn apart to be reunited, and laying down principles for rebuilding communities shattered by war, including the provision of basic needs and educational resources to children (Plattner 1984). Children's identity and family rights are also protected by Article 2(e) of the Genocide Convention, which considers forcibly transferring children from one group to another an act of genocide; and children are protected by refugee law, in theory, to the same extent as adults (UNHCR 1994).

Despite numerous legal instruments that supposedly apply to these children's human rights, serious questions must be raised about the sufficiency of these laws to secure basic survival and identity rights for children born of war. Certain of the rights in the Convention on the Rights of the Child seem to be in tension with respect to children born of war: for example, in some cases protecting children against mistreatment may mitigate their right to know their biological origins. In other respects, the Convention on the Rights of the Child might be said to be inapplicable, insofar as it does not outlaw discrimination against children born out of wedlock as a social category. (One empirical question might be this: does stigma against these children stem primarily from their "illegitimate" status or from their association with "enemy" soldiers?). As Goodhart notes in his concluding chapter, it is unclear whether the human rights discourse is necessarily a useful tool in combating social exclusion, insofar as the same discourse can be used to promote group rights, which are themselves dependent on defining group membership in exclusionary terms.

There are more general issues at stake. International law, often based on an understanding of the state and of the biological family as guarantors of rights and identities, itself is inscribed with deeply entrenched cultural norms regarding gender and ethnicity (Charlesworth, Chinkin, and Wright 1996; Wing and Merchan 1993). This may explain why there is no specific legal protection for this category of children in international law, and why the human rights of children born of war have remained ambiguous throughout the process of codifying "forced pregnancy" and "sexual slavery" as international crimes (Carpenter 2000a). Attempts to frame forced pregnancy as genocide, for example, contradict aspects of the Genocide Convention pertaining to children and reproductive rights of groups.[4] Another question to be explored, then, is whether the international rules that have evolved to protect children's rights are adequate to address the particular harms to which children of forced maternity or wartime sexual exploitation may be subject.

Formulating answers to the questions above requires more than simply a critique of existing law. It entails spotlighting local, transnational, and global social and political institutions involved in structuring, interpreting, and responding to the particular patterns we are uncovering. Numerous actors, agendas, and discourses are brought to bear in creating a context in which rape survivors throw their infants into the river (Becirbasic and Sesic 2002); in which a state prioritizes the immigration of a "war baby" for domestic adoption, while placing barriers to refugee status for the child's birth mother (Stanley 1999); in which children of rape appear in the international press to suit a particular war narrative but are absent from the agendas of global institutions concerned with war-affected women and children (Carpenter 2000a). What are we to make of these contradictions? Evaluating the way in which children born of war are constructed, represented, or rendered invisible by different sectors of the world community will generate new insights—not only on how to address the issue, but also on the intersection of global, transnational, and local norms and interests regarding gender, ethnicity, sexuality, violence, and identity.

One important area of inquiry is the way in which states respond to children born of sexual violence and exploitation as a humanitarian concern. With respect to children born of sexual exploitation, more research is needed to track the ways in which states' policies enable or produce these outcomes; the conditions under which rape becomes a political issue; and the effect of state action (or non-action) regarding these children and their mothers. As Cynthia Enloe has documented, access to local women's bodies for soldiers and peacekeeping troops is often explicitly manufactured through negotiations between countries as a normalized aspect of international diplomatic/military culture (Enloe 2000). Such arrangements have often historically been contingent on the assumption that the state of which the soldiers were nationals would bear no responsibility for children fathered by liaisons with local women (Grieg 2001). This tradition of impunity has been challenged in some recent cases, with women and older war children organizing to achieve recognition and restitution from the fathers' countries (e.g., see Reuters 2003), and with the al-Hussein report to the General Assembly on accountability in peacekeeping operations arguing forcefully for a child's right to support from his or her foreign father (UN 2005). Comparative study is needed to understand why some of these efforts are more successful than others, and what, indeed, might be considered benchmarks for "success."

With respect to mass rape campaigns, the issue may be even more complex. While children born of sexual exploitation were, until very recently, generally ignored by official bodies, children born of mass rape have sometimes been exploited for their propaganda potential (Weitsman 2003; Stanley 1999). Specific narratives linking gender, ethnicity, and identity may in some cases provide the strategic logic behind mass rape campaigns in the first place, as in Bosnia (Allen 1996), East Pakistan (Brownmiller 1976), and Rwanda (Baines 2003). Governments of populations targeted by such campaigns may exploit stories of rape to encourage international intervention or justify military retaliation (Hansen 2001); in such narratives, sexual assault may be treated as a crime not against women but against communities (Yuval-Davis 1997), and the identities of the children involved may be represented in conflicting ways by different actors (Carpenter 2000a). Weitsman's chapter in this volume documents the multifaceted use of children born of war in postwar nationalist discourses and the implications for securing the human rights of these children.

States may also play an important role in responding to the needs of rape survivors and their children, though in the past they have typically done so out of a sense of their own strategic and ideational interests rather than a concern for women's or children's rights. Weitsman notes that the Rwandan government viewed the children as a means of repopulating the country after the genocide; the new Bengali government attempted to frame survivors of the 1971 rapes as "national heroines" to counteract the stigma within communities that threatened the identity and reproductive future of the emerging nation (Rozario 1997). But even such efforts can have an ambivalent effect on the status of children born of war. Despite the Bengali government's efforts to counteract stigma against rape survivors, the government took the opposite position toward the children born of the mass rapes, possibly accounting for the futility of their efforts to reintegrate the women (d'Costa 2003). Anti-abortion exceptionalism has been documented in many contexts, where state prohibitions on reproductive rights have been rewritten to allow abortions for women carrying children "of the enemy" (Harris 1993). In some cases such discourses have empowered women in the aftermath of conflict but have also naturalized stigma against children born of war. The Kuwaiti government provided financial support to children born of war during the 1990 Iraqi occupation but denied them family names and thus various other social rights (Evans 1993). Considering the links between states' reproductive and social welfare policies and their national-ist agendas will be important for evaluating efforts to promote the rights of rape survivors and their children.

International organizations as a source of norms, discourses, and op-erational practices influencing war-affected populations must also be examined. The past decade has seen a remarkable transformation in multilateral discourses regarding gender, security, and human rights. Global institutions such as the United Nations Security Council now consider women's issues, children's issues, and the protection of war-affected civilian populations a fundamental part of their mandate (McRae and Hubert 2001); the need to "mainstream a gender perspective" is recognized, if not always implemented, within much of the humanitar-ian assistance community (Mertus 2001). In what ways does the issue of children born of war map onto or problematize these emergent norms?

At a glance there would appear to be little agenda space available for children born of war at the level of global institutions. To the extent that the gendered basis of international law has been challenged, it has gen-erally been in the context of advocacy for women's human rights. An enor-mous literature has proliferated since the end of the Cold War on the ways in which women are targeted in armed conflict, and much greater atten-tion is now being paid in international law and humanitarian policy to the psychosocial and protection needs of women and girls (Jacobs et al. 2000; Bennett, Bexley, and Warnock 1995; Moser and Clark 2001; Gardam and Jervis 2001; Mertus 2000; Lindsey 2001). Yet feminist literature on forced pregnancy and sexual exploitation has typically treated these as crimes against women only (e.g., Goldstein 1994; Copelon 1994); major docu-ments articulating women's human rights in armed conflict make only cursory mention of the need to look at children born of sexual violence (see UN 2003, 28; Rehn and Sirleaf 2002, 17–18; Lindsey 2001, 56).

A more interesting question may be the lack of such attention within the international children's human rights network. A 2004 content analysis of the children-and-armed-conflict agenda in the human security sector found no references to this category of war-affected child (Carpenter 2007). While humanitarian field manuals have mentioned the protection needs of these children in post-conflict settings for several years (UNHCR 1999; UNFPA 1999), it is difficult to identify programs in the humanitarian community aimed at implementing these guidelines. Although in 2000 the Graca Machel Review document called for an international fact-finding study entitled *Where Are the Babies?* to track and assess the needs of children born to war-rape victims during the 1990s (Machel 2000), no international child rights organization has funded such a study in the years since the report was issued. Despite a growing interest within UNICEF to address this issue more systematically (UNICEF 2005a; UNICEF 2005b), focus groups with humanitarian practitioners carried out by the Ford Institute at the University of Pittsburgh suggest a reluctance to advocate or program for this specific category (Carpenter et al. 2005).

To grapple with these various puzzles, the later chapters in this volume deconstruct existing discourse regarding human rights and post-conflict justice. Debra DeLaet considers how existing frameworks for thinking about post-conflict justice appear when examined through a lens that considers the needs of these children and their mothers, and she concludes that existing mechanisms are inadequate in many ways. Siobhán McEvoy-Levy adopts a similar approach, focusing less on justice mechanisms than on the overarching concept of human rights culture. As McEvoy-Levy points out, the development of a culture respectful of human rights broadly is a frequent aspiration of international and local actors when wars end. But, as she argues, the existing discourse of human rights culture serves to configure [children born of war] "out of the picture at precisely the moment in which they are most vulnerable." Both of these authors draw on the insights from empirical case studies to rethink the very concepts and discourse prevalent in the human rights and humanitarian action network. They encourage us to ask how well these concepts serve the needs of these children, as well as what the concepts themselves look like when viewed through the lens of their human rights.

## Advocating for Change: Toward Human Security for Children Born of War and Their Mothers

In addition to sketching the dimensions of war's impact on children born of rape and exploitation, a fundamental question motivating each of these case studies is what can or should be done. There is no consensus on this question among the working group for this project, and the goal here is to create dialogue rather than issue definitive prescriptions. Yet one tentative conclusion on which most of these authors concur is that what constitutes a best practice will most likely depend on the specific sociopolitical context in which the children are born. It remains to academics, practitioners, and local communities to better make this determination in different contexts; to draw on local capacities and cultural resources to create strategies for effective protection; and to decide how to intervene effectively on behalf of abused or neglected children born of war when such efforts fail or are for other reasons inappropriate.

One evaluative approach toward this end used by the authors in this volume has been to gather data on the indigenous resources that war-affected communities bring to bear to cope with children born of rape and their mothers. Understanding the ways in which communities interpret children born of rape is crucial to mobilizing local resources to address their protection needs. As Salzman points out, the creation of "little Chetniks" in the context of Yugoslavia could only work as a tool of genocide if the target communities internalized the assumption that babies born of rape were children "of the enemy" (Salzman 1998). Women's organizations such as Medica Zenica, as well as religious organizations, actively attempted to counter this view (Toomey 2003; Nikolic-Ristanovic 2000). Indeed, despite stories of stigma, rejection, physical abuse, and neglect in communities worldwide, there are many other stories of extended family members accepting and supporting abused women and their children (e.g., see Human Rights Watch 2002, 67).

But much more needs to be known about the circumstances under which the acceptance of previously stigmatized groups becomes possible and succeeds in the context of post-conflict reconciliation, and what actors in the human security field might do to help. The case studies presented in this book suggest that such efforts are sometimes the exception rather than the rule, and that when they occur they are often subject to critique. For example, Joana Daniel-Wrabetz points out that while women's organizations have been the most responsive to the psychosocial care of rape survivors in Bosnia-Herzegovina, they are not necessarily oriented to the best interests of children, given the tensions that arise between women's needs and children's needs in these cases and the organizations' mandate to prioritize the concerns of mothers. In her chapter on East Timor, Susan Harris Rimmer describes the Catholic church's ambivalent efforts to provide for rape survivors while promoting a gender discourse at odds with their empowerment in post-conflict Timorese society.

The chapters do not provide definitive guidance on these points, based as they are on case evidence and theoretical critique rather than systematic longitudinal research or policy analysis. But they serve to highlight important policy questions about the effectiveness of existing modes of humanitarian action and human rights discourse. Particular efforts have been made by these authors to develop creative policy solutions that think outside of existing boxes. Many of these suggestions are controversial and counter-intuitive; many of the questions raised require us to think past standard assumptions; and all are subject to further debate that must engage researchers, practitioners, and local communities.

For example, are the best interests of these children served by raising them in the communities where they are born? During the war in the former Yugoslavia, Western families mobilized to lobby for removing the children from the war-affected context and having them adopted abroad. Governments in the Balkans opposed these efforts as imperialist, many of them seeking to exploit the issue of "rape babies" for their own nationalist agendas (Weitsman, chap. 5 herein). Human rights organizations, cognizant of the risks involved in transborder adoption of war orphans, have generally been skeptical of such solutions and have supported the idea of keeping the children in situ (Williamson 1993). Yet Debra DeLaet suggests in her chapter that the humanitarian community's norm against international adoption of children out of war zones may be counterproductive to securing these children's rights.

We need to inspect more carefully the decision-making process whereby current solutions have been devised. Were they based on the best interests of the child or on other normative, institutional, and political factors? For example, to what extent were war-affected populations themselves consulted? There is some evidence that, in the Bosnian context, women's organizations believed both the children and their mothers would benefit from the babies' adoption abroad (Becirbasic and Secic 2002). In Rwanda, some mothers were eager to have their children adopted out of the country, but unlike the demand for Bosnian babies, there were few such offers and little effort to generate them (Grieg 2001, 97). By tracking and evaluating the life histories of specific children in different contexts, measured against the standards codified in the Convention on the Rights of the Child, can we confirm whether current policies constitute best practices? By interviewing adult war children, what can we learn about what such children themselves might consider to be ideal?

In conducting these analyses and generating policy recommendations, particular attention has been paid in the case studies to reconciling these children's rights with the psychosocial needs of their mothers. Many of the papers developed in workshops associated with this project, including those accepted for this volume, examine the nexus between women's and children's human rights, as well as the points of disconnect between these two issue areas, and ask difficult questions about directions for successful advocacy and change. A number of studies have suggested that post-conflict instruments such as tribunals, truth commissions, or reparations can be ineffective—or worse, counterproductive—if they fail to take into account gender hierarchies and women's experiences of war and its aftermath (see DeLaet, 2006). Should such a critique be applied in the case of children born of war as well? If so, what are the political dilemmas involved in holding members of victimized communities accountable for maltreatment of "war babies" inflicted upon them by the enemy? Several authors in this volume recognize that infanticide is a human rights violation but are reluctant to hold traumatized mothers accountable for it; this view is held by some humanitarian practitioners as well (Carpenter 2000b). Goodhart's proposal in this volume to link these crimes back to the perpetrator of the sexual violence through the legal concept of "wrongful procreation" provides one answer.

Similarly, there is an assumption among many actors in the humanitarian world, and much of the literature on treatment of rape survivors, that silence is an important protection mechanism for children born of wartime rape. If mothers deny where the children came from, both to the child and to the broader community, it is assumed this will be easier for the child psychologically and will protect the child from stigma (Aaldrich and Baarda 1994, 61). Accordingly, orphanages with such children in custody and human rights organizations have been careful to screen such children from the curiosity of journalists and researchers, under the assumption that only harm can be done by calling attention to these children as a specific category.

There are certainly grounds for these concerns. Until we conduct more careful research, however, under what conditions silence is an adequate protection mechanism and wherein lie the tradeoffs remain open questions. Giulia Baldi and Megan MacKenzie's analysis of humanitarian response in Sierra Leone questions whether universal targeting of vulnerable groups without attention to the specific dimensions of their vulnerability allows children in this category to "fall through the cracks" in humanitarian programming. Does silence or denial protect children or only ensure their marginalization? If silence about a young child's biological origins makes it easier to have that child adopted or preempts discriminatory treatment, does that offset the problems created later in life when the child or adult demands the right to know? How can a mother's desire for silence be reconciled with an older child's right to identity in such cases? How can children of rape who do experience disadvantage lobby for restitution without knowledge of the circumstances behind the stigma to which they are subject? Survivors of wartime sexual violence who have risked stigma to testify at war crimes tribunals remind us that silence protects perpetrators as well as victims; a willingness to speak out about such crimes can in some respects help to reduce stigma suffered by survivors (Human Rights Watch 2002, 67). What are the pathways for enabling children born of war to speak out about the issues that concern them without drawing attention to them in such a way as to do harm?

This brings us to a point that must remain front and center in any work that engages issues of human rights ethics and praxis: how do we gather data systematically in such a way as to empower, rather than to exploit or to marginalize, our population of concern? Julie Mertus's chapter on ethics in this volume emphasizes the ethical concerns attending all research that involves human subjects and all research with implications for political and social practice. But addressing culturally sensitive topics such as these requires particular care (Smyth and Robinson 2001). Lindner's reflections on ethnography in the Horn of Africa remind us of the potential for one's research methodology to be damaging to its subjects (Lindner 2001). Writing about the power of representations in narratives of wartime sexual violence, Mookherjee calls our attention to researchers' role in transmitting and constructing the past through the representations they create and cautions us about ethical considerations in representing the voices of survivors (Mookherjee 2003). Feminist scholars in particular have emphasized in the past decade the need for research on survivors of violence to contribute to healing as well as to fact-finding (Sharatt and Kaschak 1999), to engage those affected as participants rather than as subjects (Reinharz 1992), and for researchers to "give back" to those studied, both in person and through the uses to which the research is put (Cockburn 1998). At the same time, Goodhart (chap. 11 herein) is deeply skeptical of whether a participatory approach is appropriate when the subject population includes small children.

Thus the ethical and methodological dilemmas remain complex. That said, it has been shown again and again that to shy away from sensitive topics simply for fear of doing harm can also deprive a marginalized population of a much-needed outlet for voice and recognition (and can mask or support those whose interests are served by silences and taboos). Research itself constitutes a response and, potentially, a necessary first step to redress. Correspondingly, lack of data can be an obstacle to sensible advocacy and positive change. It seems important to undertake the process reflectively, keeping conscious of our own privilege, motives, and bias, challenging our own and one another's assumptions, seeking out alternative perspectives, and creating careful and systematic criteria for evaluating the truth-claims we present. What motivates us as researchers? To which discourses are we contributing through our choice of descriptive labels in our work? Simply choosing a term of reference—such as *child born of war*—is a value-laden move.

As researchers and activists we should carefully inspect such moves, our own and one another's, the bases on which we make them, and how they are connected to the processes we are studying or critiquing. As many critical theorists have suggested, and as both Mertus's and

Goodhart's comments on ethics and methods in this volume reiterate, such reflexivity makes research more objective rather than less, and also more likely to achieve its intended goals.

For now, these goals are modest: this book is designed to initiate a dialogue rather than to issue definitive solutions. We aim to sketch the dimensions of this issue and to create thinking space for a discussion of possible prescriptions that will engage a broad community of scholars, advocates, and policymakers. Many points of contention exist within the working group itself on the parameters of the issue, what constitutes viable policy responses, and even how to describe this population.

What can be said with some certainty is that children born of wartime sexual violence or exploitation represent a global constituency facing specific challenges from a human rights perspective. They deserve attention from scholars and policymakers alike, yet to date they have been understudied as subjects of human rights concern. The lack of systematic research on these issues is the first obstacle to successful advocacy. This collaborative project represents a step in the direction of filling this gap. Each of the authors has explored the experience of infants born of wartime rape or sexual exploitation through a children's human rights lens. We hope in so doing to generate a basis for considering and evaluating how best to respond to the sociopolitical processes that affect these children's human rights after birth, as well as to better understand the interrelationship among gender, ethnicity, and human rights in the global community.

## Notes

[1] Children of wartime rape or sexual exploitation are part of a larger group of "war children" possessing one parent from the "other" side of a conflict or from an international organization, including those whose mothers engaged in consensual liaisons with "enemy" soldiers. In each case the citizenship and family rights of the children are often complicated or denied (see Grieg 2001).

[2] This shorthand captures what is distinctive about the group as a whole without glossing over important distinctions among the children, and it lacks the negative and sensationalist connotations of various other labels such as *rape babies*. However, we acknowledge that terminology for this population remains contested among various actors, including members of this working group. A number of scholars and issue entrepreneurs are using the term *war babies* or *war children* instead to refer to this population, though these terms are ambiguous as they are also sometimes used to refer to any child affected by war. *War babies* has already emerged in the media and perhaps is a term that at least some English-speaking adult children born of wartime rape accept as a descriptive label (see Provencher 2001). However, although this working group also used the term *war babies* at the onset of the project, we found the term did not translate well

into other languages, and some activists argue that it is too euphemistic, preferring the more nuanced but unwieldy "children born of wartime rape and exploitation" (Carpenter et al. 2005). We found the shorthand *children born of war* satisfied the criteria of brevity, specificity, and neutrality better than other possibilities at this time.

[3] However, it is important to point out that women experience rape and rape-induced pregnancy within their own communities and families during conflict as well as from enemy forces.

[4] Ground-breaking legal arguments on forced pregnancy as genocide include Fisher 1996 and Allen 1996. For legal contradictions within this formulation, see Carpenter 2000b.

# References

Aaldrich, G. H., and Th. A. Baarda. 1994. "Final Report of the Conference on the Rights of Children in Armed Conflict held in Amsterdam, the Netherlands, on 20–21 June." Amsterdam: International Dialogues Foundation.

Allen, Beverly. 1996. *Rape Warfare: The Hidden Genocide in Bosnia-Herzegovina.* Minneapolis: University of Minnesota Press.

Amnesty International. 2004. *Darfur—Rape as a Weapon of War.* New York: Amnesty International.

Baines, Erin. 2003. "Body Politics and the Rwandan Crisis." *Third World Quarterly* 24, no. 3: 479–93.

Balorda, Jasna. 2004. "Bosnia's War Babies and the Search for Identity." Paper presented at the 2nd International Workshop on Theorizing War Babies' Human Rights, University of Pittsburgh, November 13.

Becirbasic, Belma, and Dzenana Secic. 2002. "Invisible Casualties of War." London: Institute for War and Peace Reporting. Available on the iwpr.net website.

Bennett, Allison. 2002. "The Reintegration of Child Ex-Combatants in Sierra Leone with Particular Focus on the Needs of Females." Available on the essex.ac.uk website.

Bennett, Olivia, Jo Bexley, and Kitty Warnock, eds. 1995. *Arms to Fight, Arms to Protect: Women Speak Out about Conflict.* London: Panos.

Brownmiller, Susan. 1976. *Against Our Will: Men, Women, and Rape.* New York: Bantam Books.

Carpenter, Charli. 2000a. "Surfacing Children: Limitations of Genocidal Rape Discourse." *Human Rights Quarterly* 22, no. 2: 428–77.

———. 2000b. "Forced Maternity, Children's Rights, and the Genocide Convention." *Journal of Genocide Research* 2, no. 2: 213–44.

———. 2007. "Setting the Advocacy Agenda: Issues and Non-Issues in Transnational Advocacy Networks." *International Studies Quarterly* 51, no. 1.

Carpenter, Charli, Kai Grieg, Donna Sharkey, and Giulia Baldi. 2005. *Protecting Children Born of Wartime Rape and Exploitation in Conflict Zones: Existing Practice and Knowledge Gaps.* Pittsburgh: University of Pittsburgh GSPIA/Ford Institute of Human Security.

Charlesworth, Hilary, Christine Chinkin, and Shelley Wright. 1996. "Feminist Approaches to International Law." In *International Rules: Approaches from*

*International Law and Relations*, edited by Robert Beck et al. New York: Oxford University Press.

Cockburn, Cynthia. 1998. *The Space between Us: Negotiating Gender and National Identities in Conflict.* London: Zed Books.

Copelon, Rhonda. 1994. "Surfacing Gender." In *Mass Rape: The War against Women in Bosnia-Herzegovina*, edited by Alexandra Stiglmayer. Lincoln: University of Nebraska.

D'Costa, Bina. 2003. "War Babies: The Question of National Honour." In *The Gendered Construction of Nationalism: From Partition to Creation*. PhD diss. Available on the drishtipat.org website.

DeLaet, Debra. 2006. "Gender, Truth-Telling, and Sustainable Peace." In *Telling the Truth: Peace Building and Truth Telling*, edited by Tristan A. Borer, 151–79. Notre Dame, IN: University of Notre Dame Press.

Donnelly, Jack, and Rhoda Howard. 1988. "Assessing National Human Rights Performance: A Theoretical Framework." *Human Rights Quarterly* 10, no. 2: 214–48.

Enloe, Cynthia. 2000. *Maneuvers: The International Politics of Militarizing Women's Lives.* Berkeley and Los Angeles: University of California Press.

Evans, Kathy. 1993. "Legacy of War: Kuwait's Littlest Victims." *Calgary Herald*, July 29.

Fisher, Siobhán. 1996. "Occupation of the Womb: Forced Impregnation as Genocide." *Duke Law Journal* 46, no. 73: 91–133.

Gardam, Judith, and Michelle Jervis. 2001. *Women, Armed Conflict and International Law.* The Hague: Kluwer Law International.

Gaylor, Albert. 2001. "The Legacy of Peacekeepers' Kids in Liberia." *Public Agenda*, March 13.

Goldstein, Anne Tierney. 1994. *Recognizing Forced Impregnation as a War Crime.* New York: Center for Reproductive Law and Policy.

Grieg, Kai. 2001. *The War Children of the World.* Bergen, Norway: War and Children Identity Project. Available on the warandchildren.org website.

Hansen, Lene. 2001. "Gender, Nation, Rape: Bosnia and the Construction of Security." *International Feminist Journal of Politics* 3, no. 1: 55–75.

Harris, Ruth. 1993. "The 'Child of the Barbarian': Rape, Race, and Nationalism in France during the First World War." *Past and Present* 141: 170–206.

Human Rights Watch. 2002. *The War within the War: Sexual Violence against Women and Girls in Eastern Congo.* New York: Human Rights Watch.

———. 2004. *Sexual Violence and Its Consequences among Displaced Persons in Darfur and Chad.* New York: Human Rights Watch.

Jacobs, Susie, et al., eds. 2000. *States of Conflict: Gender, Violence, and Resistance.* London: Zed Books.

Jordan. 1995. "Born of Rape." *Miami Herald*, July 1.

LeBlanc, Lawrence. 1995. *The Convention on the Rights of the Child: UN Lawmaking on Human Rights.* Lincoln: University of Nebraska Press.

Lindner, Evelin Gerda. 2001. "How Research Can Humiliate: Critical Reflections on Method." *Journal for the Study of Peace and Conflict*, annual edition 2001–2: 16–36.

Lindsey, Charlotte. 2001. *Women Facing War.* Geneva: ICRC.

Machel, Graca. 1996. *Impact of Armed Conflict on Children*. New York: United Nations.

Matheson, Isabel. 2004. "Darfur War Breeds 'Dirty Babies.'" *BBC Online*, December 15, 2004. Available on the news.bbc.co.uk website.

Mazurana, Dyan, and Susan McKay. 2003. "Girls in Fighting Forces in Northern Uganda, Sierra Leone, and Mozambique: Policy and Program Recommendations." Available on the redbarnet.dk website.

McRae, Rob, and Don Hubert, eds. 2001. *Human Security and the New Diplomacy*. Montreal: McGill-Queen's University Press.

Mertus, Julie. 2000. *War's Offensive on Women*. West Hartford, CT: Kumarian Press, 2000.

———. 2001. "Grounds for Cautious Optimism." *International Feminist Journal of Politics* 3, no. 1: 99–103.

Mookherjee, Nayanika. 2003. "Ethical Issues concerning Representation of Narratives of Sexual Violence of 1971." Excerpts from PhD diss., University of London. Available on the drishtipat.org website.

Moser, Caroline, and Fiona Clark, eds. 2001. *Victims, Perpetrators or Actors? Gender, Armed Conflict, and Political Violence*. London: Zed Books.

Naik, Asmita. 2002. "Protecting Children from the Protectors: Lessons from West Africa." Available on the fmreview.org website.

Niarchos, Catherine. 1995. "Women, War and Rape: Challenges Facing the International Tribunal for the Former Yugoslavia." *Human Rights Quarterly* 17, no. 4: 649–90.

Nikolic-Ristanovic, Vesna. 2000. *Women, Violence, and War: Wartime Victimization of Refugees in the Balkans*. Budapest: Central European University Press.

Nowrojee, Bianifer. 1996. *Shattered Lives: Sexual Violence during the Rwandan Genocide and Its Aftermath*. New York: Human Rights Watch.

Pine, Rachel, and Julie Mertus. 1994. *Meeting the Health Needs of Victims of Sexual Violence in the Balkans*. New York: Center for Reproductive Law and Policy.

Plattner, Denise. 1984. "Protection of Children in International Humanitarian Law." *International Review of the Red Cross* 240: 140–52.

Powell, Siam. 2001. "East Timor's Children of the Enemy." *The Weekend Australian* 1, March 10.

Provencher, Raymonde. 2001. *War Babies*. Montreal: Macumba Productions.

Raghavan, Sudarsan. 2004. "Rape Victims, Babies Face Future Labeled as Outcasts." *Miami Herald*, December 7, 2004. Available on the peacewomen.org website.

Reinharz, Shulamit. 1992. *Feminist Methods in Social Research*. New York: Oxford University Press.

Rehn, Elisabeth, and Ellen Johnson Sirleaf. 2002. *Women, War and Peace*. New York: UNIFEM.

Reuters. 2003. "Kenyan Women Stage Rape Protest against British Military." Available on the grassrootsvictories.org website.

Rozario, Santi. 1997. "Disasters and Bangladeshi Women." In *Gender and Catastrophe*, edited by Ronit Lentin. London: Zed Books.

Salzman, Paul. 1998. "Rape Camps as a Means of Ethnic Cleansing." *Human Rights Quarterly* 20, no. 2: 348–78.

Sharatt, Sara, and Ellyn Kaschak, eds. 1999. *Assault on the Soul*. New York: Haworth Press.

Smith, Helena. 2000. "Rape Victims' Babies Pay the Price of War." *The Observer,* April 16.

Smyth, Marie, and Gillian Robinson. 2001. *Researching Violently Divided Societies: Ethical and Methodological Issues.* Tokyo: United Nations University Press and Pluto Press.

Stanley, Penny. 1999. "Reporting of Mass Rape in the Balkans: Plus Ca Change, Plus C'est Meme Chose? From Bosnia to Kosovo." *Civil Wars* 2, no. 2: 74–110.

Stiglmayer, Alexandra, ed. 1994. *Mass Rape: The War against Women in Bosnia-Herzegovina*. Lincoln: University of Nebraska Press.

Toomey, Christine. 2003. "Cradle of Inhumanity." *Sunday Times*. Available on the bosnia.org.uk website.

UN (United Nations). 2003. *Women, Peace and Security. Study for the Secretary General of the United Nations, pursuant to Security Council Resolution 1325.* New York: United Nations.

———. 2005. A/59/19/Add.1. *Report of the Special Committee on Peacekeeping Operations and Its Working Group on the 2005 Resumed Session.* New York: United Nations.

UNFPA (United Nations Population Fund). 1999. *Assessment Report on Sexual Violence in Kosovo*. New York: UNFPA. Available on the reliefweb.int website.

UNHCR (United Nations High Commissioner on Refugees). 1994. *Refugee Children: Guidelines on Protection and Care*. Geneva: United Nations High Commissioner on Refugees.

———. 1999. *Reproductive Health in Refugee Situations: An Inter-Agency Field Manual*. Geneva: United Nations High Commissioner on Refugees.

UNICEF. 2005a. "A Violent Legacy of Conflict in Darfur," February 11. Available on the reliefweb.int website.

———. 2005b. "Children Born of Sexual Violence in Conflict Zones: Considerations for UNICEF Response: Final Report of a Meeting held 23 November 2005." New York: UNICEF.

Wax, Emily. 2004. "We Want to Make a Light Baby: Arab Militiamen in Sudan Said to Use Rape as Weapon of Ethnic Cleansing." *Washington Post Foreign Service*, June 30.

Weitsman, Patricia. 2003. "The Discourse of Rape in Wartime: Sexual Violence, War Babies, and Identity." Paper presented at the Annual Meeting of the International Studies Association, Portland, Oregon, February 26–March 1.

Williamson, Jan. 1993. *Bosnian Children of War: The Adoption Question*. New York: International Social Service.

Wing, Adrian, and Sylke Merchan. 1993. "Rape, Ethnicity, and Culture." *Columbia Human Rights Law Review* 25, no. 1: 1–48.

Yuval-Davis, Nira. 1997. *Gender and Nation*. London: Sage.

# 2

# Children Born of War Rape in Bosnia-Herzegovina and the Convention on the Rights of the Child

## Joana Daniel-Wrabetz

This chapter examines the societal response to children born of war rape in Bosnia-Herzegovina (BiH) during and after the mass rape campaigns of the early 1990s. After the disintegration of Yugoslavia in the early 1990s, many children, conceived in mass rape campaigns, were born to the women who survived (Williams 1993; Horvath 1993). Like thousands of other children of forced pregnancy worldwide, orphans of war rape in the Balkans are often viewed as "children of the enemy" or "Chetnik babies." The implications of this stigma for their human rights should be a concern to those committed to protecting children in conflict zones.

Although these children have already been accurately termed "secondary rape victims" (Silva 2004), the focus of attention concerning mass rape in the former Yugoslavia has been on the plight of women, their victimization, and their social exclusion in situations of rape in armed conflict. Only in recent years has research on the situation of children born as a consequence of war rape attracted the interest of academia, and still too little is known about their fate, their social integration, or to what extent their human rights are being threatened. This chapter considers how local populations perceive these children, how these perceptions affect their human rights, and what protections, if any, are available for these children and their mothers within the civil society sector in BiH.

The findings presented here are based on exploratory research conducted for the author's MA thesis between 2002 and 2003 (Daniel 2004). This research included a review of the available literature from a number of sources, such as country reports from international organizations, literature in academic journals, and press reports in magazines and newspapers. In May 2003 a fieldtrip to Sarajevo, Tuzla, Zenica, and Gračanica was made to collect testimonies about the issue from representatives of civil society in BiH. This trip included visits to women's organizations and orphanages to conduct semi-structured, in-depth interviews with the staff (primarily social workers and psychologists) of these institutions. In addition, this chapter draws on further insights developed the following year during participation in a separate exploratory fact-finding study on children born of rape in BiH sponsored by UNICEF-Sarajevo in the summer of 2004.

The extreme sensitivity of the topic, the unresponsiveness of affected communities, and the lack of reliable data on this issue represent only a few of the impediments against a better understanding of the problem. In particular, interviews with rape victims and war-rape orphans themselves were not part of the project, since such interviews require a different approach and specialized personnel to conduct them. At this point the main goal was to investigate and evaluate how the children born as a consequence of rape during war were perceived in their home country, and if and how their needs and human rights were addressed. The majority of those contacted reported unawareness about the subject, but, in certain cases, some unwillingness to provide information about such a taboo theme was also evident. This reluctance was in part motivated by previous bad experiences with journalists and researchers. Due to these factors, the findings here should be considered preliminary and tentative pending more systematic study. Only an in-depth understanding of all aspects of the subject will allow local and international actors to devise policies in support of these children and their mothers, and most important, to contribute to the improvement of their situation.

In this chapter the situation of children born of war in BiH will be evaluated against the rights applicable to all children as enumerated in international law, particularly the 1989 Convention on the Rights of the Child. In the first section a description of the particular circumstances of rape and forced impregnation in BiH is given, followed by an account of what is known about the response of various entities within BiH to these children. Particular attention is given to government policies, to orphanages and institutions for children without parental care, to women's organizations, and to the various religious communities. The international standards for the protection of all children's human rights as enumerated in the Convention on the Rights of the Child are considered, as well as the extent to which these standards have been adequately applied—

or indeed, are adequate at all—to address the particular harms to which BiH's children born of war rape are subject.

## Reactions to Children Born of War Rape and Forced Impregnation in Bosnia-Herzegovina

Although the mass rape campaigns carried out during the war in Bosnia and Herzegovina (1991–95) were treated as unprecedented at the time, it is now understood that these were part of a much broader global pattern of war-related violence against women. In conflicts all around the world, women and girls, irrespective of their age, ethnicity, or political affiliation, have been singled out for sexual violence, imprisonment, torture, execution, sexual mutilation, forced pregnancy, rape, and sexual slavery. Acts such as rape, sexual assault, sexual slavery, forced prostitution, forced sterilization, forced abortion, and forced pregnancy may all qualify as crimes under national and international law (Human Rights Watch 1999). Sexual violence is considered to be a war crime, an act of torture, an act of genocide, and a crime against humanity; forced pregnancy (or forced impregnation), recognized as a military strategy used in several conflicts, has been codified under international law as a war crime and a crime against humanity (Carpenter 2000c).

The numbers of raped women in the former Yugoslavia vary depending on the sources, ranging from twenty thousand to fifty thousand. While all sides in the Bosnian conflict have committed rapes, Serbian forces appear to have used rape on the largest scale, principally against Muslim women (Laber 1993). According to the UN Final Report of the Commission of Experts, the majority of the cases, perpetrated by soldiers, paramilitary groups, local police, as well as civilians, occurred between fall 1991 and the end of 1993.

Among several factors that substantiate the allegation of a Serbian rape policy are the five patterns of sexual violence that were identified in the UN Final Report. One of those patterns occurred in the so-called rape camps. These rape camps were established in buildings such as hotels, schools, restaurants, hospitals, factories, peacetime brothels, or even animal stalls in barns, fenced pens, and auditoriums (Salzman 1998). Frequently, the Serbian captors told the women that they were trying to impregnate them. In doing so they would create "Chetnik babies" who would kill Muslims when they grew up. Furthermore, they repeatedly said that they were following their president's orders. Gynecologists would examine the women, and those found pregnant were segregated, given special privileges, and held until their seventh month, when it was too late to obtain an abortion; at that time they were released (Niarchos 1995).

There is unquestionable evidence that rape and other forms of sexual violence were not just byproducts of the armed conflict or a form of revenge for a victorious army; rather, they were part of a well-planned and systematic policy in the context of ethnic cleansing. On January 5, 1994, the UN General Assembly adopted a special resolution stating that the "systematic practice of rape was used as a weapon of war and an instrument of ethnic cleansing against women and children in the areas of armed conflicts in the former Yugoslavia, and especially against the Bosnian women and children in Bosnia-Herzegovina" (UN 1994).

A photograph of a letter sent to the secret police chief in Belgrade from the commander of the 3rd Battalion of the Serb army reads: "680 Muslim women of ages ranging from 12 to 60 years are now gathered in the centres for displaced persons in our territory. A large number of these are pregnant, especially those ranging in age from 15 to 30 years. In the estimation of Bosko Kelevic and Smiljan Geri, the psychological effect is strong, and therefore we must continue [the rape and forced impregnation]" (Chauval 1995).

The Bosnian government estimated that thirty-five thousand women, primarily Muslim but also Croat, became pregnant from rape (Salzman 1998). According to Vesna Nikolic-Ristanovik, Serb women who were also raped and impregnated testified that their Muslim or Croat attackers made similar comments about wanting to impregnate them for ethnic reasons. According to the report submitted by Tadeusz Mazowiecki, special rapporteur of the Commission on Human Rights, the majority of these women had abortions. Although abortions are not approved by the Catholic or Orthodox churches, they are allowed among Muslim women until the 120th day of pregnancy. On the other hand, it was also confirmed that a large number of women were kept in detention until they could not have an abortion.

Ahmed Zin, director of the Egyptian Aid Agency, which was designated by the Sarajevo leadership to operate group homes for orphans, estimated that five hundred to six hundred of the children in his group homes had been born as a consequence of war rape, and he speculated that many more were trapped with their mothers in the 70 percent of Bosnian territory controlled by Serbs (Williams 1993). His interview took place in 1993, when many of the pregnant women had not yet given birth and rapes were still occurring. Some women gave birth in Bosnia, many in Croatia, and several in the countries to which they were evacuated and where they were accepted as refugees. Numbers of women were also taken in advanced stages of pregnancy to Serbia (Salzman 1998), where nobody knows their destinies. Fadila Memisevic of the Association for Threatened Peoples of Bosnia revealed that raped women who kept their babies were a tiny minority. "Many more may have wanted to do so, but the pressures on them were intolerable" (quoted in Becirbasic and Secic 2002).

Several refugee women, taken in advanced stages of their pregnancies to Croatia, delivered at the Petrovo Maternity Hospital in Zagreb. From there, according to the Centre for Women Victims of War and the Zagreb Caritas office, unwanted babies were taken to the Vladimir Nazor Orphanage or the Goljak Centre for Children with Special Needs (Becirbasic and Secic 2002). Zagreb Caritas received around 150 raped women, roughly 60 percent of whom were pregnant. The director, Jelena Brajsa, remembers the first fifteen pregnant women who arrived in 1993. All had been repeatedly raped. After delivery, just two babies were kept by their mothers, one Christian and one Muslim. Nine babies were collected by the Bosnian Embassy and Red Cross and later returned to Bosnia, where two were taken by their families, two were adopted, and five were placed in institutions. The remaining four babies, which were handicapped, stayed behind and are still in Zagreb today. The reasons behind this selection remain unclear.

In sum, the exact number of children born as a result of the mass rapes and forced impregnation is not known, but anecdotal evidence suggests that many of the war-rape pregnancies were carried to term during the war. Although many of these children left Bosnia with their mothers, some are likely to have been raised within Bosnia after the war. Of these, some were raised by their mothers, others were adopted by Bosnian families, and some have remained in institutions.

Although the Convention on the Rights of the Child, to which Bosnia is a signatory, enumerates a range of rights to which all children are entitled, regardless of "birth or other status," children born as a result of war rape may be particularly at risk of deprivations of these rights. It is not clear based on the data gathered so far whether the reaction of relevant entities in BiH has been adequate to mitigate harm.

In 1993 the Bosnian government, while claiming that 200,000 people had been killed in fifteen months of nationalistic aggression, refused to relinquish any more of its endangered citizens (Williams 1993). One of the implemented measures was the ban on the international adoption of war orphans and, among those, the children of forced maternity. This attitude, in accordance with religious principles laid down by the Muslim community, was motivated not only by the hope that relatives of these children would take care of them, but also by the desire to repopulate the country.

But it is less clear what kind of government response, if any, was available for the children born as a consequence of rape and for their mothers; how those in institutes for children without parental care are being integrated; if adopted, what follow-up measures are being taken to evaluate their integration and present situation. Such information is particularly difficult to assess by outside researchers or human rights monitors because the government does not appear to have monitored this specific group of children after the war. Rather, the conventional opinion in Bosnia appears to be that the question is not an issue. It is reported by some that no concrete measures were taken to evaluate the status of this population and to address its needs; therefore, no information is available. However, the same government officials argue that because they are not aware of cases to the contrary, the children must be doing fine.

### Institutions for Children without Parental Care

Since there are no private adoption agencies in BiH, and the concept of foster families is not well developed, centers for social work are responsible for placing the children in local orphanages or institutions for children without parental care or for organizing adoption. Children born as a consequence of rape who were abandoned by their mothers would have been dealt with through these mechanisms.

Centers for social work, state orphanages, and institutions for children without parental care are not willing to share information. Several institutions are not aware of the family history of the children because this is considered confidential by the centers for social work. On several occasions institution staff revealed that they might have among their charges children born as a result of rape, but they could not be sure because they are not aware of the children's full background.

The orphanages visited in May 2003 were very reluctant to address the question of children born as a consequence of rape. Most of the time staff members denied awareness of this particular subject, and many added that keeping records of the children during the war was extremely difficult. The psychologist of the Tuzla orphanage revealed that some children born as a consequence of rape during war were sheltered in that institution. She stated that sometimes she tried to explain to these children their origins, but they didn't understand. Nothing has been revealed regarding the relationship between these children and the other war orphans. One of the reasons, according to the orphanage workers, is that these children are not aware of their origins.

According to Advija Hercegovac of the Vojo Peric Orphanage in Tuzla, in 1993 around 700 children were admitted, although the capacity of the orphanage was only 110. "It is possible that many of those were babies of raped women, but there was a chaos at the time and we had more important tasks than keeping detailed records. Children later adopted were subject to the usual rules protecting their identities and those of their adoptive parents" (Becirbasic and Secic 2002).

Although not different from ordinary adoption procedures, the systematic lack of monitoring and assistance to adoptive children might expose children born to women raped during war, and their adoptive parents, to specific problems. The confidentiality rule can turn against

the child it is supposed to protect if social assistance and counseling become unavailable to children and parents due to the fact that no monitoring takes place after adoption.

## Women's Organizations

The main goal of the majority of women's organizations established
in BiH during and immediately after the war is the well-being of wom-
en; that is, helping them to cope with the physical and psychological
traumas caused by rape and forced pregnancy. The organizations have
special training and experience working with women's problems, including rape and domestic violence, the latter of which is a problem that has
been escalating since the end of the war. Through their work with rape
victims, these organizations are fully aware of the circumstances in which
some of these pregnancies were conceived. Given their focus on the situation of women, they are not always in a position to provide the answers
related to the destinies of the children and their integration, but some
organizations shared their experiences concerning the different types of
relationships between mother and child in cases where a client has chosen to raise her baby.

Medica Zenica is one of the few organizations that provide gyneco-
logic, therapeutic, and psychological support not only to women victims
of sexual abuse and forced pregnancy, but also to their families. Regardless of the final decision of either aborting or keeping the child, this
organization provides the necessary assistance. According to Medica
Zenica, out of 150 raped women who arrived at the center, fifteen were
pregnant and thirteen had babies. Of those thirteen, three women kept
the babies with psychosocial support from Medica Zenica. One mother
wished to keep her baby, but she did not have enough money, so the
child was taken by the government; another mother killed her baby six
months after delivery in a moment of "insanity"; and the majority of
women opted to give the children up for adoption. According to the
same organization, the majority, upon realizing that it was too late for an
abortion, wanted to have an abortion using paraprofessional methods or
even by injuring themselves. All women were extremely reluctant to accept their pregnancy, and they neglected their bodies because they were
a constant reminder of rape. One woman who approached Medica Zenica
after being raped in Brcko was accompanied by her mother, who kept
insisting that the pregnancy was her daughter's own fault (Becirbasic
and Secic 2002).

In Tuzla, Vive Zena, a women's center, provides counseling for rape
victims. Among its staff, helping several other women traumatized by
war, is a woman who was forcibly impregnated. She was six months pregnant by the time she arrived in Tuzla. Unable to have an abortion, she

had to wait until the baby was born. After an initial rejection of the baby, which was sent to the local orphanage, she reconsidered and decided to keep the baby with her. The price of this decision was high. Rejected by her family and local community, enduring the whispers and finger point-ing of other women in Zivince, the place where she started her life as a refugee, she had to go through a long fight until she could live with her son. The taboo around rape even extended to her family. Her mother, sister, and brother-in-law were supportive, but not her father or younger brother. She remained in Bosnia throughout her pregnancy, although many women who had been raped in prison camps in Northwest Bosnia were evacuated to third countries through Croatia. Tory Araldesn, the psychologist who in 1993 was overseeing the women's counseling center in Tuzla run by Norwegian People's Aid, stated that "rape here is much more taboo than it is in the West. It is so taboo that even the local thera-pists are hesitant to bring it up" (Williams 1993).

### Religious Leadership

Religious institutions became more politically relevant during and after the war in all three communities, therefore pronouncements of religious leaders on the issue of children born as a consequence of war rape have acquired particular importance. While in Republika Srpska the majority of the population of Serb origin is Orthodox, in the Federa-tion, aside from the Muslim community, those from Croat ancestry are Catholic. Although no information was obtained from the Orthodox religious authorities and their position in relation to this issue, the posi-tions of the Catholic church and especially of the Muslim leaders dem-onstrate the attempt of religious institutions to live up to their responsibilities.

The Muslim authorities, both internationally and within Bosnia, con-sidered the status and rights of the orphans of war rape early in the war. According to Muharem Omerdić, counselor for religious issues in BiH, an analysis of the problem and a study of the status of women in the Sharia Law was conducted with the intention of making sure that these women were protected. Furthermore, such study was intended to pre-pare Muslims to accept the children and to alleviate their pain. Omerdić stated that "it was particularly painful when some of the raped women were left by their husbands, even their fathers. . . . Cruel gossips about some women spread through their neighbourhoods, especially when they were left pregnant" (Omerdić 2002, 428).

In order to deal with this situation Islamic scholars from several coun-tries issued special fatwas (legal statements issued by a mufti or a reli-gious lawyer on a specific issue). According to Omerdić, several problems had to be addressed:

What is debauchery? What are the sanctions against debauchery? Are raped women unchaste? Are raped women subject of the provisions against debauchery? Are babies born by a raped mother the babies born by an unchaste woman? Whose family name will the baby carry? Who will it inherit and what will be its right in general? Who will take care of such a baby? Whom does an unwanted baby belong to by God's, natural and civil law? Are raped mothers entitled to perform abortion, and when are they allowed to do so? (Omerdić 2002, 429)

Ali D'adulhakk, the sheikh of Al-Azhar, Cairo, considered to be the greatest living Islamic authority, wrote and published a fatwa entitled "Fatwa on Children Born by Raped Women in Bosnia-Herzegovina." This fatwa, translated and published in BiH, provides important guidelines for the conduct of both women and local communities in the acceptance and integration of these women and their children as valid members of society. Emphasizing the fact that abortions after four months of pregnancy are not allowed, even for women impregnated through rape, the fatwa designates the future mother as having the main responsibility for the upbringing of the child: "She is to carry, give birth to, raise and take care of that baby" (Omerdić 2002, 430). Although these women should not be considered "unchaste" or in any other way responsible for their rape and impregnation, they will be sinners if they neglect and abandon their babies. In such a case, however, the responsibility for taking care of the child falls to the community. The society is then reminded of its duties with respect to the protection of all children, avoiding external threats like adoption in third countries: "This attitude arises from the fact that Islam obliges both society and individual to protect children, even the illegitimate ones, in order to make them useful (to mankind); their identity should not be emphasized in order to secure their social adaptation and in order not to remind them ever of their origins" (Omerdić 2002, 430).

In short, Islamic leadership urged women and communities to accept and raise war-rape orphans, to integrate them as much as possible in the communities, and, in order to "secure their social adaptation," to keep their real identities secret. It is also worthwhile to note the injunction that, in order to protect the babies of any "threat" (like being sold, enslaved, trafficked, or abused) they should not be given up for adoption, especially not to other countries. This matter is even more evident in another fatwa issued by the Muslim scholar Sheikh Ibn Baz, the former mufti of Saudi Arabia: "With regard to the children [of women who were raped in BiH and Kosovo], the Muslims are obliged to take care of them and bring them up in Islam. They must not leave them to the Christians or others."

The fact that Muslims should "not leave them to the Christians or others" is a clear expression of the conviction of the Muslim religious leaders that the interests of the child are best safeguarded within the Muslim community. It furthermore suggests that the identity of the child is Muslim regardless of the religious convictions of the biological father. This principle, however, is frequently ignored in Muslim communities.

The Islamic community in BiH also took some concrete steps to protect raped women and their children. Attention should be given to the fact that the Islamic community opposed not only adoptions by foreigners, but also the creation of special shelters and registers or records in an attempt to avoid future stigmatization (Omerdić 2002).

The approach of the Catholic authorities with respect to Croatian victims of wartime rape and forced pregnancy exhibited parallels to but also distinctions from the approach of the Islamic community. In 1993 Pope John Paul II addressed a letter to Archbishop Vinko Pulijik of Sarajevo with a message to Bosnian women who had been raped in the conflict. The aim of this letter was to appeal for these women to "transform an act of violence into an act of love and welcome" by "accepting" the enemy inside them and making the child "flesh of their flesh" by carrying their pregnancies to term. This statement raised several criticisms. One of them was from author Frances Kissling, who claims that the Roman Catholic Church is "among the harshest and most punishing of religions when it comes to understanding and respecting women's rights and needs" (Kissling 1999).

The pope's letter further states that "as the image of God, these new creatures should be respected and loved no differently than any other member of the human family . . . since the unborn child is in no way responsible for the disgraceful acts accomplished, he or she is innocent and therefore cannot be treated as the aggressor" (John Paul II 1993). The terms *rape* and *abortion* are noticeably absent from this document. It should be noted that, regarding "orphans and abandoned children," the pope only expresses "a word of appreciation to all those who are working to promote adoption procedures: when little ones lack the support of those who have given them life, it is an act of great human and Christian value to offer them the warmth of a new home" (John Paul II 1993).

Although there are several common points between the Catholic church's position and that of Islam, including an appeal for the mothers to accept their children, a clear difference exists regarding abortion and adoption policies. Muslim muftis allow abortion during the first 120 days and issue fatwas against adoption, especially by non-Muslims. The Catholic church, on the contrary, opposes abortion and welcomes efforts to provide a home to every child, regardless of religious background, for example, through adoption. The different constructions of the children's needs and rights relative to their mothers and broader communities by the involved religious authorities demonstrate the controversies in applying the concept of children's rights to this category of war-affected child and the way in which the relevant actors have struggled with various interpretations of these standards in an effort to determine the best interests of the children.

## Applying Children's Rights to Bosnia's Children Born of War Rape

During the last fifty years several documents providing rights for the protection and well-being of children have been developed in several international legal instruments. Spelling out in an unequivocal manner the rights to which every child is entitled, regardless of where or to whom he or she is born, regardless of sex, religion, or social origin, the Convention on the Rights of the Child is the most complete instrument on children's rights ever made and the first to give these rights the force of international law (Krech 1996). The Convention on the Rights of the Child includes the whole spectrum of civil and political, as well as economic, social, and cultural rights, adapted to the specific needs of children (UNICEF 2002c). The body of rights enumerated in the convention includes the rights of all children *everywhere*. The indivisibility of rights is the key to interpreting the convention. It is not enough to guarantee the right to education if children are not enrolled or cannot go to school regardless of gender or economic class (UNICEF 2002b). Likewise, it is not enough to promote family rights to children born of forced maternity if adoption is not allowed for political or religious reasons.

Focusing on children born as a consequence of rape, it is alarming to realize how most of their rights could be endangered, not only their survival rights (the right to life and to an adequate standard of living [Article 6]) but also their membership rights. According to Donnelly and Howard, "The protection of the survival rights alone guarantees only the crudest anomic existence, a life unfit for a human being; to exist as a human being, one must exist as a part of a community" (Donnelly and Howard 1988, 223). LeBlanc (1995) focuses on three particular groups of membership rights that are affirmed in the Convention on the Rights of the Child. First, the state has an obligation to respect and ensure that children are not discriminated against (Article 2); second, the child has rights to a name and a nationality (Article 7); third, there are family rights and the rights of the child within the context of the family (Articles 9, 19, and 21).

*Nondiscrimination (Article 2)*

The principle of nondiscrimination is of particular importance in the case of war-rape orphans, but to the extent that measures to address discrimination entail silence or denial about the child's origins, this may conflict with a child's assertion of his or her rights to identity later on. Some of the case studies in this volume suggest that stigma and discrimination can be specific harms that such children face. The children born as a consequence of rape in East Timor are known as sons of the enemy; in Uganda they are given names evoking their mothers suffering; in BiH they are referred to as little Chetniks. Meanwhile, both the Muslim community and the BiH government strongly oppose the adoption of these children by outsiders. For the Muslim religious community, the children are Muslims and should be raised as such; for the government they are a way of repopulating the country. But what are they for the community in which they are being raised? If caretakers manage to keep the identity of the children secret, there are no grounds for discrimination; on the other hand, the children are deprived of the right to know their identity. Are there priorities among their rights? What would be in the best interests of the child? The Convention on the Rights of the Child states frequently that state parties need to identify the most vulnerable and disadvantaged children within their borders and to take affirmative action to ensure that the rights of these children are realized and protected. But such actions could lead to new discrimination if it is not done with due discretion. It should be noted that this fact was considered in BiH by the government and also by the Muslim religious community.

*The Right to a Name and Nationality*

According to Article 7 of the Convention on the Rights of the Child, the child must be "registered immediately after birth and shall have the right from birth to a name, the right to acquire a nationality, and, as far as possible, the right to know and be cared for by his or her parents." The question of nationality is one of the most sensitive and complex issues of birth registration, and it can compromise the registration of the child. Birth registration establishes the child's identity and is generally a prerequisite for the issuing of a birth certificate (UNICEF 2002a). In the case of war-rape children, birth registration was not always done. Too ashamed to reveal the identity of the father, or unable to because the identity was not known (it could be one of several rapists), women frequently did not register their babies. Some of the orphanages visited in BiH reported that children were found simply abandoned; in these cases children were registered as NN—no name. Although some might argue that these were war-rape children, there is no proof in favor of or against this argument.

Most states confer nationality according to the principles of *jus soli*, *jus sanguinis*, or a combination of both. The different rules mean that children could possess dual nationality or no nationality at all (LeBlanc 1995). Both Bosnia and Croatia follow the *jus sanguinis* concept, which means denial of citizenship to children of Bosnian women that were born in Croatia. This situation was only changed when, in September 1996, the Bosnian government made an amendment to Article 4 of the citizenship law regulating *jus sanguinis*. The new paragraph states that if one parent is a citizen of BiH, and if the other is a citizen of a former republic of the Federal Republic of Yugoslavia, and a child was born abroad, the child should be given BiH citizenship. The inclusion of this article seems to avoid the stateless status of refugee children, especially those whose mothers were victims of rape and have no intention of keeping the babies, leaving the children to the care of local institutions.

### Family Rights

The family is often regarded as the basic unit of society (LeBlanc 1995). Its importance to the rights of the child is evident in the large number of articles concerning families included in the Convention on the Rights of the Child. Article 5 provides the basic framework. The right to know the biological parents is provided by Articles 7, 8, and 9, and Article 22 states that parties shall provide "as they consider appropriate" cooperation to protect, assist, and "trace the parents or other members of the family of any refugee child." The UN Declaration on Social and Legal Principles relating to the Protection and Welfare of Children, with Special Reference to Foster Placement and Adoption Nationally and Internationally provides that "the need of a foster or adopted child to know about his or her background should be recognised by persons responsible for the child's care unless this is contrary to the child's best interests" (UNICEF 2002b, 117). According to the holistic nature of the convention, a child who could be harmed by the discovery of his or her parents' identity should be prevented from having this information (UNICEF 2002b). The war-rape orphans case could be seen as one of the "most extreme and unambiguous circumstances" where the right to know parentage could be refused. But do the parents have the right not to be found? Does a raped woman who gives up her child for adoption have the right not to be confronted with her painful past? The children's rights to know their origins and the mothers' rights to confidentiality and protection to avoid social condemnation such as ostracism, injury, or death could be competing. Article 30 of the 1993 Hague

Convention on Protection of Children and Cooperation in Respect of Intercountry Adoption allows the state of origin of the child to deny information about the parents' identities while supporting the mother's rights. Those countries that maintain adoption secrecy in order to protect the mother should, according to the UNICEF *Implementation Handbook for the Convention on the Rights of the Child*, be able to release information to the child with the mother's permission or when she will not be affected (UNICEF 2002b).

### The Right to Alternative Means of Care

The convention emphasizes the primary responsibility of the family for the care of the child, while recognizing that under some circumstances children might become, or have to be, separated from their families, either temporarily or permanently (LeBlanc 1995). The Convention on the Rights of the Child contains two articles on alternative means of child care. Under Article 20, the state should provide "special protection and assistance" to children deprived of their family environment. These children should be given alternative means of child care like adoption or foster placement, always regarding the "best interests" of the child.

Besides the special protection, Article 20(3) is of particular importance for the present case because it presents the concept of Kafalah in Islamic law: the placement of children with relatives. Article 21 is related to the adoption of children within countries and inter-country adoptions, and it is only applicable to states "that recognise and/or permit the system of adoption." If they do, they must ensure that "the best interests of the child" are the "paramount consideration" (LeBlanc 1995, 120). Measures to facilitate adoption are, therefore, not imposed on states parties. LeBlanc further states that "delegates from some Islamic states made statements regarding the terms of both Articles 20 and 21, claiming that the articles are not binding on them because, consistent with Islamic law, they do not recognise or approve the system of adoption" (LeBlanc 1995, 120).

In BiH adoptions are the responsibility of two entities, the Federation and the Republika Srpska. Their laws and practices are basically the same; the application for adoption must be submitted to the custodial body in the municipality where the child resides, and in most cases, the responsible body is the center for social work. The center prepares an adoption case for submission to the ultimate authority, the Ministry of Social Policy, to approve adoptions by foreigners, though not for adoptions by local Bosnian citizens.

The US State Department, relating the legal requirements for adoption in foreign countries, provides information on its website about the adoption system in Bosnia: "The law stresses that there has to be overwhelming justification and exceptionally compelling reasons for a foreigner to be permitted to adopt a Bosnian child. Just what an 'overwhelming justification' might be is judged on a case-by-case basis" (US State Department 2006). The same website further informs those interested in adopting children from BiH that "neither the government of the Federation nor that of Republika Srpska considers it beneficial for native-born children to be uprooted, to lose contact with other relatives, or to lose their identity through losing their citizenship. Furthermore, in a country that is still recovering from a long and brutal conflict, it can be extremely difficult to determine if the whereabouts of a parent are simply unknown or if the child is truly an orphan" (ibid.).

### Protection Rights

Several articles of the convention deal with the need to protect children from various forms of abuse and mistreatment. Those include the protection rights enshrined in Articles 19, 21, 32–38, and 40. In addition, Article 39 establishes the obligation of the state parties to take measures to promote the physical and psychological recovery and social reintegration of a child who becomes a victim of abusive treatment.

During armed conflicts, when attention is directed at other kinds of problems, families willing to adopt children do not always go through all the legal proceedings, especially when facing a country that is willing to "get rid of" these children. The fact that children born as a consequence of war rape could face the risks of being sold for trafficking and abuse is one of the reasons why international adoption is not always seen as the best alternative. On the other hand, as mentioned above, having the possibility of being adopted by a loving, caring family is a right under the convention. The denial of this right for political or religious reasons could be seen as a violation of the right to a family and as an instance in which the bests interests of the child are not taken into account. But the Islamic concept of Kafalah, and the refusal to accept adoption as set in Articles 20 and 21, should be seen as a way of protecting children and giving the responsibility of their upbringing to their families and local communities.

### Implementing the Convention on the Rights of the Child in Bosnia

Existing international law aims to protect all children regardless of birth or other status and enumerates specific rights relevant to the particular harms to which children born of rape are likely to be subject. However, it is less clear to what extent these standards have been effectively implemented with respect to this population in Bosnia, or whether children born of rape are in fact "falling through the cracks" in existing human rights law.

The Ombudsman of the Federation and the Republika Srpska, sponsored by Save the Children Norway, created in 1997 a Children's Rights Department. As reasons for creating this department it cites

> a commitment of the state to respect the Convention of [sic] the Rights of the Child; wide range of the problems encountered by children, which requires special attention and concrete protection activities; failure to submit the Initial Report on the Situation of the Rights of the Child to the UN Committee; non-existence of a plan or program for the protection of the child at the level of the state; most serious violations of the rights of the child committed during the war resulting in physical and mental health disorders of the children." (Silva 2004, 12)

During the summer of 2004 representatives of the Children's Rights Department of the Ombudsman of the Federation and the Republika Srpska were contacted regarding the children born of rape by UNICEF's regional office in Sarajevo. The research team was unable to establish a record of initiatives designed to monitor, follow up on, or protect these specific children from stigma, statelessness, or mistreatment. Spokespersons for the Bosnian government either argued that there were no available data or refused to recognize the existence of a group of children born as a consequence of rape. As the ombudsman is allowed to act based upon specific complaints, the ombudsman's lack of awareness indicates that no such complaints were received by this institution. One can only speculate as to why this is so. But anecdotal evidence suggests that the fear of stigmatization and social exclusion might prevent women or relatives from availing themselves of this legal avenue.

## Conclusion

Like rape, forced impregnation is considered a war crime, a grave breach of the Geneva Conventions, and a form of torture, genocide, and crimes against humanity. Although recognized in international law, forced pregnancy has thus far been treated mainly as a women's issue (Carpenter 2000a). Children conceived in this way are "secondary victims," and they may suffer from varying degrees of discrimination, stigmatization, and social exclusion depending on the cultural and social context and the precise historic circumstances of their conception. Given existing global standards for protecting all children's human rights, this poses specific problems in postwar contexts.

In the particular case of BiH, rape and forced impregnation were perpetrated by all parties in the conflict. However, only the Serbian forces seem to have used rape and enforced pregnancies in a systematic fashion as a tool of war and with the clear intent of changing the ethnic composition of the population of BiH. The result has been an indeterminate number of children living with adopted families, in institutions, or with economically impoverished and traumatized single mothers within Bosnia.

This chapter has provided an exploratory analysis of some of the sequelae of mass rape in BiH by considering the human rights of the children brought to term as a result. Evidence gathered in the literature and through fieldwork within Bosnia suggests that different sectors of civil society have very different responses to the needs of these children. It is not clear whether the Convention on the Rights of the Child is fully applied or provides consistent guidance in securing their particular needs.

In the research it became apparent that the affected communities are reluctant to confront the issue openly. This might be due to sincere concern for the well-being of the children in their care; special attention to their situation might lead to stigmatization and traumatization, particularly for those children who are unaware of the conditions of their conception. In some ways, therefore, this might be interpreted as a best practice under the Convention on the Rights of the Child. However, the latent resistance to open dialogue with outside actors might also be rooted in the awareness that local authorities are not free from the same prejudices that form the basis for the discrimination against these children. The question is whether effective efforts are being made to address societal stigma without sensationalizing or marking the children, or whether the sensitive nature of the subject has become an excuse for turning a blind eye. More careful and systematic analysis of this particular case should be undertaken to build upon the results of this chapter.

The case of BiH is of particular interest also in respect to the diverse religious responses. The fact that three religious groups—Orthodox, Catholic, and Muslim—closely identified with the three ethnic parties in the conflict, are obliged to face the issue of children resulting from war rape offers the opportunity for further comparative studies. Religious communities can play an important role in helping affected communities by de-stigmatizing the victims and by providing spiritual guidance. The Muslim and Catholic positions on children born of war provide a good basis for such action. However, the lack of sustained involvement of religious authorities diminishes the positive impact of their pronouncements.

38     Joana Daniel-Wrabetz

The key to better understanding of the situation of children born as a consequence of war rape, and ultimately to devising policies to improve it, lies in the capacity of the affected community to accept ownership of the issue. Instances of denial of the problem, as documented in this chapter, make outside intervention difficult and sometimes counterproductive. Ultimately, only the communities in which these children live can create the social and emotional environment that provides for a stable and fulfilling existence.

# References

Becirbasic, Belma, and Dzenana Secic. 2002. "Invisible Casualties of War." *IWPR's Balkan Crisis Report*, no. 383, November 18.

Carpenter, Charli. 2000a. "Surfacing Children: Limitations of Genocidal Rape Discourse." *Human Rights Quarterly* 22: 428–77.

———. 2000b. "Assessing and Addressing the Needs of Children Born of Forced Maternity." Paper presented at the International Conference on War-Affected Children, Winnipeg, Canada.

———. 2000c. "Forced Maternity, Children's Rights and the Genocide Convention: A Theoretical Analysis." *Journal of Genocide Research* 2, no. 2: 213–44.

Chauval, Patrick. 1995. A War Torn Region: Bosnia-Herzegovina, Croatia, and Yugoslavia." Available on the earlham.edu website.

Daniel, Joana. 2004. "No Man's Child—The War Rape Orphans." In *Awarded Theses of the Academic Year 2002/2003. European Master's Degree in Human Rights and Democratisation*, 11–96. Venice, Italy: Marsilio Editori S.P.A.

Donnelly, Jack, and Rhoda Howard. 1988. "Assessing National Human Rights Performance: A Theoretical Framework." *Human Rights Quarterly* 10, no. 2 (May): 214–48.

Horvath, Danielle. 1993. "Children of the Rapes." *World Press Review*, June.

Human Rights Watch. 1999. *Kosovo Backgrounder: Sexual Violence as International Crime*. New York: Human Rights Watch. May.

John Paul II. 1993. "Change Violence into Acceptance." *Priests for Life, Teachings of the Magisterium on Abortion*. February 2. Available on the priestsforlife.org website.

Kissling, Frances. 1999. "Callous and Coercive Policy." *Conscience* (Summer). Available on the catholicsforchoice.org website.

Krech, Ralph. 1996. "UN Crime Prevention." In *Understanding Children's Rights*, edited by Eugeen Verhellen. Ghent, Belgium: University of Ghent.

Laber, Jeri. 1993. "Bosnia: Questions of Rape." *New York Times Review of Books*, March 25.

LeBlanc, Lawrence. 1995. *The Convention on the Rights of the Child: UN Lawmaking on Human Rights*. Lincoln: University of Nebraska Press.

Niarchos, Catherine. 1995. "Woman, War, and Rape: Challenges Facing The International Tribunal for the Former Yugoslavia." *Human Rights Quarterly* 17, no. 4 (November): 649–90.

Omerdić, Muharem. 2002. "The Position of the Islamic Community on the Care for Children of Raped Mothers." In *The Plucked Buds*, edited by Mirsad Tokaca. Sarajevo: Commission for Gathering Facts on War Crimes in Bosnia and Herzegovina.

"Pope Urges Bosnian Rape Victims Not to Have Abortions." 1993. *Los Angeles Times*. February 28.

Salzman, Todd A. 1998. "Rape Camps as a Means of Ethnic Cleansing: Religious, Cultural, and Ethical Responses to Rape Victims in the Former Yugoslavia." *Human Rights Quarterly* 20, no. 2 (May): 345–78.

Silva, Priyanthi Jayasinghe. 2004. "Docs International Law Provide Sufficiently Precise Mechanisms to Protect and Promote the Rights of Secondary Rape Victims? Bosnia's Lost Children." MA diss., School of Oriental and African Studies, University of London.

UN. 1994. "Rape and Abuse of Women in the Areas of Armed Conflict in the Former Yugoslavia. General Assembly A/RES/48/143. January 5.

UNICEF. 2002a. "Birth Registration. Right from the Start." *Innocenti Digest*, March 9.

———. 2002b. *Implementation Handbook for the Convention on the Rights of the Child*. Fully rev. ed. New York: UNICEF.

———. 2002c. *International Criminal Justice and Children*. Florence: Innocenti Research Centre.

US State Department. 2006. "Intercountry Adoption—Bosnia-Herzegovina." Available on the travel.state.gov website.

Williams, Carol. 1993. "Bosnia Bans Adoption of Children of Wartime Rape Victims." *Los Angeles Times*. July 23.

# 3

# Caring for Children Born of Rape in Rwanda

## Marie Consolée Mukangendo

In Rwanda, between April and July 1994, one of the century's worst genocides resulted in an estimated 800,000 deaths. A decade after the violence, many of the youngest victims were still struggling to survive. One of the most affected groups comprises those children born of rape during the genocide. The National Population Office of Rwanda has estimated that between two thousand and five thousand children were born of forced impregnation during the genocide and as a result of sexual violence during the unstable period that followed. According to victims' groups, the number is far higher, more than ten thousand (Wax 2004).

As in many post-conflict situations, these children face stigma. They are referred to as "les enfants mauvais souvenir" (children of bad memories) (Goodwin 1997) or "enfants indésirés" (children of hate) by their mothers and the community. Some have been even maligned as "devil's children" (Nowrojee 1996) and others named "little killers" by their own mothers (Wax 2004). As the children grow toward adolescence, they have started to question their mothers about their identity; they wonder about their fathers; and their mothers struggle to find acceptance for these children within their heart and community.

This chapter provides an overview of the problems and challenges facing the children born of rape in Rwanda. First, I briefly discuss the scope and nature of the sexual violence against women following the genocide and the period of insecurity in the refugee camps (1995–98). This is followed by an examination of the consequences of rape on women and the children born as a result. Last, I discuss policy responses to protect these children in the context of child protection more generally in Rwanda today.

## Children Born of Rape
## and Their Mothers in Rwanda

International law requires that, in a situation of war, all parties to armed conflict take special measures to protect women and girls from gender-based violence, particularly rape and other forms of sexual abuse, and all other forms of violence that occur in situations of armed conflict. Rwanda is a member and has ratified the Geneva Conventions of 1949, the Convention on the Elimination of All Forms of Discrimination against Women of 1979 and the Optional Protocol thereto of 1999, and the United Nations Convention on the Rights of the Child of 1989. In the light of such obligations, Rwanda has the responsibility to ensure the full respect for and application of international laws applicable to the rights and protection of women and girls, especially when they are civilians.

However, such laws were not implemented during the 100 days of genocide in 1994 and the period of insecurity in the refugee camps that followed (1995–98). Common patterns of violations and abuse symbolized the volatile situation, where rape was used as a premeditated act of warfare:

> Sexual rape crimes have been perpetrated through repeated violations, gang rape by soldiers and militia, or neighbors, and some rape cases of girls and women in front of the members of their family for humiliation purposes. (Nowrojee 1996, 14)

The disclosure of the 1996 report by the special rapporteur of the United Nations Commission on Human Rights, René Degni-Ségui, revealed the magnitude of the sexual violence endured by women during the genocide. The report stated that rape was "used as a weapon of war against women aged 13 to 65 and that neither pregnant women nor women who had just given birth were spared, that it was systematic and constituted the rule and its absence, the exception" (United Nations Economic and Social Council 1996, 16–20).

Many of these instances of sexual violence resulted in children brought to term. In Rwanda, in many cases men raped until women were pregnant, and sometimes they were even held as sexual slaves of the Hutu militiamen until they gave birth to the child (African Rights 2004).[1] While the exact number of children resulting from genocidal rapes is not known, estimates range between two thousand and ten thousand.

Stigmatization of mothers and their children born of rape is a hard reality for many survivors. In the cultural norms and beliefs of Rwanda, rape and other gender-based violations carry severe social stigma, and women who have been victims of rape are often marginalized by their own families and communities. Because of this, women do not dare to reveal their experience publicly. Rape survivors in general are not seen as victims, and the attitude adopted toward them is one of hostility and abandonment. In many cases they are considered outcasts by their own community, and they are sometimes accused of collaborating with the enemy.

The consequences of rape are aggravated by the fact that Rwanda is a patriarchal society; children are typically identified with the lineage of their fathers. This means that a large part of the society will perceive children of wartime rape as belonging to the enemy. This is reflected in local discourse casting the babies as "little Interahamwe" (McKinley 1996). The stigma directed at the children has led some rape survivors to hate their children even before birth because they associate the child with the perpetrator and because the child is a constant reminder of the violence they have endured. For example, in an interview a social worker with a charity group supporting 156 rape victims in Kigali declared, "We have one woman who told me her mother did not even want to see this child because she knows that the child is from Interahamwe" (McKinley 1996). A rape survivor's testimony was described in a news article:

> Some days, when she looks at her round-faced baby boy, Leonille M. feels that she no longer wants to live. It is not the child's fault. He peers back at his mother with innocent eyes. But the baby reminds her of all of her family members who died in the massacres that took the lives of at least 500,000 Rwandans, most of them members of the Tutsi ethnic minority in 1994. He also reminds her of the three soldiers of the majority Hutu group who gang-raped her. (New York Times News Service 1996)

In general, social workers have verified the heavy psychological toll on the survivors. In fact, some women suffer from extreme depression, feelings of guilt for being alive, nightmares, and in some cases violent fantasies against the babies. A UNIFEM/African Women in Crisis report stated that by January 1995, eight months after the genocide killings started in Rwanda, at least four pregnant women who had been raped during the war were showing up daily at Kigali maternity hospital requesting abortions (Laketch 1999). One of these women had been raped and impregnated by the very man who had murdered her husband and four children. Two later gave birth, prematurely, and did not want to see the babies (Hagengimana 1994).

Even though abortion is illegal in Rwanda, many rape victims desired it nonetheless. A study by the Ministry of the Family and Women's Promotion conducted after the war in just two cities found 716 cases of rape, 472 of which resulted in pregnancies. Of these, 282 ended in abortion (Angelucci 1997). Considering the high rate of sexual violence, the debate over legalizing abortion in Rwanda has been raised but has not reached a concrete solution. Opposition to any reform from the church community continues to be very strong.

Numerous victims have rejected their babies after giving birth, ashamed of carrying the child of a Rwandan Hutu militiaman (Wax 2004). Some pregnant women committed suicide rather than give birth to a "child of hate" (Goodwin 1997), and other women committed infanticide (Nowrojee 1996). These desperate acts reflect the psychological impact of the sexual violence on the women survivors of rape. In other cases women abandoned their babies after giving birth. The Family and Promotion of Women Ministry of Rwanda estimated that 80 percent of the mothers raped decided to abandon their babies (Matloff 1995). According to reporters, some women abandoned infants on the doorsteps of ministries, saying that "they are children of the state" (Wax 2004).

Those who decided to keep their children faced other problems that threatened the survival of the babies. The lack of appropriate health centers caused many women to deliver their babies in their homestead or other unsafe locations with no medical attention. Results from a sociodemographic study have shown that, looking at the country as a whole, most of the women who gave birth did not deliver in a health center. For all the known births in 1996, almost 72 percent took place in the homestead or in a relative's home. The use of existing health facilities appears to be very low, with only 18 percent of women giving birth at a health center, while the place of delivery is unknown for the remaining women (Wise 2004).

The emotional and psychological impact of rape causes long-term consequences in the lives of the women and directly affects the development of their children. We can see this in the following description of the feelings of a raped woman after giving birth:

> Hands covering her eyes, her thin legs crossed to try to stop what she could not, Eugenia Muhayimana screamed out to God as the baby pushed through her birth canal. She said she yelled and kicked during two hours of labor, hoping her heart would stop, her soul would drift away and she and her infant would pass to a world where they could live in peace. . . . Her pregnancy was not conceived in love, or in a casual encounter. It was what women in Africa call a pregnancy of war. (Wax 2004)

The pressures from the community lead the survivors to lose their marital status, and they are often chased away from their house and feel shame for what happened. These women are profoundly isolated, experiencing social rejection and ostracization (Nowrojee 1996). In many cases they lose their extended families to conflict and are left alone. A common situation of women living in such situation is poverty. Living in poverty with little support is a major constraint upon their ability to start over after the rape, and they remain utterly dependent upon the state, charitable interventions, or the goodwill of neighbors. This situation leaches away their confidence and self-esteem on a daily basis, and it also drives them to be profoundly insecure regarding the future of their family. The anguish about the future of survivors' children is reflected in an interview gathered by African Rights Working for Justice (African Rights 2004):

> I'm living in a house where I must pay the rent myself. At the moment, I'm not capable of paying the rent and the owner has given me a notice of only five days. I don't know what to do anymore, or where to go with my children after five days. It's hard for me to raise my children. But for now I'm mainly preoccupied with their future. Where am I going to leave them after my death? Who is going to look after their education? I have no idea. I don't like to be asked to testify about this history. It makes me feel as if I'm reliving it.

Another consequence of rape is the physical impact on the victims who suffer persistent health problems. According to the doctors who have treated them, the most common problem among raped women has been sexually transmitted diseases and infections, including HIV/AIDS. Another common problem is injury. Since abortion is illegal in Rwanda, doctors have also treated women with serious complications resulting from self-induced or clandestine abortions following rape-related pregnancies (Nowrojee 1996). Women have a very troubled and difficult life, and many feel their unwanted children and their survival is a form of torture, exacerbated by the fact that many of them have HIV/AIDS. Such a context has a clear impact on children, many of whom become orphans or are abandoned; others experience attachment difficulties with their caregivers.

Poverty and insecurity are complicated by women's lack of access to land and resources. In spite of new legislation entitling women to inheritance, practice has continued to favor exclusive inheritance between men. This absolute dependence has put many women in great difficulties after the war. Children born of rape are even more vulnerable, as they and their mothers (in many cases unmarried because of stigma) are chased away from their homes and have no possibilities of claiming their rights. If married, a woman may be given a piece of land by her husband; this is generally for the household's needs, but sometimes it may also be for her personal use. Single mothers, however, must rely on charity or pay rent to cultivate a piece of land.

These social currents are further exacerbated by the HIV/AIDS pandemic (MINALOC/UNICEF 2001). Although not all cases of HIV/AIDS among rape survivors can be traced to the sexual violence committed against them, the mass rapes during 1994 contributed significantly to the spread of the virus in Rwanda, particularly as rates of HIV transmission during sexual violence are believed to be high (Amnesty International 2004). According to UNICEF, of women who survived rape during the genocide, 70 percent are estimated to have been infected with HIV (Angelucci 1997, 44). Indeed, testimonies reveal that during the conflict, men who were HIV/AIDS positive deliberately infected women, using the social stigma attached to rape as an effective weapon in undermining the social fabric of the women.

> I was raped by two gendarmes. . . . One of the gendarmes was seriously ill, you could see that he had AIDS, his face was covered with spots, his lips were red, almost burned, he had abscesses on his neck. Then he told me "take a good look at me and remember what I look like. I could kill you right now but I don't feel like wasting my bullet. I want you to die slowly like me." (Nduwimana 2004)

Rwandan Law No. 2/98 has created a system of health care, the FARG (Fond d'Assistance aux Rescapes du Genocide), the "genocide survivors' assistance fund," which aims at providing assistance to the most needy genocide survivors. Victim support provided by the Rwandan government is estimated at 5 percent of its national annual budget (ICTR 2003). Beneficiaries include orphans, widows, and those handicapped during the genocide. Inspired by the right to reparation, specifically by the need for states to create national victims' compensation funds as recommended by the United Nations Commission on Human Rights (United Nations Economic and Social Council 1996, note 68), the FARG covers several basic needs, including providing schooling for orphans and lodging for widows.

However, access to life-prolonging anti-retroviral (ARV) therapy is very limited. Many rape survivors cannot afford health care due to poverty, and the system of settlements is not conducive to the accessibility of health services. This inaccessibility is related to an inadequacy of resources and to the excessively high cost of triple therapy.

According to a report of Amnesty International, policy advisers in Rwanda estimate that the number of patients clinically in need of life-prolonging ARV therapy ranges between 50,000 and 100,000 (Amnesty International 2004). As of January 2004, approximately 2,000 Rwandese were being treated with ARV therapy. Getting to major hospitals that are authorized to prescribe ARV treatment is an obstacle for the majority of women with HIV/AIDS; they live in remote areas and find the costs of medical consultation too high.

It is currently unknown how many children conceived during the genocide have themselves contracted the virus through transmission from their mothers. However, it is clear that the epidemic is depriving the survivors of their health and thereby affecting their children's rights to survive, to develop, and to be protected. Widespread poverty and severe resource constraints aggravate this situation, which makes women unable to provide their children with basic securities. Children living with a chronically ill parent face many hardships that can be detrimental to their well-being: increasing poverty, greater responsibility for household functions, less parental care, and so on. Children suffer profoundly when their parents become sick and die, and they are psychologically traumatized by the illness of their mother, often having to deal with shame and social stigma. With the mother unable to work and savings spent on care, children are forced to take on the adult role of supporting the family. The pressures of caring for parents and siblings and trying to earn an income can lead children to drop out of school even while their parents are living.

Prosecutors convicted Jean-Paul Akayesu, the former mayor of Taba, of genocide, crimes against humanity, rape, and encouraging sexual violence. The International Criminal Tribunal for Rwanda determined that rapes committed during the genocide are not only war crimes but also crimes against humanity (Donovan 2002). However, the process of trying and punishing perpetrators is still very slow in Rwanda, and most of the rape survivors are still waiting for the day their voice will be heard and justice will be done. Many cases of rape and other brutal sexual violence remain untold and unpunished. In fact, many victims of rape and other forms of sexual violence have opted to keep silent about what they endured out of the fear of being stigmatized.[2] The survivors are reluctant to trust the Rwandan judicial system, feeling trapped by the lack of accountability due to the limitations of the system to prosecute the perpetrators. Moreover, the question of the genocidaires' culpability for human rights violations against the children born of genocidal forced pregnancy has not yet been raised by post-conflict justice mechanisms.

## Status and Protection
## of Children Born of Rape in Rwanda

On January 26, 1990, the government of Rwanda signed the United Nation's Convention on the Rights of the Child and the African Charter on the Rights and the Welfare of the Child (1990); these constitute the formal obligations of the government in the field of the rights and responsibilities of the child. By ratifying the convention a year later, on January 24, 1991, Rwanda promised to provide all rights for every child under the State's jurisdiction. The obligations to the child are stipulated in the African Charter on the Rights and the Welfare of the Child (Article 31) and in Rwandan Law No. 27/2001 (Articles 25, 26, 27).[3]

Unfortunately, progress in implementing the convention was impeded immediately by the genocide, and most basic services and infrastructure needed to support children have been destroyed. While emergency relief operations were put into place to rebuild a severely weakened society, the government of Rwanda, with assistance from UNICEF and other stakeholders, undertook numerous reformulations of its ministries in order to coordinate protection strategies for large numbers of vulnerable children (Greenwell 2002). Children born of genocidal rape, however, have not been specifically constructed as a particularly vulnerable category.

A National Policy for Orphans and Other Vulnerable Children was developed by MINALOC to meet the needs of the most vulnerable children through the provision of appropriate services and protection from harm.[4] The Unité de Protection Sociale is in charge of social affairs in the ministry of local government. The main responsibilities of this department include the coordination of policies and programs for the social and economic reinsertion of vulnerable groups and the promotion of the solidarity, mutuality, and social security of Rwanda's population.

According to the Rwandan government, UNICEF, and international relief agencies such as the International Rescue Committee, approximately one million children in Rwanda are considered vulnerable. This means they are at risk of being displaced from their homes, of being unable to attend school, of being exploited in some way, of living in poverty, or of becoming sick with disease. Unfortunately, not even the state authorities know where all of these youth are living. Despite the government's commitment to meeting the needs of the most vulnerable children through the provision of appropriate services and protection from harm, a high number of children are at still at risk of being deprived of their fundamental rights.

While they are not specified as vulnerable, within this broader context, children born as a result of sexual violence and forced pregnancy face particularly difficult conditions. Poverty is one of the main causes of this vulnerability. Many of their mothers are facing drastic difficulties in taking care of their households single-handedly under extremely difficult conditions, and, as mentioned before, many are affected by HIV/AIDS. Under the circumstances it is very clear that women's and children's rights to survival, to development, and to protection are compromised. Children are more likely to be malnourished or to fall ill, and they are less likely to get the medical and health care they need. Children born of rape are often deprived of an appropriate family environment, due in part to the stigma accompanying their own and their mothers' social conditions. Children outside the family safety net are routinely denied their basic rights, such as the rights to a proper family, to food, to health, and to housing. They may also lack decent accommodation (such as a house made of long-lasting materials), may live in dwellings with no sufficient space, may lack a regular and basic education, and may have no security.

Stigmatized as both illegitimate and as enemy children, their difficult situation seems complicated. Often, the decision to keep the child causes conflicts in the family, pitting those who reject the child against those who want to raise the child:

> The babies have created deep divisions in some families. Chantal I says her uncle has threatened repeatedly to turn her out into the street unless she gets rid of her child, whose father was a member of a Hutu militia. (McKinley 1996)

Children born of rape also suffer more from the mother's instabilities and traumas caused by the rape and violence. Not all cases are negative; on some occasions the child has been raised without problems within the community (Wax 2004). Survivors may succeed in overcoming the trauma and provide their children with love equal to their other children. A survivor's testimony describes how she eventually ended up loving her child, born after she was forced to serve as a sexual slave in the Hutu militia's forest encampments:

> "I was suffering so much right until the moment I gave birth," nearly 16 months later on July 1, 1995, she said. Her fear, her guilt, her suffering all ended after the baby was born. A miracle had happened, she said. (Wax 2004)

Yet other testimonies in the same source include a mother who recognizes that sometimes "I really beat him for such petty things, and I feel I can't love anyone. . . . I try to love him. Sometimes, I don't feel like talking to anybody and I can't" (Wax 2004).

Not surprisingly, implementing the principles in the Convention on the Rights of the Child for this category of vulnerable children is a great challenge, given the great number of other vulnerable children in Rwanda and the fact that existing political mechanisms have not been designed explicitly to address the types of harms to which these particular children might be subject. To illustrate this, I briefly discuss Rwandan laws regarding birth registration and family rights.

### Birth Registration and the Right to a Name: A Policy Gap?

Children born of rape have by law the same right as any other child in Rwanda to the registration of their birth and to recognition of their identity. In fact, the Rwandan legislation makes it mandatory to register and declare the birth fifteen days after delivery, upon presentation of a birth medical certificate (Article 117 CCLI). This right complies with Article 7 of the Convention on the Rights of the Child, according to which "the child shall be registered immediately after birth and shall have the right from birth to a name, the right to acquire a nationality. . . . Failure to declare a birth in the prescribed time frame, any false declaration or any offence which may deprive the child of the possession of his/her real status including child hijacking, suppression, substitution or supposition are punishable by the Criminal Law" (Article 253–55 CPR).

These laws are significant because of the importance of birth registration as a means for monitoring implementations of other child-rights programming. A child that is not registered at birth is in danger of being shut out of society and of being denied the right to an official identity, a recognized name, and a nationality (UNICEF IRC 2002). This invisibility makes it more likely that the discrimination, neglect, and abuse they may experience will remain unnoticed and be overlooked in social development planning.

However, for some children born of rape the right to registration may not have been accomplished under article 117 CCLI of the Rwandan legislation, according to which the birth registration is made only "upon presentation of a medical certificate." Considering that in Rwanda only 18 percent of women give birth at a health center (Wise 2004), the opportunity for the issuance of a medical certificate seems compromised; the percentage may be lower among women seeking to hide a rape-related pregnancy. Therefore, the possibility of a gap of birth registrations for children born during or just after the genocide requires investigation. Some evidence suggests that children of rape were simply abandoned at birth. Some women gave false names at the hospital because they were unable to bear the idea of raising a child of the enemy who, in many cases, had killed their family members; in so doing, they deny the children's rights to identity and complicate implementation of Article 253–55 CPR of the National Criminal Law (Women's Anti Discrimination Committee 1996).

The Rwandan Civil Code recognizes the right to have a name and eventually one or many given names (Article 58 CCLI). The name may be an original or a family name. However, Article 61 of Book 1 of the Rwandan Civil Code forbids giving names that may be prejudicial to moral standards. Calling children "little killers" after the soldiers in the Hutu militia, or "les enfants mauvais souvenir," or "children of hate" is prejudicial to any moral standards and violates Article 61 of the Rwandan Civil Code by compromising and denying children born of rape their right to a nonprejudicial name and identity. There has been little effort at the political level to deal with this particular threat to children's rights to name and family.

## Conclusion

In Rwanda, the ability to protect women's and children's well-being remains a tremendous challenge. Resources to protect women and their children appear to be very limited in relation to the needs and problems that exist. According to the testimonies of some victims, of members of civil society, and of international organizations working in this area, measures introduced so far are insufficient.

Children born of rape are suffering from the critical problems affecting most vulnerable children in Rwanda. Poverty and its consequences severely curtail adequate access to food, education, and health. Rape and its impact on mothers has been a factor that has threatened, worsened, or cut short the life of many children. Abortions and infanticides have been reported in Rwanda as a direct result of mothers' rape during the conflict period. Of the children who were born, many were abandoned, while some were kept by their mothers. While some mothers managed to cope with the traumas and provide their children a life equal to other children, anecdotal evidence suggests this has been more the exception than the rule. The psychological traumas that many mothers still bear have directly affected their children, both physically and psychologically.

In addition, children born of rape face some specific problems derived from stigmatization, sometimes in their own families and/or in the communities where they live. The physical and psychological injuries suffered by Rwandan rape survivors are aggravated by a sense of isolation and ostracism that leads to inadequate care for children born of rape. Stigmatization further alienates those living in the communities.

At present, the well-being of children born of forced pregnancy is inadequately guaranteed. How can effective policy be designed to deal with such problems? Due to the lack of accurate statistical data and limited capacity and resources on the topic, it is difficult to envisage short-term solutions. The problems of children born of rape are largely similar to those of the most vulnerable children in Rwanda, which means that until more resources, capacity, and effective policy get vulnerable children out of their complicated situations, it will be difficult to find a solution to the problems of children of rape. However, special attention and psychological help, particularly from community social workers and the government, seem urgently needed to tackle the specific social stigma and problems directly associated with the condition of rape and the children born as a consequence.

---

*The views expressed herein are those of the author and do not necessarily reflect the views of UNICEF.*

## Notes

[1] Raped women have also been kept in captivity in other conflicts until they have given birth to children. As Eunice Apio documents (chap. 4 herein), the LRA has a de facto forced impregnation policy, where some abducted girls who become pregnant are taken to special camps in the Sudan and looked after by older LRA female commanders until they give birth. The children then become the next generation of LRA fighters. See also Mazurana and McKay 2001.

[2] Bianfer Nowrojee writes: "Two years after the genocide, the judicial system is still not functioning. Although the lack of justice is not reserved to victims of gender-based abuse in Rwanda, it is clear that rape victims face specific obstacles, including that police inspectors documenting genocide crimes for prosecution are predominantly male and are not collecting information on rape. Many women interviewed by our team, composed solely of women, indicated that they would report rape to a female investigator, but not to a man" (Nowrojee 1996).

[3] A more detailed list of laws and conventions can be found in Service Social International (pour MINALOC et UNICEF Rwanda), *Orientations Pour le Développement d'une Politique Familiale de Protection des Enfants Prives ou Risquant d'Etre Prives de leur Milieu Familial d'Origine* (Kigali, May 2002).

[4] A technical committee consisting of representatives of MINALOC, MINEDUC, Hagaruka, Save the Children (UK) and UNICEF carried out the tasks of guiding and supervising the development of the policy document.

## References

African Rights. 2004. *RWANDA Broken Bodies, Torn Spirits, Living with Genocide, Rape, and HIV/AIDS.*

Amnesty International. 2004. "Rwanda: 'Marked for Death' Rape Survivors Living with HIV/AIDS in Rwanda," April 6. Available on the amnesty.org website.

Angelucci, M. A., et al. 1997. *C'est Ma Taille Qui M'a Sauvé. Rwanda: De la Tragedie à la Réconstruction.* Rome: Cooperazione Italiana, Ministre Italienne de l'Enseignement Superieur, de la Recherche Scientifique, et de la Culture, and UNICEF.

Donovan, Paula. 2002. "Rape and HIV/AIDS in Rwanda." *Lancet* 360, no. 9350, Supplement: 17–18.

Goodwin, Jan. 1997. "Rwanda: Justice Denied." *On the Issues.* Fall Available on the ontheissuesmagazine.com website.

Greenwell, K. Fern. 2002. *A Profile of Children in Rwanda's Unaccompanied Children Centres: A Report Based on Statistical Indicators for 24 UAC Centres in 2000.* Prepared for UNICEF-Rwanda in partnership with MINALOC. Available on the unicef.org website.

Hagengimana, A. 1994. "Psycho-Social Trauma Management Consultancy Report to UNIFEM/AFWIC." Cited in Osei G. Kofi, *Lives under Threat: Women and Girls in Crisis in Eastern and Central Africa.* Nairobi, Kenya: UNICEF/UNIFEM, 1995.

ICTR. 2003. "ICTR Registrar Seeks Support of the African Community." Press release. Arusha, Tanzania: ICTR, May 9. Available at http://69.94.11.53/ENGLISH/PRESSREL/2003/343.htm.

Laketch, Dirasse. 1999. "The Gender Dimension of Making Peace in Africa." Paper presented at the Commonwealth Human Rights Initiative Conference on Pan-Commonwealth Advocacy for Human Rights, Good Governance and Peace in Africa, Harare, Zimbabwe, January 21–24.

Matloff, J. 1995. "Rwanda Copes with Babies of Mass Rape." *Christian Science Monitor* 87, no. 83: 1. Available on the csmonitor.com website.

Mazurana, Dyan, and Susan McKay. 2001. "Child Soldiers: What about the Girls." *Bulletin of the Atomic Scientists* 57, no. 05: 30–35.

McKinley, James. 1996. "Legacy of Rwanda Violence: The Thousands Born of Rape." *The New York Times*, September 23.

Nduwimana, Francoise. 2004. "The Right to Survive: Sexual Violence, Women, and HIV-AIDS." Montreal: International Centre for Human Rights and Democratic Development. May.

Nowrojee, Bianfer. 1996. *Shattered Lives, Sexual Violence during the Rwandan Genocide and Its Aftermath.* New York: Human Rights Watch.

MINALOC (Rwandan Ministry of Local Government and Social Affairs)/UNICEF. 2001. *Struggling to Survive: Orphan and Community Dependent Children in Rwanda.* New York: UNICEF. Available on the unicef.org website.

New York Times News Service. 1996. "Tutsi Women Bear Children, Scars, of Hutus," September 24.

UNICEF IRC (Innocenti Research Centre). 2002. "Birth Registration Right from the Start." *Innocenti Digest* 9. March. Florence, Italy: UNICEF IRC.

United Nations Economic and Social Council. 1996. *Report on the Situation of Human Rights in Rwanda, Submitted by Mr. René Degni-Ségui, Special Rapporteur of the Commission on Human Rights, under Paragraph 20 of Resolution S–3/1 of 25 May 1994.* January 29.

Wax, Emily. 2004. "Rwandans Are Struggling to Love Children of Hate." *The Washington Post*, March 28. Available on the washingtonpost.com website.

Wise, Victoria. 2004. *Nutritional Situation of Young Children in Rwanda: An Analysis of Anthropometric Data Collected by the Household Living Conditions Survey 1999–2001.* Michigan State University: Food Security III Cooperative Agreement. Available on the aec.msu.edu website.

Women's Anti Discrimination Committee. 1996. "Rwanda's Representative Calls for Establishment of Culture of Peace and Human Rights in Wake of Genocide." United Nations. February 1. Available on the un.org website.

# 4

# Orphans or Veterans?

## Justice for Children Born of War in East Timor

## SUSAN HARRIS RIMMER

All over East Timor one can find "orphans" whose parents still live, and "wives" who have never been married. These labels mask an open secret in Timorese society—hundreds of babies were born of rape during the Indonesian occupation from 1974 to 1999. In juxtaposition, as a result of the 2004 UNFPA-conducted census, there is finally data available on the current population of East Timor, and it has unexpectedly revealed a baby boom, perhaps in response to the emotional losses of the occupation. The fertility rate was found to be the highest in the world, at 8.3 babies per woman.[1] The baby as the symbol of both wound and healing is clearly at play in Timor at the present time.

Nonetheless, there is official silence on the number and treatment of the children born of conflict, a lack of attention in the transitional justice mechanisms in place in Timor in regard to the human rights violations that produced them, and no official policies to deal either with the needs of these children and their mothers or the discrimination they may face. The challenge posed by these children and women to the social fabric of Timor reveals important gaps and silences within the international human rights law framework, which might nonetheless be addressed by some fairly straightforward policy innovations.

In this chapter I argue that the status of the mothers socially and legally, as it affects the well-being and ability of the children to claim their rights, needs to be more fully addressed in transitional justice debates.

A shortened version of this chapter was the recipient of the 2006 Audre Rapoport Prize for Scholarship on the Human Rights of Women and will appear in the *Texas International Law Journal*.

Within Timor there is a definite ambivalence about the idea of these women as contributors to independence during the occupation, and there is discomfiture regarding their status as "wives" of Indonesian military. This cultural construction is both exacerbated and challenged by the ambivalent influence of Catholic teachings on East Timorese society. Nonetheless, social currents also exist that, if strategically used to reconstruct the image of these children and women, could more effectively reframe their trauma in transitional justice discourse and could contribute both to their well-being and the long-term process of reconciliation in East Timor.

The chapter proceeds in two sections. First, I provide an overview of the situation of sexual violence survivors and their children in East Timor. Second, I discuss current approaches to the children and their mothers within the transitional justice mechanisms available in East Timor at this time. I aim to shift the current approach to children born of war in Timor from covert welfare assistance by the Catholic church and NGOs to a rights-based framework under which, rather than being seen as by-products of a crime or sin, the affected children would be publicly accepted as having valid claims on the government. From this analysis it becomes clear that creative policy and legal options are required in order to assist these families with integration, status, and financial security. I conclude with one such proposal to improve the situation of these families: re-characterize the affected women and their children as "veterans" of the conflict with the same status as the former Falintil guerrillas.

## Children Born of Rape
## and Their Mothers in East Timor

East Timor is the world's newest state, but it has inherited some complex problems from its history as a Portuguese colony and an occupied Indonesian province. During the lead-up to the August 1999 referendum on East Timorese independence, which was organized and administered by the United Nations, militia forces backed and trained by the Indonesian military carried out a systematic campaign of violence. When East Timorese nevertheless opted for independence from Indonesia, pro-Indonesian militia and Indonesian soldiers initiated a scorched-earth policy, terrorizing the population and committing widespread abuses, including the rape and sexual slavery of women and girls (Coomaraswamy 2001).

There are no accurate statistics on sexual violence during this period and consequently during the period of forced deportation and internment in West Timor. However, a wealth of anecdotal evidence shows that gender-based international crimes in Timor have been widespread since 1975 and were rife in the 1999 violence. Testimonies to this effect have been collected by the United Nations (Security Council Mission 1999; Special Rapporteurs 1999; International Commission of Inquiry on East Timor 2000); by human rights NGOs such as Amnesty International (Amnesty International 2001); the Indonesian Human Rights Commission KPP Ham (KPP-HAM 2000); Australian journalists (McDonald et al. 2002); and most important, East Timorese NGOs themselves (Godinho 2001; Fokupers 2000). The most comprehensive overview of sexual violence in Timor appears in Chapter 7.7 of the report by the CAVR entitled *Chega!* The CAVR recorded 853 cases of sexual violence but added:

> The Commission notes the inevitable conclusion that many victims of sexual violations did not come forward to report them to the Commission. Reasons for under-reporting include death of victims and witnesses (especially for earlier periods of the conflict), victims who may be outside Timor-Leste (especially in West Timor), the painful and very personal nature of the experiences, and the fear of social or family humiliation or rejection if their experiences are known publicly. These strong reasons for under-reporting and the fact that 853 cases of rape and sexual slavery, along with evidence from about another 200 interviews were recorded lead the Commission to the finding that the total number of sexual violations is likely to be several times higher than the number of cases reported. The Commission estimates that the number of women who were subjected to serious sexual violations by members of the Indonesian security forces numbers in the thousands, rather than hundreds. (CAVR 2005, 109)

While statistical data on rape is difficult to find, there is no data at all on how many children have been born of rape or how many orphans are in East Timor at the present time.[2] However, anecdotal evidence points to perhaps hundreds or even thousands of children born of war who have been kept and raised by their mothers despite the stigmatization and rejection of these women and children by their families or villages. Some individual examples can be cited of forced maternity in Timor— one of the earliest is contained in a report to the UN special rapporteur in 1997 (Aditjondro 1997)—but a full study has never been undertaken. Available evidence suggests, however, that children have resulted both from slavery-like conditions and forced marriage prior to independence, as well as from mass systematic rape used as a tool of terror during the post-referendum violence that engulfed East Timor in 1999. The *Chega!* report recounts testimony from survivors about how the "branding of women and their children not only resulted in social isolation, but also often resulted in severe psychological problems within the family" (CAVR 2005, 100).

Prior to 1999, an unverifiable number of Timorese women were abducted, raped, and impregnated by Indonesian soldeirs; these women were often kept captive under slavery-like conditions and later rejected by their families. An example of this pattern of violence is revealed in the testimony story of Beatriz Guterres, one of fourteen East Timorese women invited to Dili by the CAVR to participate in the commission's third national public hearing held April 28–29 on the theme of women and conflict:

> In 1991 another Kopassus soldier, Prada M, had duty in Lalerek Mutin. When my friends and I were in the rice field he shot in our direction. My friends pressured me so that I would become his wife in order to save myself. Because I was ashamed I stood and said, "OK. I'll cut myself in half. The lower half I'll give to him, but the upper half is for my land, the land of Timor." They said to me, "Don't be afraid, don't run. You probably must suffer like this because your husband was murdered, whereas you are still alive. . . . Our lives are the same." Then Prada M. walked with me and I answered each of his questions only with, "Ya." . . . I was just re-signed to my fate. We lived as husband and wife and I had a child. (Campbell-Nelson 2003)

Beatriz Guterres's story contains many common elements with other women's experiences of gender-based persecution during the Indonesian occupation of East Timor from 1975 to 1999. She was targeted and interrogated by the Indonesian military due to her husband's political activities, her husband was murdered, and her child died due to illness. She was forced into "marriage" and sexual servitude to three Indonesian soldiers over the following decade. She had two children and a miscarriage as a result of this servitude, and she was abandoned by the soldiers. In an independent East Timor, Beatriz was then stigmatized by her own family and village, and her children were not accepted.

A more acute form of gender-based violence occurred during the post-referendum violence in 1999: the systematic rape of East Timorese women in the context of the forced deportation of over 250,000 people into camps in West Timor. A leading women's NGO, Fokupers, has documented forty-six cases of rape during the 1999 violence: nine of them by Indonesian soldiers, twenty-eight by pro-Jakarta militias, and nine of them joint attacks by militias and soldiers. Eighteen were categorized as mass rapes (AFP 2000). "Many of these crimes were carried out with planning, organization and coordination," a Fokupers report states. "Soldiers and militias kidnapped women together and shared their victims" (AFP 2000).

In the camps in West Timor, where tens of thousands of women were forcibly deported, a fact-finding team in one study alone found 163 different cases of violence against 119 women and noted serious effects of sexual violence on women's health (Tim Kemanusiaan Timor Barat 2000). There is still a serious campaign by activists, including the new first lady of East Timor, Australian Kirsty Sword Guasmo, to obtain the release of several young women in the refugee camps of West Timor who are thought to be held against their will as "war trophies" by militia leaders (Farsetta 2001). The special rapporteur on violence against women, during a joint fact-finding mission in November 1999, together with the special rapporteur on extrajudicial, summary, or arbitrary executions and the special rapporteur on the question of torture, found evidence of widespread violence against women in East Timor during the period (from January 1999) and concluded that "the highest level of the military command in East Timor knew, or had reason to know, that there was widespread violence against women in East Timor" (Special Rapporteurs 1999, 24). They reported:

> Rape was used by the military as a form of revenge, or to force the relatives out of hiding. Much of the violence against women in East Timor was perpetrated in the context of these areas being treated as military zones. . . . Rape by soldiers in these areas is tried in military tribunals, and not before an ordinary court of law. Under Indonesian law, for a rape to be prosecuted it required corroboration—including the testimony of two witnesses. Women lived in a realm of private terror, for any victims or witnesses who dared to take action were intimidated with death threats.

As in the cases of sexual slavery of East Timorese women during the period 1975–99, children were born to women raped during or after the forced displacement. Sian Powell gives an example from the camps in an article entitled "East Timor's Children of the Enemy," published in *The Weekend Australian* on March 10, 2001:

> His mother is Lorenca Martins, now 23, a wistful East Timorese woman with eyes only for her child. His father is Maximu, a militia thug and rapist. Maximu raped Martins in a refugee camp near Atambua, over the border in West Timor, where she was exiled for six months. A member of the notorious Besi Merah Putih gang (Red and White Iron), he first violated her on December 8, 1999, in broad daylight, in the jungle. "It happened to many women (in

the camps)," she says. "If they saw a beautiful woman, they just took her." . . . A child of the new nation of East Timor, five-month-old Rai, is much loved by his mother. He is one of the first generation born free, yet his past will imprison him.

Rai is one of an unverifiable number of children born as a result of both the systematic sexual slavery and forced marriage of women under the occupation, as well as the mass rapes of the 1999 post-referendum violence. Although no systematic attention has been given to their status and rights relative to other children affected by the political violence in East Timor, anecdotal evidence suggests such children are at risk of abandonment to orphanages and likely to experience ostracization and impoverishment if kept by their mothers, due to the mothers' low social status in post-independence East Timorese society.

There is contradictory evidence regarding the relative likelihood of child abandonment due to forced maternity in East Timor.[3] The article by Powell suggests that no one who works with raped women in East Timor can recall women who have abandoned a child because it is the product of rape. But it seems unlikely that the author would have interviewed everyone working with such women, and women who have received services and support from NGOs may not be representative of the broader population of forced maternity survivors. The *Chega!* report details that there was at least once case of an unsafe abortion procured by a mother (CAVR 2005, 95). However, there is also some anecdotal evidence of close identification and loving acceptance of the mothers with these children, despite the extremely traumatic circumstances of conception (Daniel 2002, 34–35).

To give one example, the first wife of Xanana Gusmão, Emilia Baptista Gusmão, bore a child by an Indonesian army officer after one of the many interrogations she was put through to try to influence her husband to surrender (the Indonesian military routinely targeted the wives of guerrilla leaders to monitor any communications with the husbands in the mountains and to compromise the women as "unfaithful" wives, thereby isolating them from community support). The child died, and even after she had been forced to flee Timor for Australia and her relationship with Gusmão had broken down, Emilia said publicly that she would carry the grief of the dead child all her life "because that child was my child" (Aditjondro 1997, 12).

This willingness and ability of mothers to bond to children conceived under such circumstances rather than to define them as "of the enemy" may be explained by the low status of Timorese women and the fact that status may only proceed from motherhood in some circumstances (Sissons and East Timor Human Rights Centre 1997, 8).[4] It also may be due to the influence of Catholic teachings in Timor, as explored below. However, comparative work should establish how representative these anecdotes are of the population and to what extent they reflect instead the particular media framing of this conflict.

Despite some East Timorese survivors' proclivity for keeping their babies born of rape, it is nonetheless clear that numerous children of rape have been abandoned by their mothers. A nun, Sister Maria, is quoted whispering to a journalist that "a truth openly voiced in East Timorese society," is that in a Catholic orphanage "most of the children are mixed race, the babies of women raped by Indonesian soldiers." She notes that in the early years following the Indonesian invasion, orphanages were filled with "genuine" orphans because so many adults had been killed in military operations. Another complicating factor is that "genuine" orphans (the children of Timorese parents) generally are not treated well by ordinary Timorese; for example, many families take one to work as a house slave. Now, many of these are children of rape.

Those children of rape or sexual slavery that have been kept by their mothers are reportedly stigmatized by the wider community. Special Rapporteur Coomanaswamy's report asserted that "many of the women who were raped as virgins are single mothers who have suffered stigma in their communities after giving birth to children of Indonesian soldiers."[5] Media reports confirm that the "victims of militia rape and sex slavery continue to bear the scars of post-ballot violence in East Timor, facing ostracism on their return home" (AFP 2000). Abuelda Alves of the Timorese NGO Fokupers said bluntly of the women who are able to return home, often with babies who are the product of rape: "They are viewed as rubbish. Their families are embarrassed. Women who were already married, their husbands reject them" (AFP 2000). In this context the extremely low rates reported by Timorese women, especially those returning from forced deportation to the West Timor camps, is unsurprising (Powell 2001). Generally, women will only speak to nuns or priests, or, as lawyers assisting Timorese asylum-seekers have noted, they will not speak to anyone at all (Aditjondro 1997, 2).

The pervasiveness of the stigma against rape survivors and their children in East Timorese society is demonstrated by the euphemistic language associated with the issue. According to the translator's notes for the book *Buibere*, Timorese people "speak in hints"; there is not a clear Timorese word for rape. When used regarding women, the Portuguese words *violacáo* (violation) or *estraga* (damaged or destroyed) are used. The implication is that "victims of rape have had their whole sexuality, their 'womanhood' damaged, and they will never be the same again" (Winters 1999, 36).

In part, the stigma against survivors of rape and sexual slavery in East Timor derives from the unwarranted or misunderstood association with prostitution, which is deeply stigmatized in Timorese society. During the occupation East Timorese girls and women were perceived to have become prostitutes as a consequence of rape by Indonesian soldiers, high levels of unemployment, and the need to support themselves and their children, often in the absence of their men, who were away fighting or had been killed (Aditjondro 1997). These women are treated as prostitutes in terms of status, but they are called "wives" in "marriages" because under Indonesian criminal law, it is not possible to rape your wife.[6] This characterization also holds deeper meanings for a strongly Catholic society, which shall be examined further below. As evidenced above, another euphemism commonly used in Timor is that of orphan to refer to children born of rape. It is difficult to determine whether such obfuscation and use of euphemism is a strategy of denial, of benevolent protection against the stigmatization of illegitimacy, or stems from a genuine belief that marriage is not meant to be consensual. It is clear that the victims are often ascribed to have agency in a situation against all the evidence before a community. "One young woman I knew had four babies. I kept asking her why this had happened again and she just said there was nothing she could do" (Williams and Lamont 1999).

The picture that emerges, then, is that survivors of militia rape in East Timor and children brought to term as a result are experiencing a degree of hardship specifically related to society's construction of the sexual violence and its sequelae. The physical, economic, and psychosocial situation of the children is intricately bound up with the social status of their mothers, and vice versa.

Coomaraswamy's report concluded that the Indonesian state should take responsibility for these children. It is not clear what form the special rapporteur expected this responsibility to take, whether offers of citizenship, compensation, or even the facilitation of paternity suits, or how this would be taken forward in the absence of willingness on the part of the mothers to identify themselves for fear of communal stigmatization. This exemplifies the problem that despite the fact that widespread and systematic sexual violence has finally been acknowledged as prevalent in recent conflicts such as Bosnia, Rwanda, and Sudan, and that gender persecution is subject to international criminal sanction, unless the crime of genocide can be established, there is no clear position in international law for the offense of forced maternity on behalf of the mother, or any offense on the part of the child (Carpenter 2000).[7] This has resulted in a conceptual gap in the transitional justice mechanisms in East Timor, as well as a lack of appropriate programming attention by civil society actors. In the section below I briefly review existing responses to this issue in East Timor before suggesting some specific policy innovations that might be brought to bear to address more constructively the difficulties faced by these women and their children.

## Assessing Existing Responses to Children Born of War and Their Mothers in East Timor

The response to rape survivors and their children in East Timor has ranged from denial and silence to efforts to respond to their acute survival needs on the basis of a welfare paradigm that has reproduced conservative cultural conceptions of mothering and domesticity. Below, I describe both the lack of recognition of gender-based violence by existing transitional justice mechanisms and the ambivalent and somewhat problematic discourse associated with the Catholic church's response to the children and their mothers. Both of these patterns could be constructively improved, I then argue, by incorporating recognition of these women's and children's status as "veterans" of the war into discourse and practice in post-conflict East Timor.

### Gaps in Transitional Justice Mechanisms

The situation in East Timor has unfortunate resonances with other post-conflict societies in this regard: the plight of children born of war, defined as children born of rape or exploitation in an armed conflict situation, is generally met with silence or avoidance by transitional governments.[8] A quotation from Bishop Belo is paradigmatic. Belo wrote of "the path to freedom" and asked the international community to take heed of "the legacy of the past" when watching Timor struggle toward a democratic society "founded on the values enshrined in the Universal Declaration of Human Rights." He wrote, "Up to 3,000 died in 1999, untold numbers of women were raped and 500,000 persons displaced—100,000 are yet to return" (Belo 2001). The phrase "untold numbers of women" is poignant and literal—the story of women's experience before, during, and after the 1999 violence remains largely untold despite the extraordinary efforts of Timorese women advocates.

This silence both reflects and helps perpetuate a situation in which women are not being consulted or not participating adequately in transitional justice processes. Key decisions about the transitional justice model have been determined primarily by the transfer of power between male elites with very little democratic consultation. Key questions over what type of society East Timor should be in the future have been determined so far by reference to a limited and gendered focus on the personal and economic security of men in the society. As a Timorese editorial stated in mid 2001:

Women have played a critical role in East Timor's struggle for national independence. Both inside the country and in the diaspora, they courageously challenged the Indonesian invasion and occupation, as well as the international support that made these possible. East Timorese women have survived Indonesian military campaigns of violence, including forced sterilization, rape, and sexual slavery. They have shown themselves as leaders, though they are often pushed aside in political discussions. And women have continued to struggle for equality throughout the United Nation's administration of East Timor. Unfortunately, women's liberation is not a natural outcome of national liberation. (The La'o Hamutuk Bulletin 2001)

East Timorese women should have been in a better historical position than other groups to benefit from precedents in international criminal law. The jurisprudence of the Nuremberg and Tokyo tribunals after World War II has been strengthened by the practice and judgments of the ad hoc International Criminal Tribunal for the Former Yugoslavia and the International Criminal Tribunal for Rwanda. The Statute of Rome, which created an International Criminal Court to try genocide, war crimes, and crimes against humanity, is a reality at last. There are also several credible models of truth and reconciliation tribunals, such as those in South Africa and Chile. There are new hybrid "internationalized" criminal tribunals, such as that for Sierra Leone. Many states have implemented domestic legislation to cover war crimes such as genocide and are exercising universal jurisdiction, as in the case of Belgium.

In relation to prosecutions for gender-related crimes in international criminal law, the precedents have been even more revolutionary. The international criminal tribunals for both the Former Yugoslavia and Rwanda have successfully indicted, prosecuted, and convicted defendants for gender-based crimes for the first time in history, including rape as a crime against humanity and an element of genocide in the *Akayesu* case before the International Criminal Tribunal for Rwanda,[9] and the *Celebici*, *Furundzija*, and *Kunarac* cases relating to rape as torture, sexual slavery, and sexual acts as inhumane treatment before the International Criminal Tribunal for the Former Yugoslavia.[10] Article 5(g) of the new International Criminal Court Statute explicitly enumerates rape as a crime; in his April 29, 2004, report to the Security Council, the secretary general wrote, "In its resolution 1410 (2002), the Security Council stressed the critical importance of cooperation between Indonesia and Timor-Leste, and with UNMISET, to ensure that those responsible for serious crimes committed in 1999 are brought to justice."

In terms of the transitional justice process so far, this aim has not been realized. There is no real prospect that Indonesia will pay reparations or compensation to the victims of the occupation from 1975 to 1999. There is hope that the truth commission process and UN trials in

Dili will go some way to at least creating an accurate historical record of human rights violations in the territory, although this effort was set back by the acquittals in the Jakarta ad hoc trials. Expectations are dwindling that the United Nations will create an international tribunal that could force the Indonesian military to stand trial despite the recommenda tions by its own appointed commission of experts in 2005. There has been one successful verdict of rape as a crime against humanity in the Dili Serious Crimes Court, but it is against a low-level Timorese militia member who may soon be freed if the amnesty legislation is passed as expected as a result of the agreed Joint Truth and Friendship Commission with Indonesia. The Serious Crimes Unit finished its mandate in May 2005, having filed eighty-seven indictments accusing 373 individuals, but most of the accused remain at large in Indonesia.

Even with this bleak prospect of justice for violations in East Timor, rape of women has become so commonplace there as to be perceived almost as a non-issue. Few women have been prepared to bear the shame and horror of recounting their appalling experiences; the fourteen women who did find that courage before the Reception, Truth, and Reconciliation Commission were both brave and exceptional. So the ability of East Timorese victims of rape to gain justice remains low. As Hilary Charlesworth notes, "The players in international law crises are almost exclusively male. . . . The lives of women are considered part of a crisis only when they are harmed in a way that is seen to demean the whole of their social group" (Charlesworth 2002, 389).

Elsewhere I have analyzed the *Leonardus Kasa* and *Lolotae* cases, and I concluded that justice for women during the period of Indonesian occupation will be hard won through the courts. In the *Kasa* case, the special panel of the Dili District Court, in spite of the principle of universal jurisdiction, declared that it held no jurisdiction on the case as the rape had been perpetrated in West Timor, thereby precluding all further cases of women who had been forcibly removed from East to West Timor from being tried (Harris Rimmer 2004). Indeed many initial cases seem to have been addressed by domestic rather than international law, thereby leading to narrow court decisions and the exclusion of pioneering case precedents from the international stage. Even if there were to be a successful prosecution, it is unlikely that a judgment would result in the type of integration and financial outcomes that might be required for these families.

The United Nations could have initiated a precedent-setting trial through the Serious Crimes process, under which forced sexual slavery or forced impregnation would have been charged as a war crime, torture, or crime against humanity, and this process would have properly considered the idea of compensation or reparations for victims. According to Articles 7 and 8 of the Rome Statue and Sections 5 and 6 of

UNTAET (United Nations Transitional Administration in East Timor) Regulation 2000/15, the courts are entitled to prosecute the war crimes and crimes against humanity of rape, sexual slavery, enforced prostitution, forced pregnancy, enforced sterilization, or any other form of sexual violence of comparable gravity. Forced pregnancy was listed for the first time as an international crime in the Rome Statute, copied by the UNTAET Regulation. It is defined as "the unlawful confinement of a woman forcibly made pregnant, with the intent of affecting the ethnic composition of any population or carrying out grave violations of international law." This definition is strongly based on the practice of Bosnian Serbs forcibly raping and then detaining Muslim and Croat women so that they would bear Serbian children (MacKinnon 1994). Barbara Bedont and Katherine Hall Martinez comment that the forced pregnancy provisions were the most contentious part of the state negotiations around what should be included as an offense in the Rome Statute:

> While some negotiating took place on the other gender crimes, such as enslavement and gender-based prosecution, none of them was the subject of such intense opposition as forced pregnancy. (Bedont and Martinez 1999, 67)

Bedont and Martinez report further that the Vatican and a core group of Islamic states objected to inclusion of the offense due to their belief that the aim was to "criminalize the denial of abortion services"; they attempted to limit the offense to ethnic cleansing. The additional ground of violations under international law was added on the penultimate day, due to the weight of the example that during the Second World War, Jewish women were forcibly made pregnant so that they and their fetuses could be used for medical experiments (Bedont and Martiniez 1999, 68).

Kelly Askin argues that the phrase "other violations of international law" could include the intent to persecute, discriminate against, or torture the victim (Askin 2005, 144). She does not address the requirement of unlawful confinement. Many Timorese victims were not confined in a detention facility (although many Timorese women were raped while in detention).

Forced maternity in Timor was not an afterthought or unintended consequence. However, proving intent under the test required under the Rome Statute may be very problematic for women unless overtly genocidal intent is present. Prosecuting forced maternity only as genocide or where some other violation is present that harms the group diminishes the fact that the violation is against the woman herself, first and foremost (Dixon 2002, 702). An interesting idea is whether a criminal case could be brought on behalf of a child born of rape, rather than on behalf of the mother, and what the possible charges could be (Daniel 2002).

The question remains, however, whether trials are the preferred outcome for women survivors of violence or for children born of war. Many of the contributions to this volume raise the same dilemmas of breaking down the stigmatization involved with making claims public. Julie Mertus notes that court trials are inherently counter-narrative (Mertus 2000), despite the best efforts of investigators and prosecutors. The purpose of a trial is to prosecute and punish major war criminals for violations of the Geneva Conventions. Subsequently, a war-crimes trial can "only do so much" (Mertus 2000). Victims of sexual violence, for instance, if they are actually chosen to give testimony at an international criminal trial, only get to tell a piece of their story. Further, those experiences remain cloaked in secrecy, given that, out of necessity for protection and safety, the court sessions are often in private. The physical and psychological wounds as a consequence of rape and sexual abuse are also not part of accepted rape testimonies, and thus women's experiences are obfuscated, as emotions have no place in the courtroom. Further, the reconstruction of the story will entail reliving the traumatic event and may induce retraumatization (Herman 1992). In addition, the nature of a court trial is to discredit the evidence of the witness, which may exacerbate the devaluation of raped women who have come to testify at an international criminal proceeding (Henry 2003).

This leads us to question whether a war-crimes tribunal is the appropriate context for sexual violence survivors per se, let alone mothers of children born of war. Given the inherent limitations of a war-crimes trial (that a women's story is only partially told, that most survivors do not have access to this forum, that those who do may face ostracism upon return to their communities, and that retraumatization is a common response), perhaps a war-crimes trial is not the appropriate context for sexual violence survivors to reconstruct their stories and thus to recover from their traumatic experiences. On the other hand, testifying at an international criminal proceeding is potentially an empowering process for survivors, given that it constitutes a measure of justice because of its legal weighting, and it is, after all, an international proceeding that is broadcast to the whole world (Stanley 2003). There is mixed evidence presented in the CAVR report of the healing power of testimony: most of the testimony is in fact being given under false initials, although the courage of the fourteen women who testified at the National Public Hearing on Women and Conflict in April 2003 was applauded (CAVR 2005, 5).

Moreover, the outputs of a prosecutorial system are sentencing and reparations that usually focus on the offense of rape itself, not even on the offense of forced maternity, and do not relate to the status and maintenance issues faced by the mother and child in the longer term.[11] Reparations may be capable of being geared toward the future needs of children born of war (Wandita, Campbell-Nelson, and Leong Pereira 2006). There are excellent recommendations in Part 11 of the final CAVR report dealing with reparations that specifically identify as priority beneficiaries "children born out of an act of sexual violence whose mother is single" (CAVR 2005, 41). It is prefaced by this anonymous quotation from a CAVR interview with a victim of sexual slavery in Uatu-Lari, Viqueque, September 18, 2003:

> Because of the war I was used like a horse by the Indonesian soldiers who took me in turns and made me bear so many children. But now I no longer have the strength to push my children towards a better future. (CAVR 2005, 35)

### The Role of the Church

Since 1999 the church has carefully defined its role in Timorese politics. Bishop Belo stated in a circular on February 11, 2001, that "the whole process of formation of this people as a nation, all the problems which it will meet, all the challenges it will face, are the problems and challenges of the church. The church is one with the people in the gigantic task of building a new East Timorese nation" (in Walsh 2001).

That the church has played and, given its influence, is likely to continue to play an important role in shaping the culture of the newly independent country is undoubted. The question of the extent to which that influence will be of benefit to women is far more controversial. In many ways the struggle that the women of East Timor face in their dealings with the church is a microcosm of the complex way in which the Catholic church generally both supports women against certain types of oppression and aids in perpetuating other forms of oppression. Since the Second Vatican Council of 1962–65 (if not earlier), the church has increasingly been prepared to criticize governments for abuses of human rights. This is particularly the case when a predominantly Catholic population faces domination by a non-Catholic regime—a situation faced in Catholic Poland by Pope John Paul II during his younger days and a situation in which the East Timorese found themselves during Indonesian occupation.

But while the church and its leadership have been prepared to call upon leaders acting in the public sphere to behave in compliance with human rights, it has been far more ambivalent in respect to abuse visited on women within the private spheres of Church and home, where women have generally been exhorted to be passive and patient in response to their suffering.

Both of these phenomena can be seen in East Timor. Where women's suffering under Indonesian occupation can be equated with that of men, the church has been responsive and supportive of justice for victims. The church has stood in solidarity with those who suffered so greatly under the occupation and has resisted the attempts by the government to ignore past injustices. Yet when women's oppression has been gender specific—involving rape by occupying forces or domestic violence in the home—the church has often sided with the violators rather than the victims. This demarcation between the public and private realms to the detriment of women is reinforced by the response of international law to the transitional justice process in East Timor.

Thus, in the area of sexual offenses against women the church's influence has been ambivalent. On one hand, church leaders have advocated the importance of reparations for women who have been raped. They have also stood against the notion that women are to be regarded as sinful or impure by virtue of being raped. One member of the CAVR is a Catholic priest, Father Jovito, and he has consistently sided with women who were victims of the occupation. By his participation in the commission, he and the church can offer pastoral care and also learn about the gendered experience of occupation. One participant in the Women and Conflict hearings expressed concerns about the status of her marriage since her rape by a militia commander in 1999, and she was reassured by Father Jovito that rape cannot nullify her marriage (Campbell-Nelson 2003). Such reassurance by a leading Catholic priest on the question of law and morality could prove invaluable for the particular woman, but the story should also bring home to the church hierarchy the concern many women feel about these issues.

This understanding has spread to some of the population as well. A story reported from a 1999 "women to women" visit of the World Council of Churches and the Christian Conference of Asia details a horrific set of rapes, assaults, destruction of property, and a state of constant fear for the wife of a Falintil soldier:

> Fortunately her husband understands that it was not her fault. He told her that they all face risks for the sake of freedom, and that she too, as a woman, needs to face risks.

What she said sounded like a theological statement:

> This experience has given me a new perception of my womanhood and my power. I know that almost every other woman in my village has had a similar experience of violence. I am determined to fight for the life of other women. Men may fight with guns, but as a woman I will fight with the power

that I have gained out of my suffering, by raising my voice.
(WCC/CCA 1999)

However, while the official position of the Church is not to blame
women for the sexual crimes committed against them, the Church nonetheless has some degree of complicity in creating a culture in which
victims of sexual crimes, as well as children born of such violence, are
mistreated. It is reported in one village, for example, that Church workers refused to allow baptism for the babies born of rape or confession
for their mothers (Mydans 2001). More generally, the conservativism
of Timorese Catholic society, particularly in relation to issues of sexuality, is partly generated from a religion in which sexual purity, particularly for women, is given such significance. In light of this, it is
understandable that Ms. Laura Abrantes of Fokupers would note that
the culture of East Timor is in large part to blame for the reluctance of
rape victims to speak out, as publicity means shame and humiliation.
"Our culture does not allow women to speak out. For some it is very,
very difficult. They feel great shame, they are shy and cry" (Asia Human
Rights News 2001).

Thus, while the church has the potential to catalyze a progressive
response to victims of rape and their babies, in reality it has played a role
in contributing to the culture of East Timor that more generally leads to
women being blamed for their victimhood and discouraged from being
assertive of their rights to physical integrity. While the church has officially encouraged women to stand up to those linked to the occupation
who committed sexual violence, it has discouraged women from standing up to abuse and violence (including rape) within the home and family. The church is itself a patriarchal institution wedded to ideas of
hierarchy and obedience, and it has supported the patriarchal structure
of East Timorese society. Despite the genuinely heroic struggle of the
church against the occupation and the fight by the church for the rights
of all victims of the occupation, it must accept some responsibility for
creating a society in which women grow accustomed to violence and are
blamed when they try to escape from abusive relationships. In such circumstances it is hard to tell women who have been encouraged to be
subservient in their private lives suddenly to stand against the violence
of the occupiers.

This failure to understand the often grim realities of women's lives
reflects the church's difficulty in coming to terms with the role of wom-
en, outside the family—the concept of the woman as more than wife and
mother. The church does not permit the ordination of women and women
are excluded from its leadership and decision-making hierarchy (Offices
of the Congregation for the Doctrine of the Faith 2004).

This concept of womanhood resonates deeply with segments of East Timor's patriarchal population and serves to legitimate male control of and dominance over the household, including the use of violence to perpetuate that control. Even Father Jovito has admitted that Catholic doctrines can be mistaken in supporting the idea that men are dominant and that women should be "spiritual law educators" (Conway 1998). Yet the potential for the church to play a positive role in helping to transform East Timorese society remains significant:

> The Catholic faith is indeed deeply ingrained in the culture of East Timor. This makes the Church and its leaders, if not the strongest political entity, certainly the strongest moral authority in the land. With its non-partisan voice, the Church could do much in the struggle to end violence between youth gangs, between political parties and within homes. Or, it could continue to prioritize dogmatic ritual and emphasize the spiritual while largely ignoring the physical. How the Church chooses to use its enormous power in East Timor will be one of the great determining factors in the future of this nation. (Gabrielson 2001, 8)

At times the church and women's groups have spoken in unison, particularly on the issue of justice for victims of the occupation. Sadly, despite this coalition, it seems that the likelihood of formal justice for crimes under the occupation is beginning to look remote (see CAVR 2005, 101–2).

Yet, despite the end of the occupation, violence against women continues in East Timor. And when the church has been faced with husbands and fathers rather than occupying military or militia as the abusers, its response has been muted. It has been more concerned about shaming women who leave their husbands than in asserting the rights of those women to physical integrity and safety. However powerful a voice for women the church might have been over justice issues, its interests are not always the interests of women. Groups such as Fokupers recognize the need for women to speak with their own voices and through their own groups rather than relying solely on the church. Strategic alliances can and have been made between the church and women's groups, but until the church is prepared to see women as independent citizens and holders of rights in all contexts—including the home—then the positions of the two groups are likely to continue to diverge over time.

### From Orphans to Veterans? A Modest Proposal

Given these gaps and silences and the specific needs of this population, it is necessary to explore creative legal and policy options that would have as their aim the long-term integration, improved status, and financial security of these affected mothers and children. This, in turn, may have important benefits for the future of East Timor itself. Arguably, integration of these families into Timorese society and a transitional justice process that is durable and inclusive are critical to avoid generational conflict. In the end, it could be that, by following such a course of action, the government is more able to achieve its goal of economic survival in a sustainable manner. The image of a Timorese baby may come to symbolize a secure future rather than a tragic past. Likewise, the Catholic church has an opportunity to transform itself to oppose abuse and violence in all its form and to reconceptualize the role of women in East Timorese society. Should the church seize this opportunity, it could have an enormously beneficial impact on the women of East Timor for whom religion and the church continue to play an important personal and spiritual role.

Yet what are the available policy options in this regard, given the conservative nature of Timorese society, the cultural ambivalence toward women's sexual involvement with foreign troops, and the cross-cutting nature of the harms to be addressed? One simple but perhaps far-reaching proposal might be to expand the definition of "veteran" in the draft legislation currently before Parliament to include both the affected women and children as veterans of the conflict with the same status as the former Falantil guerrillas. This would serve the purpose of providing a pension to them and acknowledging the contribution these women made through their bravery on the path to independence. It would also have the effect of putting the situation of these families squarely into current transitional justice debates in Timor.

This does not mean that women and children should become combatants in the traditional sense of taking up arms. It means instead that the idea of contributing to the independence of the nation should be defined by more than the holding of a weapon or a formal commission, especially when the protection of noncombatants is breaking down. It is clear in assessing the patterns of sexual violence in Timor that rape was not a personal, sexual crime committed by individuals in an opportunistic manner. Mario Carrascalao, former governor of East Timor, was asked by the chair of the CAVR National Public Hearing on Women and Conflict what he thought the objective of violence against women was. He replied simply, "The aim of this violence against women was to reduce the power of the resistance."[12]

The issue of proper support for veterans and the question of what makes a veteran has been a hot debate in Timor since independence. The main source of tension is that the UN Mission did not convert the majority of Falantil veterans into the new standing army or reserve. Instead, the East Timor Defense Force is a small but well-trained army comprising fifteen hundred regulars (thirty-one of whom are women) and fifteen hundred reservists. Over seven thousand people applied for the last round of 428 places, leaving many disgruntled veterans without a position (Havely 2002).

On June 8, 2004, President Gusmão formally presented to the National Parliament the report of the Veterans Commission, which recommended forms of recognition and material benefits to the veterans identified through a long registration process. More than thirty-seven thousand people have been registered as having fought for independence during the occupation; nearly all are male combatants. Tensions about the long process led to a demonstration led by Cornelio Gama (known as L-7) of 120 veterans on July 19, 2004, outside the Parliament. The demonstration was dispelled by tear gas (UNMISET 2004). An August 2004 interview with President Gusmão shows a government willing to empathize and negotiate with this group:

*Gusmão:* I can understand the position of those former veterans, you know they previously were very clear about who the enemy was, it was the Indonesian military. They had a role as heroes in fighting against that enemy. Nowadays who are they? You know they haven't been given any special recognition from government, they're not clear about what their role is in determining the future of their country. So I think it's very understandable that they are feeling marginalized now and disgruntled with the government and expressing that through demonstrations.

*Werden:* Well what do you think the government should do with people like L-7?

*Gusmão:* I think it's really important that the government sit down and listen to what they're saying and really make a special effort to respond in some way, either with training or employment opportunities for these people, not just because they have the potential to disrupt stability in the future, but because they really are genuinely deserving of attention and special support. (ABC Radio Australia 2004a)

In short, this group of veterans has links with the leadership and the ability to make itself heard, but children born of war and women survivors do not. And yet, why should combatants be given priority over these women and children?

Such a proposal, if implemented, could work to counter the prevailing inertia and patriarchal attitudes that account for many of the hardships these survivors and their babies face, while drawing strategically on other nationalist imagery currently at a premium in post-independence East Timor. In part, the reluctance to incorporate a concern with gender-based violence into existing mechanisms for legal redress in East Timor is due to ambivalence about the idea of women as fighters for independence during the occupation and the discomfiture regarding their status as "wives" of Indonesian military. The language still used to describe these women is filled with euphemism and the assumption of consent through formal rituals such as "marriage" and "wives"—even more pronounced than terms like "comfort women." Likewise, the language used to describe the babies is, at worst, one that invokes shame and illegitimacy and at best, one that evokes pity for their status as "orphans," despite the fact that they may be in the custody of their mothers.

Policy proposals that would reconstruct these mothers and their children as wartime veterans or symbols of post-conflict reconciliation rather than as the bearers of shame and stigma will not resolve their situation overnight. However, it may provide a language and a framework in which women's groups and progressive elements within the church can engage in work to promote greater social inclusion for these families, and such terminology may be validating to the survivors and their children themselves. In addition, a step such as this would go a long way toward meeting some of the economic as well as social needs of the women and children.

## Conclusion

This chapter argues that the well-being and ability of children of rape to claim their rights is related to the social and legal status of their mothers, and this status needs to be addressed in transitional justice debates. Within Timor, there is a definite ambivalence about the idea of these women as contributors to independence during the occupation and discomfiture regarding their status as "wives" of Indonesian military.

This could be changed by simple policy choices; one discussed above would be to redefine veteran status to include victims of rape and sexual slavery as well as the children born as a result. Another solution might be to convene a special hearing of the Truth Commission (or its successor) or the Parliament to deal with the rights of children born of rape. The government of East Timor, with international donor funding and encouragement, might also institute a special assistance program for affected families that includes a public antidiscrimination campaign. There is a precedent for such a campaign in the domestic violence program run in 2003. International donors and humanitarian organizations working in East Timor could help to advocate for such an initiative.

The first imperative is to gain qualitative and quantitative data on the situation of these children and their mothers. Such work should endeavor to shift the approach from a covert welfare program to a rights-based framework and to approach the children as rights-bearers and the subjects of analysis rather than byproducts of a crime or sin. The position of the women of East Timor is not static, and there are some causes for optimism. When Natércia Godinho-Adams addressed the UN Security Council, she pointed out that, while the Indonesian occupation had been a tragedy for the women of East Timor, the crisis had also created a number of new opportunities for them:

> Men's and women's roles changed substantially during the years of conflict and social disruption since 1974. A significant number of women assumed active roles in the clandestine liberation front and the armed resistance. They were soldiers, they smuggled medication, food, armament, and information to the resistance movement hiding in the mountains. . . . In the absence of the male household head, women assumed new responsibilities in traditional male income generation. East Timorese women want to build a society that will respect their newly acquired post-conflict roles, and will not force them to return to traditional powerless roles. (Godinho 2001)

Thus, the position of women and, correspondingly, of their children is fluid. While in many ways East Timor remains a patriarchal and traditional society, there are social forces that suggest that women could start to play a greater role in post-conflict reconstruction and governance. The question is whether the society can shed the euphemistic veil that lies over a substantial social and moral issue in East Timor—that of the reintegration and acceptance of women who have suffered human rights violations and the right of their children to a future.

## Notes

[1] UNFPA statisticians used the latest satellite technology to record the addresses of every household to make sure everyone in the country was counted, using several thousand workers with GPS systems (ABC Radio Australia 2004b).

[2] On April 28, 2003, Mario Carrascalão, former governor of East Timor, stated in his testimony to the CAVR National Public Hearing on Women and Conflict that in 1985 there were forty thousand orphans in Timor.

[3] Future comparative work on this topic would need to establish both how prevalent child abandonment is in this context relative to other cultural contexts

and how prevalent it is for children born of forced maternity relative to other conflict-affected children in East Timor.

⁴ Note the comment by a young refugee woman to Sissons that "women are always second. Women are trusted only to have children and feed them."

⁵ The well-being of children born of rape and raised by their mother is inextricably bound up with the social status of the mother herself. The special rapporteur's report continues: "The women are having a very difficult time, not only because of poverty, but because the sight of these children often reminds them of rape" (Coomaraswamy 2001).

⁶ Chapter XIV, "Crimes against Morals," in the Indonesian Penal Code (KUHP) contains the relevant sections dealing with rape and sexual offenses. There is no official English translation of the code. In the 1999 report to the Commission on Human Rights by Radhika Coomaraswamy, special rapporteur on violence against women, the section on the causes and consequences of rape and sexual offenses, Article 285 of the Penal Code, was translated: Any person who, by using force or threat of force, forces a woman to have sexual intercourse with him out of marriage, shall, being guilty of rape, be punished by a maximum imprisonment of 12 years" (E/CN.4/1999/68/Add. 3, 21 January 1999). See also Scott and Cristalis 2005, 100.

⁷ Even in domestic criminal law there are no parallels. There have been cases of "wrongful life" suits brought against doctors for negligent advice in torts law where a sterilization has not been successful, and there is the possibility of pursuing a father who has abandoned a child for maintenance in family law.

⁸ As Carpenter notes in the introductory chapter, this silence is also still evident within international law and the international community.

⁹ Prosecutor v. Jean-Paul Akayesu, 2 September 1999, ICTR-96–4–T.

¹⁰ Prosecutor v. Dragoljub Kunerac, Radomir Kovac, and Zoran Vukovic, Judgement, Case No. IT-96–23/1–T, 22 February 2001; Prosecutor v. Anto Furundzija, 10 December 1998, ICTY-95–17/1–T.

¹¹ For example, on April 12, 2006, a domestic court in the Democratic Republic of the Congo made history by convicting seven soldiers to life imprisonment for rapes treated as crimes against humanity based on the application of the Rome Statute provisions. The court fixed an amount of $5,000 reparations payable to each victim of the rapes. On the evening of December 21, 2003, the FARDC battalion based in Songo Mboyo raped at least 119 girls and women (International Justice Tribune 2006).

¹² Testimony given April 28–29, 2003, in Dili.

# References

ABC Radio Australia. 2004a. "East Timor: First Lady Calls on PM Alkatiri to Respond to L-7." *Asia-Pacific.* Australia: ABC.

———. 2004b. "East Timor's Population Is on the Rise." *Asia Pacific.* Australia: ABC.

Aditjondro, George J. 1997. *Violence by the State against Women in East Timor—A Report to the UN Special Rapporteur on Violence against Women, Including Its Causes and Consequences.* Newcastle: East Timor Human Rights Centre.

AFP. 2000. "Scars of Vote Violence Remain Real for Many East Timor Women," November 19.

Amnesty International. 2001. *East Timor: Justice—Past, Present and Future.* London: Amnesty International.

Asia Human Rights News. 2001. "East Timor: Sexual Violence Including Rape Was a Deliberate Military Strategy against East Timorese Women." Available on the ahrchk.net website.

Askin, K. 2005. "The Jurisprudence of the International War Crimes Tribunals." In *Listening to the Silences: Women and War*, ed. H. Durham and T. Gurd. Leiden: Martinus Nijhoff.

Bedont B., and K. Hall Martinez. 1999. "Ending Impunity for Gender Crimes under the International Criminal Court." *The Brown Journal of World Affairs* 6, no. 1: 65–85.

Belo, Bishop Carlos Filipe Ximenes. 2001. "To Forge a Future, Timor Needs Justice for the Past." *The Sydney Morning Herald*, August 28.

Campbell-Nelson, Karen. 2003. "East Timor Women Must Tell of Atrocities by Indonesians." *The Jakarta Post*, June 9–10.

Carpenter, Robyn Charli. 2000. "Forced Maternity, Children's Rights and the Genocide Convention: A Theoretical Analysis." *Journal of Genocide Research* 2, no. 2: 213–34.

Charlesworth, Hilary. 2002. "International Law: A Discipline of Crisis." *The Modern Law Review* 65: 377–92.

CAVR (Commission for Reception, Truth, and Reconciliation). 2005. *Chega! Final Report.* Dili: CAVR.

Conway, Jude. 1998. "Fokupers: Report of Women's Seminar Dili 25 November 1998." Dili: Fokupers.

Coomaraswamy, Radhika. 2001. *Report of the Special Rapporteur on Violence against Women, Its Causes and Consequences, Ms. Radhika Coomaraswamy, Submitted in Accordance with Commission on Human Rights Resolution 2000/45.* Geneva: United Nations Commission on Human Rights.

Daniel, Joana. 2002. *No Man's Child: The War Rape Orphans.* Master's thesis, Ludwig Boltzmann Institute of Human Rights, University of Vienna, Vienna.

Dixon R. 2002. "Rape as a Crime in International Humanitarian Law: Where to from Here?" *European Journal of International Law* 13, no. 3: 697–719.

Farsetta, Diane. 2001. "East Timorese Refugees in Militia-Controlled Camps." In *The Devastating Impact of Small Arms and Light Weapons on the Lives of Women: A Collection of Testimonies*, ed. M. H. C. Pua. New York: WILPF for International Action Network on Small Arms (IANSA) Women's Caucus.

Fokupers. 2000. *Gender-based Human Rights Abuses during the Pre- and Post-Ballot Violence in East Timor.* Dili: Fokupers.

Gabrielson, Curt. 2001. "The Church in East Timor." *Institute of Current World Affairs: Letters*, August 1.

Godinho, N. 2001. *UN Security Council "Arria Formula" Meeting on the Implementation of Security Council Resolution 1325.* New York: United Nations.

Harris Rimmer, Susan. 2004. "Untold Numbers: East Timorese Women and Transitional Justice." In *Global Issues, Women, and Justice*, ed. S. Pickering and Caroline Lambert. Sydney: Federation Press.

Havely, Joe. 2002. "Timor's Army Marches out of the Jungle." *CNN.com*, May 19.

Henry, Nicola. 2003. "Secrecy, Silence, and Sexual Violence in International Criminal Proceedings." Paper presented at Activating Human Rights and Diversity, Byron Bay NSW, Australia, July 1–4.

Herman, J. 1992. *Trauma and Recovery: The Aftermath of Violence from Domestic Abuse to Political Terror*. New York: Basic Books.

International Commission of Inquiry on East Timor. 2000. *Report of the International Commission of Inquiry on East Timor to the Secretary-General*. New York: United Nations.

International Justice Tribune. 2006. "Seven Congolese Soldiers Sentenced to Life." Justice Memo. Paris: International Justice Tribune.

KPP-HAM. 2000. *Full Report of the Investigative Commission into Human Rights Violations in East Timor*. Jakarta: KPP-HAM.

The La'o Hamutuk Bulletin. 2001. "Editorial: Women and the Reconstruction of East Timor." *The La'o Hamutuk Bulletin*, August.

McDonald, Hamish, Desmond Ball, James Dunn, Gerry van Klinken, David Bourchier, Douglas Kammen, and Richard Tanter. 2002. *Masters of Terror: Indonesia's Military and Violence in East Timor in 1999*. Canberra Paper #145. Canberra: Strategic Defense Studies Centre, Australian National University.

MacKinnon, C. 1994. "Turning Rape into Pornography: Post-modern Genocide." In *Mass Rape: The War against Women in Bosnia-Herzegovina*, ed. A. Stiglmayer. Lincoln: University of Nebraska Press.

Mertus, J. 2000. "Truth in a Box: The Limits of Justice through Judicial Mechanisms." In *The Politics of Memory: Truth, Healing and Social Justice*, ed. I. Amadiume and A. An-Na'im. New York: Zed Books.

Mydans, Seth. 2001. "Sexual Violence as Tool of War: Pattern Emerging in East Timor." *New York Times*, March 1.

Offices of the Congregation for the Doctrine of the Faith. 2004. "Letter to the Bishops of the Catholic Church on the Collaborations of Men and Women in the Church and in the World." Vatican: Congregation for the Doctrine of the Faith.

Powell, Sian. 2001. "East Timor's Children of The Enemy." *The Weekend Australian*, March 10.

Scott, Catherine, and Irena Cristalis. 2005. *Independent Women: The Story of Women's Activism in East Timor*. London: Catholic Institute for International Relations.

Security Council Mission. 1999. *Report of the Security Council Mission to Jakarta and Dili*. New York: United Nations.

Sissons, Miranda E., and East Timor Human Rights Centre. 1997. *From One Day to Another: Violations of Women's Reproductive and Sexual Rights in East Timor*. Melbourne: East Timor Human Rights Centre.

Special Rapporteurs. 1999. *Report on the Joint Mission to East Timor Undertaken by the Special Rapporteur on Extrajudicial, Summary or Arbitrary Executions, the Special Rapporteur on the Question of Torture, and the Special Rapporteur on Violence against Women, Its Causes and Consequences: Situation of Human Rights in East Timor*. Geneva: United Nations.

Stanley, Elizabeth. 2003. "Torture Silence and Recognition." Paper presented at Activating Diversity and Human Rights, Byron Bay, NSW, Australia, July 1–4, 2003.

Tim Kemanusiaan Timor Barat. 2000. *Violence against IDP/Refugee Women— Report of TKTB (Tim Kemanusiaan Timor Barat) Findings in IDP/Refugee Camps in West Timor*. Jakarta: Tim Kemanusiaan Timor Barat.

UNMISET. 2004. *Progress Report of the Secretary-General on the United Nations Mission of Support in East Timor (29 April to 13 August 2004)*. S/2004/669. New York: United Nations.

Walsh, Pat. 2001. "East Timor's Political Parties and Groupings." *Briefing Notes*. Canberra: Australian Council for Overseas Aid.

Wandita, G. K. Campbell-Nelson, and M. Leong Pereira. 2006. "Gender and Reparations in Timor-Leste." Forthcoming case study in *Engendering Reparations: Recognising and Compensating Women Victims of Human Rights Violations*, edited by Ruth Rubio-Marin. New York: International Center for Transitional Justice.

Williams, Louise, and Leonie Lamont. 1999. "Rape Used Over and Over as a Systematic Torture." *The Sydney Morning Herald*, September 11.

Winters, Rebecca. 1999. *Buibere: Voice of East Timorese Women*. Darwin, N.T.: East Timor International Support Center.

WCC/CCA (World Council of Churches/Christian Conference of Asia). 1999. *Women to Women: A Solidarity Visit to Indonesia and East Timor, 23 June–1 July 1999*. Geneva: World Council of Churches.

# 5

# Silent Identities

## Children Born of War in Sierra Leone

## Giulia Baldi and Megan MacKenzie

According to a recent study by Physicians for Human Rights (PHR), 215,000–257,000 women and girls may have been affected by sexual violence in Sierra Leone's ten-year civil conflict (PHR 2002). Of these assaults, an estimated 9–10 percent resulted in pregnancy, with more than 20,000 newborns. One might argue that the immediate human rights issue is the physical and mental health of these raped girls and women, not the children born out of the horrific experience of rape. This might be seen as particularly the case when these women are children themselves, at times twelve or thirteen, who had been abducted from their home by rebel forces, repeatedly raped by several men—sometimes child soldiers of their same age—and sometimes forced to become the "wife" of one of the rebels. Although the first concern for young mothers is easily justifiable, the babies born from rape still exist, and their presence is manifest in Sierra Leone. These children will be a part of the generation growing up right after the war, and they deserve the same right to a life with dignity as the rest of the population, the right to survive and thrive, to receive an adequate education, to have access to medical treatment, and to have a family who loves them and takes care of them.

Our case study of Sierra Leone builds on the broad definition of children born of war conceived in the first chapter of this volume. Our work confirms the validity of a framework that does not limit the category of children born of war to those born of rape but also includes those born of violence and exploitation. We do this by arguing that there are common stigmas attached to, and fluid boundaries between, children born as a result of rape that occurred during the war, children born in captivity to girls and women abducted into armed groups (both those raped

78

and sexually enslaved and also the children of consensual unions) and children being raised only by their mothers. Children born as a result of rape from either civilians or rebels, as well as children born of consensual relationships with men from the rebel forces, are sometimes referred to locally as "rebel babies." A child born from a relationship that was considered illegitimate by the community or by family members, such as a consensual relationship between male and female soldiers who were not married, may face the same stigma and rejection from the family and community as a child born as a result of rape. Therefore, the stigma of "rebel baby" is linked both to the act of rape and to the paternity of the child. Throughout our analysis, when we refer to children born of war we include this broad category of children that are marginalized because of their paternity.

An endless number of questions and issues could be raised around this complex topic; many of these are taken up elsewhere in this volume. This chapter focuses on three central themes: first, the limited existing knowledge about children born as a result of sexual violence; second, the obstacles to obtaining information about these children; third and finally, how interviews with mothers of children born during the war in Sierra Leone enhance our understanding of the experience and needs of the children and shed light on the gaps in the international response to the issue.

Although information is available and attention is beginning to be paid to this issue, children born as a result of sexual violence largely remain an invisible category in existing human rights discourse. There is hardly any literature focusing on children born from rape in Sierra Leone, either as a specific study population or as direct right-holders under international law. This is an indication that these children are still in the shadows, are hidden behind the statistics of pregnancies as a result of rape. Much of the qualitative and quantitative data on these children can be found only in epidemiological evidence and gray literature concerning sexual violence in conflict situations.

Given these constraints, we base our analysis on a triangulated approach of textual analysis of existing literature on sexual and gender-based violence in Sierra Leone, supplemented by semi-structured interviews with humanitarian practitioners in the region, and open-ended, first-person interviews with former women and girl soldiers conducted in Sierra Leone between October and December 2005. The women interviewed were all former soldiers who are now in a training program operated by CARITAS, a Catholic organization, in Makeni, Sierra Leone. Fifty women between the ages of eighteen and thirty-two were included in the specific population of interviewees. The women had been involved in various factions of the fighting forces in Sierra Leone in a range of capacities and were from diverse regions in the country. The women were asked a variety of questions, including the number of children they had, the age at which they gave birth, where they gave birth, who the father was, where he is now, if the father accepts and supports his child, what they will tell their children about their father (particularly for those mothers who admitted to having a child from a rebel), and if their families accept the children.

We acknowledge that former female soldiers are only one group of women that experienced sexual violence and gave birth to children as a result; however, there is diversity in the children of our interview population in terms of the circumstances of their birth, the paternity of the children, the relationships of the women to the children's fathers, and the relationships between the children and their mothers. For example, within this population some of the children were described as products of rape from rebels and were identified as "rebel babies"; some children were products of legitimate relationships with rebels; and some children were born as a result of rape by civilian men. Thus, although we admit the specificity of our sample population, we argue that the range of circumstances surrounding the birth of their children sheds light on some of the overlapping experiences and child protection issues for the broader population of children born of violence during war.

Our study is one of the first that offers both a comprehensive analysis of the existing data about children born from sexual violence in Sierra Leone and testimonies from mothers of some of these children. We acknowledge that the perspectives of the mothers are not the same as the perspectives of children themselves; however, we believe that the mothers interviewed for this case study provide rare insights into the needs and experiences of the children they gave birth to during the war. Therefore, our case study is offered as a unique perspective on the issue of children born of violence during war.

We begin with a historical analysis of the use of sexual violence during conflict in Sierra Leone and what is known about the number of pregnancies that have resulted. Following this, we look at the obstacles to gathering information about children born as a result of violence. A discussion of the layers of stigma associated with children born as a result of violence is given. An overview of the humanitarian response to sexual violence, pregnancy, and children born as a result of violence is followed by an analysis of the gaps in terms of the response to the protection needs of these children and some recommendations.

## Conflict and Sexual Violence in Sierra Leone:
## Background

The ten-year civil conflict in Sierra Leone has been described by human rights organizations as one of the most brutal in human history, characterized by particularly inventive atrocities, including high-profile massacres, abductions, and mutilations. The estimated death toll from this war ranges from thirty thousand to seventy thousand. Amnesty International reports that "abduction and sexual violence against girls, often very young, have been among the most abhorrent and distressing features of the conflict" (Amnesty International 2000). Although mainly perpetrated by the Revolutionary United Front, rape was used as a tactic of war during the civil conflict in Sierra Leone by all factions of the fighting forces.

As in many conflicts, rape was used to terrorize populations, to shame families, and to divide communities; in Sierra Leone it was also used strategically to violate and undermine various social norms. For example, in order to sever young soldiers' ties with their families, and to demonstrate their loyalty to the armed group, some boys and young men were forced to rape their sisters, mothers, and even grandmothers. Fathers were made to watch while their daughters or wives were gang raped. Young girl virgins were targeted and raped. Mothers were raped in front of their children. Pregnant women were raped with objects to try to abort the fetus (Amnesty International 2000; Human Rights Watch 2003).

In many instances girls and women were rounded up by rebels, brought to rebel camps, and then subjected to individual and gang rape. Although women of all ages were victimized, young girls under seventeen—those thought to be virgins—were particularly targeted. Rebels would threaten to kill parents if they did not turn over their children. PHR reported that "in many cases the abductees were gang raped, beaten, starved, tortured, forced to walk long distances carrying heavy loads, and told they would be killed if they tried to escape" (PHR 2002). A recent report by Mazurana and McKay that focuses on girls in military and paramilitary groups paints a picture of systemic sexual violence against girls in particular. Among the 48,216 estimated total force of child soldiers in Sierra Leone, 7,500 are estimated to be girls. Most girls and young women reported that their primary roles were as cooks and fighters, followed by porters, "wives," and food producers. All respondents who reported their primary role as fighter also reported that they were forced to be "wives" (Mazurana and McKay 2003). These are a few examples of the horrors that females and males had to endure during the conflict in Sierra Leone.

The statistics of war rape in Sierra Leone are staggering. Some studies estimate that between 70 and 90 percent of abducted women and girls were raped during the war. One study conducted by Medicins Sans Frontiers of 1,862 female victims of sexual abuse found that 55 percent had been gang raped and 200 had become pregnant. PHR conducted a comprehensive study on sexual violence in Sierra Leone, sampling 1,048 households in three internally displaced persons (IDP) camps and one community with a large number of IDPs: Mile 91 Township. The camps/locales included in this study represented 91 percent of the registered IDP population in Sierra Leone. Of the respondents, 9 percent (ninety-four) reported one or more war-related sexual violence experiences. Study participants also reported sexual violence among 8 percent (396) of females and one-tenth of one percent (six) of male household members. One hundred fifty-eight additional women did not report sexual violence, but either became pregnant or experienced vaginal bleeding, pain, swelling, uterine pain, vaginal discharge, or sexually transmitted diseases. If these women are included in the statistics on war-related sexual violence, the percentages may be as high as 11 percent (554 out of 5,001). Respondents also reported that the majority of the abuses occurred between 1996 and 1999, with most of these occurring in 1999.

Despite its widespread use, there has been considerable silence surrounding wartime rape in Sierra Leone. This silence has serious consequences for the victims and for children brought to term as a result. In terms of health, it is reported that the majority of girls who returned from the fighting forces have STDs, including syphilis, gonorrhea, chlamydia, and HIV/AIDS. STDs are sometimes treated, especially when demobilization is conducted through a rehabilitation or interim-care center, or if an NGO has established primary health-care services. HIV/AIDS is a significant threat to the women and their communities. Testing is seldom available or may not be offered unless requested. If the girl is HIV-positive, no treatment exists at this time (until antiretroviral therapy is available) other than supportive counseling. This also has major implications in terms of the risk of mother-to-child transmission of HIV (Mazurana and McKay 2003, 27). Health concerns such as HIV/AIDS are compounded for many mothers by lack of access to basic health care, food, shelter, and clothing.

## Children Born as a Result of Sexual Violence in Sierra Leone

The starting point for many analyses of children born of violence is statistics on war rape. It is known, for example, that while sexual violence occurred throughout the ten-year civil conflict, the majority of sexual violence was committed between 1997 and 1999. From this, it can be inferred that children born as a result of violence during the war may be between the ages of four and fifteen, with a majority of the children between six and nine. Prevalence data on sexual violence gives some indication of the number of such children. For example, as noted above, PHR has estimated that 70 to 90 percent of females who were abducted by the fighting forces were raped, and the total number of women and girls thought to have experienced sexual violence in Sierra Leone in the broader population is between 215,000–257,000 (PHR 2002). Rape-related pregnancy rates inferred from the sources cited above are consistently in the range of 9–11 percent. Given even this conservative approximation, the number of resulting pregnancies following the possibly 215,000–257,000 rapes would be close to 20,000.

However, records have not been kept for how many of the rape-related pregnancies resulted in live births. As a result, accurate statistics about the number of children born as a result of sexual violence are unavailable. There has been no exhaustive study on the number of babies born as a result of rape in Sierra Leone. Official statistics on sexual abuse during the war in Sierra Leone remain relatively speculative, both because of under-reporting and because of cultural factors, fear of retaliation, and distrust of authorities and the justice system. Until the rebel offensive in Freetown in 1999, there were no statistics kept on rape and no programs—governmental or nongovernmental—designed to treat victims of sexual assault.

Another source of information about children conceived from sexual violence may be found in statistics relating to infant mortality and abortions. Knowledge about both the number of pregnancies due to rape that are brought to term and the level of care given to the children when they are born is key to understanding the issue of children born of sexual violence in Sierra Leone. There are anecdotal links to sexual violence between the increases in both the infant mortality rates and the number of abortions in Sierra Leone. A recent mortality survey conducted between 2000 and 2001—one year after the major escalation in violence in the Sierra Leone conflict—by the International Rescue Committee (IRC) in Kenema District showed a dramatic increase in child mortality, especially neonatal and infant mortality, compared to 1999 data. Neonatal mortality rose to 50 in 1,000 live births, while infant mortality was 330 in 1,000 live births, probably due to an increase in the incidence of diarrhea, malaria, measles, and ARI within these age groups. In regard to the 21 percent of child deaths in which the child did not receive any treatment by a health provider, it would be interesting to know how many of these children were born from rape during the war. This information could provide a possible proxy for health-care-seeking patterns for children born of rape by their mothers, at least within the district covered by the survey.

In addition to the increased rate of neonatal mortality, the trend in the rate of abortions would also be useful to know in order to have a better idea of the destiny of the children of rape. Anecdotal reports suggest an increased trend (Human Rights Watch 2003). An abducted nurse who was interviewed in the report explained that, although there was an increase in the number of women who wanted to abort their fetuses, a large number of women were forced to carry their pregnancies to term by their rebel husbands or captors:

> Many women and girls became pregnant as the result of the rape[s] they were subjected to. Although some women were reportedly able to abort without the knowledge of the rebels using traditional herbal treatments, the majority had no choice but to carry the child to full term. . . . Medical personnel were instructed by a rebel doctor, Dr. Lahai, not to perform abortions, distribute birth control, or advise that traditional herbal treatments be taken, as the rebels felt that too many people had died and they needed to increase the population. Many women did have miscarriages because of the brutal rapes and trauma they were subjected to by the rebels, as well as the difficult conditions in the bush. (Human Rights Watch 2003)

Dangerous childbirth practices during the conflict were also reported, especially for pregnant girls who participated in fighting, such as pushing on the pregnant girl's abdomen when labor contractions were strong and beating the mother when she was giving birth. Numerous maternal and infant deaths in the bush were reported (Mazurana and McKay 2003, 15). In Sierra Leone there are also reports that babies were left behind (for example, at a clinic or with captor husbands in the bush), died in the bush, or were killed by rebels—sometimes by cutting them out of the pregnant girl's body. Many girls died in the bush from abortions induced by the girls themselves, by nurses and doctors in rebel forces, or by traditional birth attendants.

There are several obstacles to identifying and gathering information beyond rape and health-care statistics that help to shed light on the complexity of the issue of children born of sexual violence in Sierra Leone. First, the number of women in Sierra Leone that continue their silence surrounding both rape and the paternity of their children due to stigma make it difficult to identify children born as a result of sexual violence and to gather information about their circumstances and vulnerabilities. Second, although there was a significant escalation in sexual violence between 1997 and 1999, sexual violence was used during the entire period of conflict in Sierra Leone. This has meant that, unlike cases such as those in Bangladesh, there is no limited specific time period in which mass rapes occurred and no massive cohort of children that are identifiable as war babies.[1] Third, the issue of ethnicity was not a factor in the use of war rape in Sierra Leone. Unlike the situations in Rwanda and Bosnia, rape was not used as a form of ethnic cleansing or to force the birth of children of a particular ethnicity. Further, intertribal marriage is common, and there are few and subtle physical differences among different ethnic groups in Sierra Leone. As a result, children cannot confidently be identified by their physical characteristics as products of rape, and their paternity can easily be hidden. It would seem that the widespread knowledge of the use of rape in Sierra Leone over a long period of time, and the inability to distinguish babies born as a result of sexual violence by their physical features, would decrease the stigma for both the children born of sexual violence and their mothers. However, despite the fact that it is almost impossible to identify children born as a result of sexual violence by their physical characteristics, there is often a supposition that single, young mothers, or mothers who had children at a very young age, were likely victims of sexual violence. This is particularly true for women who admit to having had a relationship with a soldier or a rebel during the conflict. Because rape was widely used as a tactic of war, sexual relationships during the conflict are often assumed to have been coerced.[2] The impact of this for children born during conflict is that they may have a greater chance of being stigmatized if they are born to a single mother from a consensual relationship than if they remain in a two-parent family, even if in the latter case their mother was forced to marry her former rebel captor or the man who raped her. Thus, it is not only the specific category of children born as a result of sexual violence that is stigmatized and will face social obstacles in Sierra Leone; rather, a broader population of children born to young mothers or to single mothers may be given the local "rebel baby" stigma.

In addition to stigma from the larger community, many single mothers in Sierra Leone face obstacles such as poverty and rejection by their families. The layers of their marginalization directly affect their children; therefore, it is important to consider the factors that have contributed to, and the circumstances of, single motherhood in Sierra Leone in order to better understand the conditions in which children born during the war will be raised. Of the fifty women interviewed in Sierra Leone, over 50 percent were single mothers, and 30 percent admitted that the father of at least one of their children had left them and was not helping to care for the child. Only 23 percent of the fathers lived in the same town as the mothers, and 19 percent of the fathers were dead. According to the women interviewed, the reasons they were raising their children alone include the fact that the large number of deaths that occurred during the war meant that many fathers had died; some women were abandoned by the fathers and do not know where they are; the displacement of people that occurred during the war and during the disarmament, demobilization, and reintegration process often physically separated fathers from their children; and women may have escaped from their military captors and may have avoided the fathers of their children.

Even children born during conflict to single mothers that later marry may also experience stigma. One source of stigma is from men within the community who father a second or third child with mothers who have had children during the war. Twenty-four percent of the women interviewed admitted that they had children born from at least two fathers. One woman in particular explained that she had a child from a rebel and then had married the father of her second child after the war. She disclosed that her first child lives with her mother because her husband will not accept the baby as his. Historically in Sierra Leone, it is not uncommon for women to remarry or to marry after having a child with another man. Typically, the new husband accepts the other children as his. However, since the end of the conflict in Sierra Leone, some men have refused to accept a woman's child if he suspects that the baby is a result of rape or has a father that is from a particular armed faction. The implications for children born from sexual violence are significant. In a society where it has been commonplace for men to accept children born before their marriage to a woman, when they choose to reject a child because of the possible circumstances of his or her paternity it stigmatizes the child.

In addition to the problem of stigma, certain children born during the conflict face massive social obstacles. One obstacle is that many of their mothers—whether the children are born as a result of rape or not—have limited parenting skills because they were involved with the fighting forces from childhood and have never been "mothered" or parented themselves. Many girls were abducted at an early age by rebels, and some lost both their parents through displacement or death during the conflict. For example, 23 percent of the women interviewed in Makeni gave birth before the age of fifteen. Some of these women were abducted at such a young age that they cannot remember life before they were with the fighting forces. This phenomenon is not only true for former girl soldiers; due to violence and displacement, large portions of the general population lost, or were separated from, at least one parent.

Despite this, women are the ones who most often take responsibility for raising children born during the conflict based on the gendered assumption that women "naturally" have the skills they need to parent. It cannot be concluded that women and girls who were never parented will naturally have skills necessary to parent a child. Although some organizations like CARITAS and the Conforti Welcome Home help teach women basic parenting skills, such as how to breastfeed, it needs to be acknowledged that a generation of children will be raised by women—many of them alone—who have little knowledge of simple parenting skills. To say this will have lasting social impacts on this generation of children is an understatement.

Two additional points of concern for these children are the relationship between them and their mothers and the information that they will be given about their fathers if they were born from sexual violence or from rebel fathers who have abandoned them. In terms of the relationships of the children with their mothers, from the interviews conducted with women in Sierra Leone, the bond between mothers and their children does not seem to have been affected negatively by the paternity of the children. Despite the fact that these children may have been born due to rape or sexual slavery, most women explained that they had no problems bonding with their children. Only one woman admitted that things were "strange" between her and her child and that she had a hard time accepting the child because of his paternity.

Another distinctive pattern in Sierra Leone, in comparison to other cases described in this volume, relates to the children's eventual knowledge about their paternity. When asked what they will tell their children about their fathers, the majority of the women admitted that they planned on divulging the truth. In response to this question, one woman looked confused as she explained, "I will tell her the truth . . . that her father was a rebel." Although CARITAS and other local organizations are trying to encourage community members to avoid using terms like "bush baby" and "rebel baby," little attention has been given to the role mothers play in informing children about their paternity. This is most likely due to the fact that few organizations are spending time interviewing women and asking them how they will approach the issue of paternity with their children. We are not recommending that women be encouraged to lie to their children about their fathers; however, some attention must be given to the fact that many children born during the conflict will be informed about the violent circumstances of their birth. Efforts must be made to understand how such knowledge will influence this second generation of war-affected children and to provide assistance in helping them cope with this information.

## The Humanitarian Response
## to Children Born of War
## in Sierra Leone

There are no agencies that deal exclusively with children born as a result of sexual violence during the conflict in Sierra Leone. These children have generally been dealt with indirectly through programs directed at victims of sexual violence, displaced persons and orphans, or homeless women and girls. Organizations that have been effective at addressing sexual violence include UNICEF, the IRC, and CARITAS; issue-specific international NGOs such as the Marie Stopes Society (MSSSL); and local or regional NGOs, including the Forum for African Women's Educationalists (FAWE). One example of organizations that deal with children born from rape indirectly is the IRC, which provides comprehensive maternal-child health services and sexual violence services and is operating an interim care center for former child soldiers in Kenema District. The IRC was the first international NGO to focus on sexual violence and has been providing sexual-violence services under the umbrella of a safe motherhood program that addresses basic reproductive health. Similarly, CARITAS operates interim care centers for former child soldiers and provides training for former girl soldiers while offering child care for their babies.

Organizations that focus on more specific issues related to children born during the conflict include MSSSL and Leonet. MSSSL, an international NGO headquartered in the UK, focuses on reproductive health matters. Many sexual violence survivors are among the seven thousand women treated every month at the three MSSSL outpatient clinics in West, Central, and East Freetown. The organization accepts referrals for abandoned children and rape survivors in need of delivery services through the Child Protection Committee on Sexual Violence. Like other members of the committee, MSSSL does not test patients for HIV, partly because of concerns over the lack of an official national policy on confidentiality of test results. This is of particular concern for children born of sexual violence because, although MSSSL's concerns regarding confidentiality are valid, hundreds of pregnant women are passing the disease to their babies even though transmission could be prevented through medication.

Leonet is an American NGO that works with unwanted and street children, many of whom are sexual-violence and abduction survivors. Leonet has been assessing young girl abductees who have been rejected by their families due to resulting pregnancies. UN agencies, government ministries, and NGOs refer the "most hopeless" cases to Leonet. In 2000, the organization was operating day-care and skills-training centers in Kissy, the eastern part of Freetown, which was hardest hit by the January incursion of 1999, and it was also operating in Port Loko. The building was given to the organization by the community and was open to other single mothers and their babies; however, the program is at a standstill because of lack of funds. The suspension of this program is partly due to the difficulty in attaining funding for programs that do not address what are considered "immediate and direct" post-conflict concerns. Children born as a result of sexual violence are not considered a direct security concern or an emergency issue for most agencies in Sierra Leone.

FAWE is another organization that has focused more directly on children born from sexual violence. FAWE is a pan-African NGO that has been successful in promoting education for girls; however, it has also addressed the issue of pregnancy and childbirth as a result of sexual violence. FAWE expanded its mandate to respond to the needs of rape victims after the January 1999 incursion by rebels in Freetown and, because there was a vacuum, became the primary organization providing medical and counseling services to rape survivors. Its ultimate goal, in service of its mandate, is to get these girls back to school. As of March 2000 FAWE had been 100 percent effective in negotiating with parents of girls who had babies as a result of rape to keep them in school. One of the greatest successes of FAWE, in terms of its attention to children born from sexual violence, has been the work it has done to sensitize the community at large to accept girls who have become pregnant as result of rape and to accept their children.

The Italian NGO COOPI (Cooperazione Internazionale) is an excellent example of a program response to children born of sexual-violence survivors at the country level.[3] COOPI is an Italian NGO that has been working in Sierra Leone since 1967. One of the three interim-care centers created within COOPI's social reintegration program for sexually abused girls, the Conforti Welcome Home has been one of the most effective programs in addressing the needs of children born as a result of sexual violence. Conforti Welcome Home was set up in Freetown as a temporary facility for pregnant girls and child-mothers who could not go home for reasons ranging from the inaccessibility of their area of origin to fear of rejection by their families. Entirely supported by UNICEF, the home hosted 200 mothers and 193 children (there were seven miscarriages) from 1999 to 2002. The primary objective of the Conforti Welcome Home was both to reunite the mothers and their babies to their families and communities and to help the mothers and their children overcome stigma and possible initial rejection. A family-tracing and reunification program was run within the center, which successfully reunited 75 percent of the cases.

What is particularly interesting about COOPI are the unique tools it used to try to create awareness and to discourage stigma about children born of rape, including extensive radio campaigns, one to two TV appearances, community involvement, and the creation of community child welfare committees composed of local authorities, politicians, education and health practitioners, and the police forces. Community leaders and NGO workers, including those from the IRC, CARITAS, and UNICEF, praised the effectiveness of these methods in informing a broad population about the negative effects of rejecting and stigmatizing children born of rape and in encouraging community members to accept all children born during the conflict.

## Conclusion

There are exceptionalities to the Sierra Leone case study that add breadth to an understanding of the complexities of the issue of children born of war. Certain parallels can be drawn among our analysis and others in this volume, including the challenges in gathering information beyond health-care and rape statistics about children born during conflict—particularly due to the silence surrounding wartime rape. Our case study is distinguished from some analyses of war rape by the fact that there was an extended use of war rape with no short-term incursion of mass rapes and no single identifiable group of children born of rape. This fact, combined with the reality that there are few and subtle differences among ethnic and tribal groups in Sierra Leone, has meant that children born of war rape cannot be identified by their physical features.

The interviews with mothers in Sierra Leone greatly contributed to a deepened understanding of children born of war. Although we do not argue that the needs and experiences of children are identical to those of their mothers, clearly there is much knowledge to be gained about lives of children born of war from the women who gave birth to them. Specifically, children who are unwanted by mothers either because they are products of rape or because they are not accepted because of their paternity may be neglected, abandoned, killed, or aborted. Also, for those children raised by their mothers, the care that they receive is affected by the fact that many of the mothers have not been parented themselves; they may have been raised either by extended family or by rebel groups. In addition, the information that mothers give their children about their paternity will directly influence how children born of war identify themselves.

Perhaps the most valuable insights about children born of sexual violence during war, inferred from interviews with fifty mothers, relates to the fluid boundaries between who is stigmatized as a "rebel baby" and who is not. Our analysis outlines the overlapping vulnerabilities of children born from rape by militant forces or civilians, and children born from consensual relationships that were considered illegitimate by the parent's family or community members. It is not only children born of rape that are marginalized, abandoned, and isolated in Sierra Leone. Our conclusion substantiates the framework of this volume, which broadly conceives of children born as a result of sexual violence and exploitation rather than focusing narrowly on children born as a result of wartime rape. This framework provides room within which to investigate a broad category of children and war in Sierra Leone and the complexities of the issues of stigma and marginalization within post-conflict communities.

It is only when this compound relationship between paternity and stigma is understood that effective practices regarding the care and protection of children born of war can be developed and evaluated.

Our overview of the international and national response to the issue of children born as a result of sexual violence helps highlight some of the common gaps that need to be filled in post-conflict Sierra Leone. The first gap is the more general issue of the lack of international funding for women and girls in post-emergency contexts. Specifically, children born as a result of sexual violence are not viewed by organizations and donors as directly affected by the conflict; thus, they fall out of most post-conflict aid beneficiary categories. Funding often follows the big waves of emergencies, and once a conflict and its immediate aftermath are over, funds tend to disappear. This common trend makes it difficult to gain funding and attention for a "silent emergency," such as children born of sexual violence, or for long-term issues such as stigma and the reintegration process of these children and their mothers within their communities.

Related to the issue of funding is the lack of follow-up monitoring of the conditions of children born as a result of rape from a child-protection and health perspective. There is an urgent need for longitudinal studies on this target population, especially post-conflict. The long-term mechanism through which stigma operates should be investigated. There is also an ethical issue that should be carefully considered: while it is necessary to collect individual information on the children and their mothers in order to look at specific outcomes such as morbidity, mortality, any proxy for stigmatization and marginalization of children, adoption, institutionalization, and the proportion of street children, it is extremely important not to violate privacy and therefore risk creating even more stigma around these children.

More research must also be focused on the impact of the outreach tools used by COOPI to encourage accepting children born as a result of rape and children born as a result of consensual relationships with rebels—both are referred to as "rebel babies"—into the communities. Mazurana and McKay have looked at these "sensitization" tactics as well as some traditional and religious rituals that can also be used to impose community normative behaviors—such as forbidding girls and their babies to be called "rebel wives" or "rebel babies." Mazurana and McKay argue that when they are contextually appropriate and safe, produce no further trauma, and do not contravene international human rights standards, rituals can be an important part of the healing process when children return to their communities (Mazurana and McKay 2003, 29). More information needs to be gathered about the effectiveness of awareness campaigns and traditional rituals in relation to decreasing the stigma attached to children born during conflict.

Perhaps the most glaring gap in the response to children born as a result of sexual violence is the continued silence surrounding the category of children born of sexual violence during war. Even though agencies and organizations like FAWE, UNICEF, and COOPI have indirectly addressed the issue of children born during the war, there still seems to be a reluctance to identify these children as a separate category of beneficiaries. Children born of violence are only provided for indirectly through programs designed to deal with sexual violence. The result of this is that these children remain a hidden category, and concern for their welfare has not been mainstreamed into child-rights programming in conflict situations (Carpenter, et al. 2005). These children must be identified as a specific category of war-affected child who possess human rights and are worthy of being direct beneficiaries in post-conflict policy and programming.

## Notes

[1] The term *war babies* is borrowed from media coverage and scholarship on Bangladesh's children born of rape after the genocide (see d'Costa 2003).

[2] This supposition is contested by testimonies from interviewees who explained that it was not uncommon for women and men to fall in love during the conflict—even while fighting as soldiers together—and have legitimate, consensual relationships. Women resent the fact that they have had to justify their relationships with soldiers or rebels.

[3] Information on the experience and achievements of the Conforti Welcome Home was gathered through a phone interview with Phillip Kamara, its former coordinator.

## References

Amnesty International. 2000. "Sierra Leone: Rape and Other Forms of Sexual Violence against Women and Children." London: Amnesty International. Available on the web.amnesty.org website.

Carpenter, Charli, Kai Grieg, Donna Sharkey, and Giulia Baldi. 2005. *Protecting Children Born of Wartime Rape and Exploitation in Conflict Zones: Existing Practice and Knowledge Gaps*. Pittsburgh: University of Pittsburgh Ford Institute of Human Security.

D'Costa, Bina. 2003. "War Babies: The Question of National Honour." In *The Gendered Construction of Nationalism: From Partition to Creation*. PhD diss. Available on the drishtipat.org website.

Human Rights Watch. 2003. "'We'll Kill You If You Cry': Sexual Violence in the Sierra Leone Conflict." Human Rights Watch report 15:1(A). Available on the hrw.org website.

Mazurana D., and S. McKay. 2003. *Girls in Fighting Forces in Northern Uganda, Sierra Leone, and Mozambique: Policy and Program Recommendations*. Montréal:

Canadian Agency for International Development and International Centre for Human Rights and Democratic Development.

PHR (Physicians for Human Rights). 2002. "War-Related Sexual Violence in Sierra Leone. A Population-Based Assessment." *Journal of the American Medical Association* 287: 513–21. Full report also available on the phrusa.org website.

# 6

# Uganda's Forgotten Children of War

## EUNICE APIO

In Uganda today, armed conflict directly affects some 300,000 children. The effects of the conflict are widespread—affecting livelihoods, access to basic services, infrastructures, and family life, with child abduction topping the list of major abuses of children, often with long-term consequences for their lives and communities (Witter 2002). In Uganda from 1986 to date, the war between the Lord's Resistance Army (LRA) rebels and Government of Uganda (GoU) has inflicted immense suffering and an almost complete breakdown of socioeconomic systems that served to regulate the livelihoods of the local people. An entire generation of children has grown up with no knowledge of peace; the terror of war has been their daily reality, underlining every aspect of their lives and preventing them from gaining access to the most fundamental services—health care and immunization, a sufficient diet, and schooling (Knox-Musisi 1998).

Generally, authors on the northern Uganda conflict have agreed that children have borne the brunt of the northern war greatly, but no deliberate mention has been made of those children who have emerged as a consequence of the war. Such categories may include children born as a result of abduction and sexual abuse by their mothers' captors, the rape of women by soldiers at internally displaced persons' (IDP) camps, children born at army detachments, and others. Therefore not much has been written particularly on these children born in military units, notably the case of children born of girls abducted and forced into "marriages" among the LRA rebel ranks. Whereas various authors hold a

---

I gratefully acknowledge the financial support of the Belgian government through the Belgian Technical Cooperation in Uganda, which funded my master's thesis.

common view that child mothers returning from the LRA enclaves are indeed more traumatized than those returning without children, little is mentioned regarding the status of the children who come back with them.

In northern Uganda the LRA/GoU war has seen over twenty-five thousand children abducted since the onset of the war, with at least half said to be girls (Human Rights Watch et al. 2003). These girls are forced to become "wives" to the LRA ranks.[1] By mid 2001 these girls had reportedly borne thousands of children in captivity.[2] These children, born in the bushes of southern Sudan or northern Uganda, sometimes find their way back, along with their mothers, to the world of "freedom." Sometimes mothers escape, and other times they are released.[3] Upon their return there are measures in place to facilitate their assimilation into family and community. The children born in captivity, however, have been largely overlooked by organizations reintegrating child soldiers.

This chapter presents the findings of a study conducted in the Gulu district located in the northern part of Uganda. The goal of this study was to unearth the experiences of children born in conflict situations in northern Uganda between 1990 and 2003, with a special focus on children born of the LRA. The research aimed to assess the impact of captivity on these children and to evaluate whether programming to reintegrate children born of the LRA into Ugandan society is effectively addressing the particular needs of these children. Given its geographic limitation, the study has no claim to be generally representative.[4] However, the findings here provide preliminary and long overdue information on the most forgotten category of children in armed conflict.

The study relied on one-on-one interviews (structured and unstructured in-depth interviews with children born of the LRA and their formerly abducted mothers), focus-group discussions, key informants, and documentary probes. Families/guardians of the mothers, staff of nongovernmental agencies, and individuals working and/or interacting with former child soldiers, as well as the cultural/traditional leadership of the Acholi tribe, were interviewed. Questionnaires helped the researcher gather relevant data; the subjects were asked a number of questions relating to psychosocial status and experiences of children born in captivity as well as those born in the Acholi settlement, who served as a control group. Data was gathered on sixty-nine children born in captivity, with thirty-six younger than one year and thirty-three older than one year. Thirty-two were male and thirty-seven female. The mothers and/or guardians of these children were also interviewed, and the data were compared with those of a sample of eighteen children born in families within the Acholi settlement.

As discussed by both Carpenter and Mertus in this volume, research on sensitive topics carried out in ongoing war zones must involve ethical and methodological constraints. In this case, for example, the inhabitants of Gulu Municipality were suspicious of most people and too resignedly traumatized to contribute significantly and easily to change. Poverty also characterized this part of Uganda to the extent that every new face was viewed as a potential source of quick revenue and/or handouts. Preliminary rapport with key agencies in the area and local cultural leadership overcame such hurdles and lent legitimacy to the study as a potential platform for international concern. Perhaps for elite contacts, especially the politicians, it was a relief to know that the research was purely academic and not aimed at affecting the political situation in the district and/or country.

Direct interviews with the children and their formerly abducted mothers also presented the risk that singling them out would contribute to their marginalization. Preliminary interviews, however, suggested this risk was primarily salient outside the reception centers. Direct interviews at reception centers were much easier and less ethically problematic, as the interviewees easily identified themselves with all in the center community. In the centers they belonged with one another and spoke freely, as though they were still with the rebels. Thus, in the end, interviews with child and mother associated with the LRA were restricted to inside the centers.

An additional risk involved safety for mothers who had escaped captivity rather than being released by the rebels. These young mothers feared revealing certain aspects of their background lest the rebels gain access to that information and trace them and their families. The assurance that the media and the rebels would not have access to the data garnered the confidence of the respondents in support of the study. To protect the identities of the respondents, numbers rather than names were associated with each interview transcript.

The findings detailed below indicate that in the northern Uganda context, both the formerly abducted and those born in captivity experience trauma requiring particular attention upon integration. Yet there are scarcely any specialized measures in place to support the assimilation of these children into Ugandan society once their mothers leave the LRA enclaves. Children born of the LRA face both the traumatic impacts of life in captivity and of subsequent rejection when introduced in their mothers' families and communities. The provisions in place to assist with assimilation tend to be directed only at formerly abducted people rather than to the children brought to term in captivity.

This chapter is organized as follows. In the first section I provide a background to the conflict in northern Uganda and outline the specific rights violations evident against children born in captivity as well as the particular situation faced by their mothers upon escape from the LRA. In the next section I describe the services available for reintegrating and rehabilitating child soldiers in Gulu with an eye toward children born in captivity and their mothers. I conclude by suggesting the need for additional programming and fact-finding in this area.

## Background to the Conflict

Gulu Municipality is located in the Gulu district of northern Uganda. From the colonial days until recently, Gulu was the provincial headquarters of northern Uganda.[5] The majority of the inhabitants are members of the local Acholi tribe. Gulu is in the center of a war that has raged on relentlessly between the GoU/Uganda People's Defense Forces (UPDF) and the LRA since 1986.[6] The war traverses an entire region of northern Uganda, directly affecting more than two million people and resulting in mass displacement into camps and neighboring districts (CSOPNU 2006). The camps are characterized by very poor living conditions and mounting insecurity.[7] Still characterizing the conflict is abduction, with the majority of victims under the age of eighteen; those abductees are used as porters, combatants, sex slaves, and cooks. This situation has continued for almost two decades, spilling over to all the districts of northern Uganda and some parts of eastern Uganda. Given the levels of extreme insecurity, schools have closed and many other social amenities are not operational.

As described in several recent reports, every life in Acholi land has been affected by the war, with abducted children, mourning families and communities, and IDPs features of the landscape (see, e.g., Foundation for Human Rights Initiatives 2002; Brumaci and AVSI 2001). But perhaps one of the most outstanding facts about this war is that completely new categories of children have emerged in northern Uganda. Thousands have been born during or as a direct result of the conflict, including (1) children born in IDP camps out of rape; (2) children born in army/UPDF detachments or war fronts; (3) children born of the LRA and largely mothered by abducted girls who have now returned to freedom; and (4) children born of the LRA and still with them.

This case study focuses on children born as a result of abduction by girls into the LRA ranks. Over twenty-five thousand children have been abducted and re-abducted by the LRA since the onset of the insurgency eighteen years ago (Human Rights Watch et al. 2003). According to Human Rights Watch, abducted girls are distributed to rebel leaders as sex slaves, a fact confirmed during the interviews with former child soldiers at the reception centers. By mid 2001 these girls had given birth to thousands of children in captivity, excluding those who returned from captivity with children or pregnant.[8] By some estimates this figure would form approximately one-quarter of the children held by the LRA. According to Human Rights Watch, by the late 1990s more than eight hundred children had been born to the LRA "wives" at Jebelein camp alone in southern Sudan. This view is reinforced by Brumaci and AVSI, who argue that girls as young as twelve are given to rebel commanders as "wives," and many have now given birth in the LRA enclaves in Sudan (Brumaci and AVSI 2001).

Although it is increasingly acknowledged by human rights organizations that the sexual slavery of girls results in babies, human rights organizations have been slow to give explicit or systematic attention to the status of children born in captivity; where such references are made, they are often based on conjecture rather than fact-finding.[9] This chapter argues that children born as a result of sexual slavery in armed conflict do exist and are among the most forgotten and vulnerable groups of war-affected children. As the primary research below confirms, these vulnerabilities are heightened when they return with their mothers into communities affected by the very conflict that saw their emergence.

## Physical and Psychosocial Difficulties of Children Born in LRA Captivity

Children conceived as a result of their mother's abduction into the LRA may be categorized into three groups: those still in captivity; those born in captivity but demobilized with their mothers; and those conceived in captivity but born after demobilization. The research suggests that these sets of children have had different experiences.[10] Yet despite this variation, children born as a result of sexual slavery in the LRA as a whole are particularly vulnerable to a number of both physical and psychosocial deprivations. In the sections below I compare the health and psychosocial situation of those children demobilized with their mothers both to children within the broader Acholi settlement and to international standards for health and development in order to illuminate their particular traumas, needs, and vulnerabilities.

### Physical/Health Impacts of Birth in Captivity

Based on the data gathered, it is evident that children born in captivity are deprived relative to children within the broader population in terms of food, medical care, and other basic means of life. They have also been exposed to violence and the threat of death since birth, and some have lost their mothers. All of these factors have an impact on the child physically and developmentally.

As children fathered by LRA soldiers, these children originally formed part of an outlawed group in danger of confrontations with the UPDF, especially during Operation Iron Fist, a GoU effort to flush out the LRA once and for all. At the same time, other LRA enemies, including the SPLA (Sudan People's Liberation Army) and sometimes Sudan government troops, posed a great threat to the security of the children during confrontations. During such ventures many children's lives were lost alongside those of the mothers and the LRA. Some children clung to their dead mothers' bodies, and many may have remained undiscovered, at the mercy of the wild; others sustained bullet wounds. To strap a baby on one's back and turn around to open fire at an enemy was not uncommon for abducted girls turned mothers.

All the children born of the LRA have suffered starvation and lack of proper food during the entire length of time spent with the LRA.[11] For children born within the enclaves of the LRA, food was scarce right from birth because the breastfeeding mothers did not have enough to eat. Supplementary foodstuff was also hard to come by in the unfriendly jungles of southern Sudan and northern Uganda. The situation was often worsened by the need to be constantly on the run from opposing forces, including the UPDF. This has had an impact on the rate of growth and the general health conditions of the children.

Comparatively, the eighteen children born in the Acholi settlement (the control group) were better off, with adequate sources of food except in Unyama IDP camp, where families lived mainly on relief handouts. That some children born in captivity suffered starvation in the hands of the LRA is further suggested by the twenty children who mentioned food as the thing they love most.

Medical attention for these children while in the bush was also compromised relative to children in the Acholi settlement. Of the sixty-nine children born in captivity, sixty-six were not immunized until their return. Two other children were not yet immunized at the time of the research because they had only just returned from captivity with their mothers. One other child was immunized back in the Sudan LRA camp because he was the son of a high-ranking commander and thus benefited from the preferential treatment of accessing health facilities in Khartoum.[12]

The eighteen children not born in captivity had all been immunized as recommended by the Ministry of Health guidelines in Uganda, which is in line with World Health Organization guidelines. This implies that the health of children in the enclaves of the LRA was jeopardized relative to the broader population. Exposure to immunizable diseases (including tuberculosis, poliomyelitis, diphtheria, tetanus, whooping cough, hepatitis B/haemophilus influenza type B, and measles) could threaten the child's survival and development.

Some children born in captivity and now back in the Acholi community are growing to maturity without having undergone immunization. These are children who bypassed reception centers and joined their families immediately upon return. Since the majority of abducted children are from less educated families, the families may not take it upon themselves to follow up on the child's health.

The sixty-nine children born in captivity all had near-uniform responses about basic issues affecting the lives of children in captivity. According to the child mothers interviewed, parenting in the confines of the LRA enclaves was a most difficult experience. One hundred percent of the mothers sampled acknowledged that life in captivity before motherhood was extremely harsh, with inhumane conditions ranging from disease, starvation, thirst, rape, and arbitrary punishment to imminent death. Sixty-four percent (forty-four) of the mothers emphasized that life was even worse when one became a mother; still, 36 percent (twenty-five) of mothers thought life had a brighter lining for them the moment they became mothers while with the LRA. The forty-four mothers gave examples of worsening conditions that included the extra responsibilities associated with raising a child: feeding, clothing, fleeing from enemies, tending to a sick child, having no access to pre- and post-natal services and, as a result, the agony of watching one's infant struggle to overcome imminent death. The 36 percent of mothers claiming a better life in captivity as a mother pointed out that mothers were sometimes exempted from drastic tasks like going into battle, arbitrary punishment, and, for mothers attached to high-ranking LRA commanders, young maids or helpers (young captives) to support them.

One hundred percent of the children interviewed mentioned a severe lack of basic needs (food, medicines, water, clothing, and shelter). The children witnessed dreadful sights, suffered from horrible diseases that were in most cases never treated (particularly mentioned were diarrhea, cholera, malaria, and worms), had no knowledge of school whatsoever, and had to accompany their mothers to the battlefields. Upon return to their communities the children often continued to lack basic needs because their mothers are economically insecure.

### Psychosocial Effects of Birth in Captivity

In addition to physical deprivation, children born in captivity face a number of specific forms of psychosocial difficulty based on practices such as stigma, lack of parental care, negative labels, lack of security, and lack of the ability to play.

All sixty-nine children sampled had been fathered by members of the LRA. Their mothers were girls abducted from northern Uganda and forced to become "wives" to the LRA ranks. All these children had returned to freedom fatherless, either because their fathers had been tallied among the battle casualties (thirty-nine children) or were still marauding in the bush of southern Sudan and northern Uganda (eighteen).[13] This means fifty-seven percent will never set eyes on their fathers again, while forty-three percent may, depending on what prevails later in terms of peace: whether their fathers surrender or come out of the bush, whether they become interested in and manage to trace the children, and whether mothers are willing to acknowledge their paternity.

Typically, unless killed or lost during battle, mothers are with their children. But these mothers are not receiving the support they need to parent effectively or to raise their children. A few children who have no parents at all have been discovered. Some later reunite with their mothers when they come back; for some others, their grandparents are traced and involved (discussed later in this section under integration).

Naming practices affect these children's identity, sense of self, and ability to reintegrate. All of the sixty-nine children sampled had acquired names upon birth. This complies with the legal provision that every child has the right from birth to a name (Convention on the Rights of the Child). However, forty-nine of them had names with meanings depicting the plight of their mothers. Such names included Komakech (I am unfortunate), Anenocan (I have suffered), Odokorac (Things have gone bad), and Lubanga Kene (Only God knows why this happened to me).[14] These names compile all the bad experiences of a mother into a name and give it a life in the nature of her baby. In this way the baby is turned into a living reminder of her sufferings. This affects her integration as well, as the scars of her captivity will be by her side in the form of her child and reinforced by the child's name.

For the child, the name can lead to self-chastisement; the child may consider himself or herself an accident that brought overwhelming suffering to his or her young mother. At the reception centers the social workers attempt to give these children new names, for example, Komakech is converted to Komagum (I am fortunate) and Odokorac to Odokober (Things have turned good). The mothers, however, are reluctant to pick up these changes. They prefer the old names.[15]

Nine of the children had ordinary names, not associated with their mother's predicament. These children were conceived in captivity and delivered in reception centers upon their mother's return. The officers at the reception centers gave them ordinary names, mostly after relations of the mother. Another eleven children conceived or born in captivity had names given, for example, by the LRA father after his relatives, himself, or his Arab friends, or were named after LRA leader Joseph Kony as a tribute. Except for the name Joseph Kony, which is associated so much with suffering in Acholi, such names have no negative implications.

In terms of nationality, all of the sixty-nine children, based on the responses given by their mothers and the humanitarian agencies, are considered Ugandans. The traditional leadership in Acholi also stressed this fact. All these people backed up their responses by the GoU's 1995 Constitution, which specifies citizenship by birth. Both the LRA and the mothers of the children are citizens of Uganda by birth, and thus their children are also Ugandan citizens. Children allegedly picked up from battlefields by UPDF or others are also citizens of Uganda, since they were found within battlegrounds either in Uganda or in southern Sudan confrontations with rebel LRA who are also Ugandans.

The interviews sought to evaluate what recreational games if any, these sixty-nine children enjoyed. This is in line with the internationally codified right to play, which is designed to ensure proper growth and development. Of the children, forty-nine played games associated with violence: tying up playmates and marching them away, pretending to administer strokes of a cane onto a stubborn child, opening up imaginary gunfire on playmates, and hurriedly tying up luggage to flee from an imaginary raid.[16] The remainder engaged in ordinary childhood games like imitating phone talk, racing, football, peddling tires, blowing balloons, and playing parent or were too young for significant play.

The children interviewed singled out several issues that gave them a sense of insecurity, especially following their return from the LRA enclaves. Interestingly, none of the children sampled mentioned darkness as a cause for fear; ordinarily, children are afraid of darkness. Finding solace in darkness suggests a concern for survival in these children; only under cover of darkness could they go unnoticed and thus be safe.

Over half of the children mentioned the military as their greatest fear. Ordinarily, the military is meant to protect civilians and other innocents from enemies. The LRA has been terrorizing the Ugandan populace for close to two decades, and it has, in turn, been under persistent fire from the UPDF. It is therefore not strange that these children fear the military above all else; they are part of the LRA, and therefore they have been hunted down by the UPDF, whom they see as an enemy. Whereas a few of the sampled children were too young to respond, one-third of the sample mentioned other causes of fear, ranging from death, strangers, losing mother, starvation, and wild animals. The eighteen children born in the Acholi settlement (the control group), by contrast, mentioned lack of school fees, fear of abduction, losing a parent, and death. It can be concluded that nearly all children born in captivity have emerged in Ugandan society with a variety of physical and psychosocial vulnerabilities.

Upon integration into Ugandan society, these children and their mothers face a variety of reactions from the communities. Nineteen mothers interviewed acknowledged a good reception in the community, but nine reported a negative reception, including one mother who stated that the community nearly lynched her as a rebel; she was rescued by the UPDF, which fired into the air to disperse civilians.

Twenty-two mothers indicated that children they have borne in captivity are treated differently from those not born in captivity. Despite the fact that 94 percent of the child mothers expressed joy at being out of captivity, they also described negative consequences of integration, including, above all, the negative reception accorded their children born in the enclaves of the LRA. In two cases mothers mentioned the option of going back to the LRA because of the stigma they were experiencing outside LRA captivity; they thought life was better for them and their children under the LRA. They said that while they were with the LRA nobody discriminated against their children because all babies there belonged to the LRA. They added that they had easy access to basics because they did not need to buy them but rather plundered them from the civilian populace.

The fact that these children were forced on innocent girls with impunity has contributed most in isolating these children from enjoying the privileges of normal growth and development. Also, the endless sufferings on their families and communities that the LRA has meted out does not auger well for them. The children of the LRA symbolize these almost two decades of long suffering: rape, defilement, cold-blooded murders and massacres, abductions, pillage, wreckage of the once peaceful and progressive society, displacement of whole communities, and disruption and stoppage of social services. These children are therefore automatically and unanimously blamed for the acts of their parents. Each grows up being seen as a rebel, a thief, a murderer, an accident, an outcome of rape and defilement, a Joseph Kony.

The stigma suffuses the entire community where they live. In these communities the children are regarded with disdain; they exist as evidence of atrocities committed on the community by their parents as members of the LRA. They are stigmatized even if a family decides to treat the child well. Such families then carry the burden of prejudice from the community to the extent that they are accused of sympathizing with the LRA father.

## Agencies Supporting Assimilation of Children Affected by Armed Conflict in Gulu

Integration refers to the process of assimilating into the life and customs of the group or society that one lives in so that one is accepted fully. This may include both short-term and long-term activities, for example, health counseling, medical care, general education, and job counseling.

There are a number of agencies in Gulu carrying out activities in support of children of armed conflict. Two organizations, GUSCO and

World Vision, run reception centers. Others, notably CPA, run follow-up programs for children reunited with their families. Some others, like the SOS children's village in Gulu, have taken in a few children and thus keep them in the village.

The research sought to evaluate whether existing programs (1) specifically target the particular needs and vulnerabilities of the children born in the enclaves and (2) adequately address their needs. The key finding is that while some programs, mainly pilot projects, are in place to support child mothers returning from the enclaves of the LRA, little psychosocial programming is directed at the children themselves.

A closer look at the GUSCO center reveals that the children fall into three categories: children may be born in captivity and come back unaccompanied; they may accompany their mothers back; or they may be born upon arrival of mothers who escaped while pregnant. In the case of unaccompanied children, GUSCO's response emphasizes connecting them to caregivers. So far, GUSCO has received forty-six unaccompanied children between the ages of two months and eight years. A concerted effort to trace relatives has enabled twenty-six of these children to be handed over to members of their mother's family. Twenty are still at the centers without any clue who their mother or her relatives are.

While they are at the center, GUSCO attaches these unaccompanied children to child mothers returning from LRA captivity. This temporarily fills the gap of no special provision for such children. Then the tracing effort ensues. In the case of the twenty-six already united, the maternal grandparents were traced and contacted. Grandmothers are normally encouraged to come and stay at the center so that they can get used to the children and also acquire basic skills on reproductive health, especially regarding HIV/AIDS. Over 95 percent of the reunions took place with relatives on the maternal side. The children's maternal relatives were easier to locate than their paternal relatives. Also, in Acholi, children born out of wedlock customarily belong to the maternal side.

In the case of children returning from captivity with their abducted mothers or while their mother was pregnant, GUSCO makes an effort to trace the parents of the mother. Pregnant girls start receiving prenatal support and do not permanently leave the center until after giving birth. Upon arrival, children start receiving immunization and medical attention. Upon successful tracing, the mother and her child are visited by the relatives. The young mother, however, stays in the center for psychosocial support until she is considered better; then she is handed over to her parents. Tracing is also done for the father's family. In the event that they both are successfully traced, the two sides are brought together. Thus, both parties will sit and iron out their differences. Reunion of the girl and her "husband," if it occurs at all, is not undertaken by the center but handled by the two families.

The emphasis on reconnecting girl mothers and their babies to their families leaves a number of gaps. Many of the girl mothers do not wish to be treated as children now that they have children of their own. Fifty-one of mothers wanted to be empowered economically. This, they said, would go a long way toward making ends meet for themselves and their children. They would then not be destitute and dependent on charity, which is hard to come by. None of the sixty-nine mothers indicated a desire to depend on her family or on any agency for her needs and the needs of her child.

Often, too little attention is given to whether the baby will be accepted by the girl's family. The fact that families find it difficult to cope with these children is very evident. One indicator is that most girls who come back pregnant are held in the centers until after they give birth precisely so that families do not force them to abort their unborn babies. Some child mothers who already had been reunited with family returned to the reception centers citing unfriendly terms with family as their reason. One child mother had no immediate relations alive. She was reunited with the family of the LRA fighter who had fathered her child as the only option. This girl escaped back to World Vision center with her son after a month-long ordeal of life-threatening experiences.

Other mothers want to return to the LRA, claiming it is a much better life. These examples are only the tip of the iceberg. The prevailing cultural norm is that children born out of wedlock are illegitimate. This subverts the assimilation of these children into the community, even if some families become supportive.

Some Acholi cultural practices could be of use in counteracting this stigma. One such practice currently being used to assist in integration of abductees is a ceremony called *dwoko ayo*. A domestic animal, such as a goat, a cock, or a sheep, is slaughtered to ward off the evil spirit. As the animal's blood cools the earth and the troubled heart of the returnee, the evil is sent away with the "eye of the setting sun" *(wang cent otero ci otero)*. To open this ceremony, the returnee steps on an egg. This symbolizes the entrance of the returnee back into the family and keeps evil at bay. So far, this ceremony is specifically targeting returnees, not their children, although they presumably benefit along with their mothers.

Hope still hinges on an equally old Acholi cultural practice that such a child legally belongs to its mother's clan. A father can only claim fatherhood of a child born outside marriage upon payment of a heavy fine, normally in the form of herds of cattle or goats. This avenue can be pursued by empowering traditional leadership in Acholi to encourage returned LRA fighters, and the girls attached to them who may be willing to continue the relationship, to adopt this practice. Such couples then need tailor-made programs in order to support them to lead normal lives.

In short, while there are mechanisms in place for the assimilation of children of armed conflict back into fairly normal lives, such programming is inadequate to support the assimilation of children born in the enclaves of the LRA. This, in turn, has implications for the mother; the rejection of children by families and communities will directly negate efforts to assimilate the mothers. Mothers whose children are rejected prefer to stick with their pregnancies and babies rather than with their families and communities. For an effective reunification of mother, family, and community, programs are needed for children born in captivity. Efforts to draw on and support local cultural practices that support healing and integration could help. In cases where such transformation is ultimately not possible, however, the mothers themselves require economic support in order to live independently.

## Conclusion

It is increasingly recognized that challenges associated with the assimilation of children born in armed conflict require more systematic study. The United Nations commissioned a study on women, peace, and security in the year 2000; it yielded a report that was published in 2002 (United Nations 2002). This study acknowledged that children who are born of forced pregnancy by girls in armed conflict are one of the basic impacts of armed conflict on women and girls. But it also mentions that little is known about these children and how they can integrate with their mothers back into their communities. Moreover, conflicts where girls are used as sex slaves are found the world over, in most cases resulting in the birth of children.[17] This study, therefore, has the utmost importance in aiding the processes of programming and planning for the incorporation of such children into communities.

The phenomenon of young girls being abducted by insurgents and forced to become pregnant was a fairly new one for the people of northern Uganda. So too are the complex details associated with the plight of the children they bear. The complexity does not end with experiences gained while still with the LRA but increases with their emergence into the local Acholi communities. These communities have suffered the blows of the rebellion and are discomforted by the scathing reminder of their suffering in the form of a strange child suddenly appearing with a once abducted daughter. This results in bitter rejection of the children. This is further compounded by the culturally rooted practice that shuns children born out of wedlock.

Agencies and programs directed toward supporting the assimilation of children of armed conflict into normal life do exist. These programs, however, are geared toward psychosocial support to children in general rather than ones tailored according to specific needs. The only somewhat specialized one is a recently incorporated program for child mothers. Some programs are still in their pilot stages and focus only on the mothers. The psychosocial needs of the children they come back with are barely supported. Yet the psychosocial welfare of these children greatly affects their mothers' psychosocial status as well. If the children are not helped to integrate, then the mothers cannot do so successfully. This means if the children are not welcome within a certain circle, their mothers will feel left out as well.

# Notes

[1] Oral interviews with Concerned Parents' Association in Gulu. This estimate is contested by others however, including UNICEF, which puts the estimate of girls at a quarter of the abducted, not half.

[2] Concerned Parents put the estimate at three thousand by mid 2001 as the number of babies still with the LRA, excluding those returned with mothers. If this is anything to go by, then the estimate could go up by a few hundreds to make a quarter of all children held by the LRA.

[3] Interview with GUSCO and World Vision reception centers for child soldiers in Gulu, northern Uganda. January 2004.

[4] It was infeasible to conduct interviews with members of the LRA or inside southern Sudan, and therefore this study of returnees was confined to Gulu Municipality.

[5] Uganda gained independence from the British colonialists in October 1962, but the administrative system (including provincial jurisdictions) remained in place to the early 1980s. The northern province comprised the Lango subregion of the Lango people in the present districts of Apac, Lira, Oyam, and Dokolo. Also in the north was the Acholi subregion of the Acholi tribe, covering the current districts of Gulu, Pader, and Kitgum. Gulu was then the seat of administration.

[6] The present conflict in Acholi grew from a number of oppositional forces since August 1986. These include UPDA, Lakwena, Lubanga Won (God the Father) led by Severino Lukoya, father to Lakwena and uncle to LRA's Joseph Kony. The LRA is viewed as an Acholi problem rather than a national problem; international involvement has escalated the conflict, and spiritual influence has played a role too.

[7] In mid 2003, the eighteen-year-long conflict finally spread to Teso in eastern Uganda, causing thousands to flee to camps. Thousands were abducted or killed.

[8] Oral interviews with the Concerned Parents' Association in Gulu. The association was formed in 1996 by parents whose daughters were abducted on October 10, 1996, from the Catholic secondary school, St. Mary's Aboke, by the LRA. Its aim was to form a lobby group for the unconditional and immediate release of these children from captivity.

[9] For example, the previously cited Human Rights Watch report only briefly mentions the rejection of children born in captivity, explaining this away as a result of custom and kinship structure of the Acholi (Human Rights Watch et al. 2003, 30). The report argues that the child belongs to the father, and that since the father in these cases of gang-rape is not known, or the father is an LRA rebel, the mother's kin may not accept the child. This simplistic interpretation contradicts the same Acholi custom that observes that a child born outside marriage belongs strictly to the girl's family, and therefore should be named after her family and treated as part of her family unless the father pays a fine (luk). Even so, the child would still bear the original name from the mother's side, signifying lineage.

[10] Children conceived in captivity but born upon their mothers' return to safety seemed better off than those born in captivity in terms of social behavior, acceptance, and health status. This group escaped the scathing environment of the LRA and was fortunate enough to be born and start growing up in a deserving environment (of freedom and at least minimal medical care). While it was impossible to collect primary data on those children still with the LRA, it is hypothesized that they are worse off compared to the other groups, as they are exposed to a culture of war, crime, death, deprivation, and destruction.

[11] Children interviewed all detailed the dire need for food in terms of quantity (they had been forced to depend on wild leaves and roots at times while in the Sudan, facing starvation) as well as quality (no variety; varieties often accessed only by the commanders while in the Sudan camps).

[12] Interviews with child mothers at GUSCO reception center and Unyama IDP camp.

[13] Interviews with child mothers at Unyama IDP camp and staff of GUSCO and World Vision reception centers in Gulu.

[14] Interviews with child mothers and staff of GUSCO, World Vision reception centers, and the SOS children's village, January 2004.

[15] Verbal interview with staff at World Vision center, January 2004.

[16] Observed in GUSCO and World Vision reception centers.

[17] Other contemporary conflicts that used children are exemplified by the DRC civil wars of the late 1990s and the Sierra Leone civil war.

# References

Brumaci, Gina, and AVSI. 2001. *Unearthed Grace: Stories from Northern Uganda*.
CSOPNU (Civil Society for Peace in Northern Uganda). 2006. *Counting the Cost: Twenty Years of War in Northern Uganda*. Kampala: CSOPNU.
Foundation for Human Rights Initiatives. 2002. *The Defender* (Kampala, Uganda) 7, no. 2.

Human Rights Watch, Human Rights and Peace Center, LIU Institute for Global Issues, and Human Rights Focus. 2003. *Abducted and Abused: Renewed Conflict in Northern Uganda* 15, no. 12(A).

Knox-Musisi, Anne. 1998. *Where Is My Home/Children in War*. Kampala: AVSI, GUSCO, Red Barnet, UNICEF, and World Vision.

United Nations. 2002. *Women, Peace, and Security: Study Submitted by the Secretary-General Pursuant to Security Council Resolution 1325 (2000)*. New York: United Nations Publications.

Witter, Sophie. 2002. *The Silent Majority, Child Poverty in Uganda*. London: Save the Children.

# 7

# Children Born of War
# and the Politics of Identity

## PATRICIA WEITSMAN

Assumptions regarding identity, biology, paternity, and genetics underpin policies of rape during warfare. These assumptions are discernible in the discourse surrounding rape and in the debates regarding the fate of the children who are the consequences of the assaults. For example, the mass rape in Bosnia by Serbian troops was actually encouraged by the Serbian government and military. It was viewed as a means of ensuring that Bosnian Muslim women would bear Serbian rather than Bosnian Muslim babies. This stands in contrast to Nazi policies during World War II that prohibited military personnel from raping Jewish women, as the act would not only defile the rapist, but any ensuing pregnancy would perpetuate the "inferior" race. In other words, there are dramatic differences in the way identity is constructed. As a result, there are profound differences in the way the children conceived during wartime are perceived. The rape of French women by German invading soldiers during World War I prompted national debate regarding the legalization of abortion, so that the French government could effectively prevent the birth of "children of the barbarian." In contrast, children born of rape in Bosnia were not allowed by the Bosnian government to be adopted overseas, as they were viewed as a central means of repopulating the country (Williams 1993).[1]

In this chapter I argue that children born of rape during wartime, a subset of what the authors in this volume call children born of war, raise

I would like to thank J. Samuel Barkin, Amy L. Bernath, David L. Hoffmann, and George Shambaugh for their comments on various versions of this essay. R. Charli Carpenter provided innumerable and invaluable edits, insights, and insertions for which I am deeply grateful.

important issues about the way we conceptualize identity. They also inform us about the way those ideas about identity are disseminated through institutional structures including warring communities, the transnational scholarly community and media, and post-conflict governments. I begin with a discussion of the assumptions that underpin the construction of national, ethnic, and religious identity. I then analyze how these assumptions affect the context in which political actors engage, make sense of, and respond to mass rape campaigns. I examine the ways in which discourse and representations of these conflicts contribute to collective understandings about identity. I then link those processes and representations to the post-conflict response of governments to the children born of rape during wartime. I conclude by arguing that the state, society, and media all play an important part in generating the assumptions about biology, ethnicity, genetics, and gender that construct a permissive environment for sexual violence during war and the perceptions of the children who are born as a consequence.

## The Construction of Identity

Beliefs about the derivatives of identity are variable and are driven by social and historical forces. These beliefs matter, despite the fact that they are socially constructed, and the ramifications are manifold. The tendency of groups and individuals to set themselves apart in regard to certain social categories affects their behavior in ways that validate and perpetuate their identities (Fearon and Laitin 2000, 7, 47). Not only do these identities generate social conflict between groups, but they give rise to national identities: nation states evolve as a consequence. Very sophisticated, complex, and nuanced laws develop around these identities, particularly in regard to citizenship and nationality, in other words, who belongs and who does not. These laws and institutional structures support and perpetuate socially constructed concepts of national identity (Sarup 1996, 182; Coser 1968).

The representations of these identities reveal assumptions about gender, ethnicity, and race that are deeply rooted in society. The discourse of Western media and academics informs public understandings of the conflicts. These collective understandings often have important ideas about identity embedded within them. The depictions of policies of rape in wartime as ethnic cleansing or racial hygiene, or of children born of rape as genocidal babies, all perpetuate myths about identity—that it is genetically determined, that it derives from the father, that it derives from the mother, that some blood is purer than other blood, and so forth. These discursive practices, by becoming an essential part of the historical record, perpetuate permissive environments in which thinking about identity in these ways can continue. One consequence is then to accept as normal or expected pervasive discrimination against specific social groups, acts of violence against women, or neglect of children who are born of rape during wartime.

The media, popular discourse, norms and customs, and institutional and governmental practices are all purveyors of these myths about identity. The narratives that are used to convey information help communicate what society is to take as the most important aspects of an identity. In many of the narratives described below, for example, being a woman is intertwined with the central questions of political passivity and ethnic belonging.

During wartime questions of identity become outlined in even sharper relief. Persecuted groups, or any social group confronting external hostility, will have a heightened sense of self identity. Drawing together as a group and becoming more cohesive will validate the group's identity (see Sarup 1996, 3; Coser 1968). The source of cohesion and disintegration in any societal group derives from sentiment, and the best way to manipulate and construct sentiment is discourse (Lincoln 1989, 10). As we seek to identify others through whom we are not (our enemies, our "others"), our ethnicities, races, citizenships, religions—all become tools of exclusion.

This is certainly true in the case of the children of "mixed heritage" who result from rape during wartime (see Carpenter 2000). The children born of rape in Bosnia are called a generation of children of hate (Branson 1993). In Kosovo, they are known as the children of shame (Smith 2000). In Rwanda, they are called children of bad memories, children of hate, and unwanted children (McKinley 1996). Children born of US fathers to women in Vietnam during the war were known as children of the dust (McKelvey 1999). In Darfur, children born to ethnic Africans in the aftermath of the large-scale rapes by government forces in Sudan are called janjaweed by their mothers, or devils on horseback (Polgreen 2005). These are just some examples, all of which reveal a disturbing stigma attached to these children, even though they themselves are obviously not the ones who have the bad memories, nor are they the ones who hate. Yet their identity becomes constructed in a way that is inextricably linked to their rapist fathers, even though it is others who raise them (Carpenter 2000). In contrast, the babies born in Britain during World War I to unwed mothers and fathered by departing soldiers led to a call for reform in "bastardy laws." These children were considered the result of "self or race preservation" and were not to be condemned. These babies were considered "unborn children . . . left to us in trust by our soldiers" (Grayzel 1999, 96; Grayzel 1997).

Part of the challenge posed by children born of rape during wartime is that they entail elements of both self and other. The inability of those around them to disentangle them from the circumstances of their conception manifests itself in their uncertain status as well. Identity revolves necessarily around difference and is understandable only through contrast. Children born of war become a prism for these differences. While technically a combination of the self identity as well as the "other," the way they are perceived does not always reflect that reality. Instead, these children are often viewed purely as "other," despite their birth mothers' identities, and despite the fact that they are usually raised by members of their mothers' ethnic group.

The sections below identify the construction and reproduction of these identities in three sites around the war-babies problematique: the rape campaigns themselves, the depictions of mass rape in scholarly literature and the media, and state efforts to respond to babies brought to term in the aftermath.

## The Role of State Apparatuses

The role of the state or state officials in shaping ideas regarding identity is paramount. The links among genetics, culture, gender, and identity are embodied in policy prescriptions that drive behavior and shape outcomes. These norms and ideas are pervasive and hard to change once embedded in the culture in question. These images are manifest in the treatment of the children conceived in wartime as well.

The state plays an important role in creating and sustaining particular views of identity. Official policy in regard to the rapes and the children who result from the assaults is very telling in reference to social beliefs about identity, both its construction and propagation.[2] For example, in the cases where rape and forced impregnation and maternity were encouraged by authorities in order to "ethnically cleanse" a territory, the link between paternity and identity is held above all others. This appears to have been the case for the rapes perpetrated by the Serb militias in Bosnia. Accounts by rape victims and rapists indicate that these were violations not only sanctioned by Serbian officials but ordered by them. According to a Deutsche Press-Agentur account on July 2, 1996, soldiers, police, and paramilitaries who systematically raped women and girls in Bosnia said that they "had been instructed to make chetnik babies" ("Mass Rape in Bosnia" 1996). Another interview in the *Toronto Star* found that

> 95 out of 105 young women held at a rape camp at Kalinovik, south of Sarajevo, say they were gang-raped by the members of the "White Eagles" militia with the specific purpose of making them pregnant. . . . One woman held prisoner in the camp for two months

has described how bearded Serb gunmen shouted, "You are going
to have our children—you are going to have our little Chetniks."
. . . She said women who were expecting babies were left unmo-
lested because they could not be made pregnant (Fisk 1993).

These reports were confirmed by other sources as well; women and girls
were raped repeatedly until pregnant, then left alone. One man who
raped "10 girls in their 20s and killed six of them" said he was "forced to
rape the women under orders from his commanders" (Branson 1993).
Another Serbian militia rapist told his victim, " I must [rape you]. If I do
not they will hurt me. Because they have ordered me to" (Rodrigue 1992).
According to Roy Gutman, prize-winning journalist for *Newsday* maga-
zine, Bosnian Muslim rape victims were told that their captors wanted
to "plant the seeds of Serbs in Bosnia" (Gutman 1993, 76).[3]

In sum, the policy of forced impregnation implemented by the Serb
militias during the war in the former Yugoslavia was a conscious policy
dictated by the Serbian government. The policy was predicated on a
notion of identity that privileged paternity and largely denied a biological or cultural connection to the mother in establishing the identity of a
child.

In contrast, the Nazis viewed identity as determined by both parents.
The rise of National Socialism in Germany was accompanied by "scien-
tific" concern regarding "racial hygiene." Ultimately, racial hygienists
advocated sterilization in order to ensure that the "genetically diseased"
would not reproduce (Proctor 1988, 95; Weindling 1989). While this
eugenicist movement was not limited to Germany,[4] it had the farthest-
reaching implications there. By September 1935, marriage and sexual
relationships between Jews and Germans were prohibited (Proctor 1988,
103). The reproductive role women play was paramount in Nazi Germany, but only for those women who were deemed racially desirable.[5] In
fact, these women were given awards for producing many children, were
prohibited from curbing their fertility,[6] prevented from joining certain
professions, and were only given job security in official postings after the
age of thirty-five. All of these measures would ensure healthy breeding
stock of women (Proctor 1988, 124). By contrast, coerced abortions by
the Nazi government on women producing undesirable offspring en-
sured that only the "genetically correct" would perpetuate the next generation (Grossmann 1997, 41). The point here is that "'Jewishness' could
never be bred out of a population unless there was strict segregation"
(Weindling 1989, 531). In summary, while Nazi views of women were
problematic, they saw identity as genetically determined by both mother
and father. Policies of sexual reproduction, prohibitions of sexual contact, and forced sterilizations were thus predicated on this construct of
identity.

While rape was unquestionably a weapon of the war in Rwanda, forced impregnation or maternity was not always the intended goal as it was in the former Yugoslavia. As one Tutsi survivor reported, the Interahamwe repeatedly yelled to her and the other women in her group, "Kill them, you have to kill them. They will make Tutsi babies" (Human Rights Watch 1996, 27). Tutsi women were the specific target of the Hutu militia group's violence. Propaganda generated by the organizers of the genocide argued that Tutsi used their women to infiltrate and control Hutu communities. Extremist newspapers and radio stations, supported by government and military officials, continually broadcast warnings about Tutsi women. Stereotypes represented Tutsi women as believing themselves to be superior, arrogant and manipulative, using their sexual prowess to dominate and control Hutu men. Representations of Tutsi women as tools to demean and control Hutu men became increasingly pervasive in the extremist propaganda. Anyone in the military seeking to marry a Tutsi woman was expelled from the military. And when the violence began to unfold in 1994, the rape of Tutsi women occurred on a massive scale (Human Rights Watch 1996):

> Most of the women interviewed described how their rapists mentioned their ethnicity before or during the rape. Rape survivors recounted comments such as: "We want to see how sweet Tutsi women are"; or "You Tutsi women think that you are too good for us"; or "We want to see if a Tutsi woman is like a Hutu woman"; or "If there were peace, you would never accept me." When asked why rape was so widespread, one Rwandan woman who works with a nongovernmental organization in Kigali said, "Hutu men wanted to know Tutsi women, to have sex with them." Tutsi women were supposed to be special sexually. Other women noted that their attackers said, "You Tutsi girls are too proud," apparently setting the stage for their degradation.[7]

An estimated 250,000 Tutsi women were raped by Hutu militia groups. Many of these women were held as sexual slaves—sometimes collectively, sometimes as the private property of one individual. Some were held for days, others for years. The violence directed against these women was catastrophic. Estimates of the number of children born as a consequence of these rapes range from two thousand to more than ten thousand, some women held as sexual slaves bearing more than one (Wax 2004; Mukangendo, chap. 1 herein).

Genocide is one type of "social engineering" designed to construct a society deemed perfect or improved over its current status. In the Holocaust this meant truly eradicating the genome (hence, genocide) of certain "races," as the Nazis called them, a very different approach than that in the former Yugoslavia or in Rwanda. After all, to wipe a "race" of people from the face of the earth, one must kill the children, not bring more of them into the world (Bauman 1989, 90). The cases also reveal that the way in which the government frames the identity issue, both in terms of ethnicity and gender, will be an important determinant of how sexual violence manifests as a consequence.

## The Language of Rape in Wartime

Governments are the key actors in constructing and implementing identity policies. Yet transnational actors become important as well, since the way history is recorded institutionalizes certain ideas about identity. In other words, the way conflicts are represented in the scholarly literature and journalistic reports drives our collective understandings about identity.

On the one hand, very important advances have been made in the ways in which the heinousness of war crimes has been assessed in contemporary warfare. There is less of a tendency now to be dismissive of certain war crimes, such as rape or forced impregnation, than there was fifty years ago. And yet, on the other hand, while these war crimes have been getting more attention in the media and in scholarly literature, the ways in which the issues are framed raise questions as well. The discourse that is used reflects and perpetuates normative assumptions regarding women as actors and as cultural symbols. In the reports examined here, women are represented as being devoid of agency in warfare, of being completely passive and the mere spoils of war; they are portrayed as vessels, able to perpetuate offspring, which take on the identity of the father, without imparting any of their own selves. These representations cloud the issues associated with the trauma of rape, forced impregnation, and forced maternity,[8] as well as the provision of necessary support to the resulting children. Further, the discourse that surrounds these events helps institutionalize certain views of identity.

One noticeable tendency in scholarly and media portrayals of the women victims of rape during wartime is that women are assumed to be passive actors in men's wars. Consider the following from the *Irish Times*: "Impregnated by Serbs, Bosnian Muslim women become the pawns in genocidal warfare," or the headline from an article in *The Times* (London): "Caught in the Crossfire," and the opening sentence of the article, "They may not be in the front line firing bullets, but around the world women are dealing with the daily devastating fallout of war" ("Perfect Gentleman" 2002; Danziger 2002). To be pawns or caught in the crossfire suggests that the women in question have no agency themselves or are passive bystanders in wars fought by their husbands, brothers, and fathers. For example, as Catherine Niarchos observes:

> Although warfare, by biology or circumstance, is the male habit, tragic numbers of women are the victims of men's wars. Women's suffering in war is specifically related to gender—women are raped, forced into prostitution, forcibly impregnated. The war in the former Yugoslavia is the most recent episode in a long history; in that war, women have endured what women in all wars endure. Rape in war and rape in peace exist on a vastly different plane, but the connection is clear. In both situations, women are reminded that they are vulnerable, unequal, and exist only by man's good graces. (Niarchos 1995, 689)

Yet wars are not simply a male preserve; even women who stand opposed to a war are actively engaged in it. Further, women who are raped during wartime, forcibly impregnated, or coerced into becoming mothers, can only be caught in the crossfire or become pawns if they exist exclusively as property of their combatant men. If a woman raped in war is merely a pawn, the implication is that the injury to her matters less than the injury to the men of her society. Similarly, if a woman who is raped during wartime is "caught in the crossfire," then the rape itself has meaning only to the extent that it affects the male combatants of her culture. Further, it suggests that the rape itself is directed at the enemy men, not at the women who survive the assaults. In essence, the women are common sexual property, and the rapes represent the symbolic emasculation of the fighting men.

While Niarchos is correct to emphasize the gendered aspect of violence directed against women during wartime, she overstates the case, and in so doing ultimately perpetuates the image of the woman as passive victim during wartime.

An additional striking tendency in the media and scholarship on forced impregnation during wartime is to view the act as genocidal or a consequence of so-called ethnic cleansing.[9] Anne Tierney Goldstein makes this point:

> For at least the nine months it takes to carry the rapist's child to term, a woman is incapable of conceiving and bearing a child of her own ethnicity. If she is nearing the end of her child-bearing years, if she encounters complications in pregnancy that impair her future fertility, or if as a result of her pregnancy she is rendered unmarriageable within her community, the enforced pregnancy may

preclude her permanently from having a child of her own ethnicity or genetic heritage. (Tierney Goldstein 1993, 34; see also Carpenter 2000)

While the children born of rape during wartime may bring up painful memories for their mothers, and certainly may be rejected because of those memories, they actually are half the mother's genetic heritage, and, if raised by her, then culturally even greater than that in regard to their ethnicity. Claiming that children born of war are not of the mother's ethnic or genetic heritage actually validates the Serbian government's thinking that drove the policy of forced impregnation in the first place.

Further, as R. Charli Carpenter, Vesna Nikolić-Ristanović, and others have pointed out, viewing children born of rape as a product of genocide or "ethnic cleansing" is tantamount to denying the genetic link between mother and child (Carpenter 2000; Nikolić-Ristanović 2000, 67). In fact, if we examine the words *ethnic cleansing*, the suggestion is that it is the male contribution to the reproductive process that not only forms the genetic and cultural heritage of the child, but somehow "cleanses" or abnegates the mother's contribution to it. And yet there is wide acceptance of this interpretation of forced maternity. "As they try to ethnically cleanse Kosovo, paramilitaries—often aided by masked Serb neighbors—systematically searched villages for girls of prime, childbearing age. It was about power and control, humiliation and revenge. What better way to damage the enemy's morale than to hit at his family?" (Smith 2000). Here the women of childbearing age are the tools of "ethnic cleansing," and they are, again, merely pawns—a way of striking at the real enemy, the men. The rape itself takes on meaning only to the extent that it is directed against the enemy men; the crime itself is secondary.

Todd A. Salzman defines ethnic cleansing as a "means [of] rendering an area ethnically homogenous by using force or intimidation to remove persons of a given groups from the area" (Salzman 1998, quoting UN 1994). Forced maternity can only completely remove people of a given ethnic group if one reproduces the thinking of the perpetrators, that is, that maternal identity is unimportant in regard to her offspring. This is the thinking replicated in the media as well. For example, in an article about the rape camps in Bosnia, a report stated that a gynecologist from Bosnia "has completed a comprehensive list of the names and ages of every woman raped in the Kalinovik camp—perhaps the most detailed record yet compiled of the most evil aspect of Serbia's 'ethnic cleansing' in Bosnia" (Fisk 1993).

Even more pointed is an article that ran in the *St. Louis Post-Dispatch* on March 20, 2000, covering the rape case at the International Criminal Tribunal for Yugoslavia: "Since the battles of ancient Greece, commanders have given soldiers license to rape women, who were seen as a spoil of war. But what distinguished the Bosnian war was that women were prime targets in 'ethnic cleansing' campaigns because of their role in propagating identity" (Socolovsky 2000). In this case, women are mere vessels—propagators of the identity of any impregnator, consensual or not. The article continues, quoting an author of a book on the war: "What is new, and extraordinarily horrifying, is that many of the rapes committed in the territory of the former Yugoslavia (were) . . . committed with the intent to impregnate, in an effort to destroy a particular ethnicity" (Socolovsky 2000).

Similarly, a report in *The Gazette* (Montreal) stated that "girls were systematically being impregnated and imprisoned past the three-month abortion deadline, so that they would be forced to bear Chetnik babies. Many women said their captors seemed to gloat over the prospect of making them pregnant. Besima recalled the drunken, bearded rapists saying: 'Now you will be getting a little Chetnik. You can't kill us all. We will multiply'" (Rodrigue 1992).

These ideas regarding identity are socially constructed. The complete destruction of a race or ethnicity should not entail trying to bring about half-Bosnian Muslim babies; yet the idea that identity is linked exclusively to paternity is so pervasive that it makes sense to a wide audience when explained in that way. Yet there is a critical difference between Hitler's "Final Solution" to the Jewish problem and the forced pregnancies in the Former Yugoslavia. While Salzman argues that the "research, planning, and coordination of rape camps was a systematic policy of the Serbian government and military forces with the explicit intention of creating an ethnically pure state" (Salzman 1998, 356), "ethnically pure" to Hitler meant that anyone with a drop of impure blood needed to be eliminated; reproduction by Jews and others who were ethnically impure was prohibited. As noted above, sexual relations between Aryans and Jews, whether consensual or not, were therefore expressly forbidden.[10] To Hitler, maternity was a condition to be reserved for women deemed racially appropriate. The Nazi genocide was designed to eradicate ethnic undesirables by not allowing children of mixed heritage to survive. This is certainly in contrast to the numerous accounts of Bosnian Muslim women being forced to bear "Chetnik babies."

The way violent conflicts are reported by the scholarly literature and the media is important in establishing the recorded history of events. These depictions further contribute to collective understandings of what happened and why. They institutionalize ideas about identity. The discourse that surrounds these events may even inform debates surrounding human rights violations (Salzman 1998, 276–78).[11] These understandings often perpetuate the thinking that gave rise to the policies in the first place. Language in reporting must offer alternative understandings, challenge the assumptions embedded within such depictions, or at a minimum, bring those implicit assumptions to the fore.

## Post-Conflict Responses to Children Born of War

Ideas regarding the source of identity translate into policies to deal with babies who are conceived by rape during wartime. For example, ethnically undesirable women were allowed free access to abortions in Nazi Germany; in East Timor, Indonesian soldiers would take their pregnant victims to clinics in West Timor and force them to abort their pregnancies when they conceived, although numerous babies were nevertheless born (Grieg 2001, 37). The large-scale rape of French (and Belgian) women by the invading German armies in World War I sparked national debate on the legalization of abortion. The children conceived of rape were considered "children of the barbarian" (Harris 1993). These babies were considered of mixed race, although in the discourse French blood of the mother could make the child French (Grayzel 1999). Interestingly, the Germans offered to take the babies and pay mothers (Grayzel 1999, 60). Although the "children of the barbarian" were considered by many to be racially undesirable because of their German paternity, the government did not entirely propagate this view. In fact, the French Ministry of the Interior offered full support to the women who chose to raise their children, and the news reported the irony that "children who nursed with milk of hate could become the ones to avenge their outraged mothers" (Grayzel 1999, 54).

What is interesting to note here is that while children conceived by rape in wartime are frequently considered to assume the identity of the father by the perpetrators, the victims' states do not necessarily adopt that view.[12] Even when the mothers consider their babies to be "monster" babies (see MacKenzie 1999), the state itself may not follow suit. In both Bosnia and Rwanda, where recent wars yielded numerous children born of rape and where mass rape was used as a deliberate weapon of war, the governments have refused to allow the children to be adopted overseas (see chap. 2 herein). In both cases the children were seen as an important means of repopulating the countries. As one newspaper report stated, "The Rwandan government classifies them as 'genocide orphans' and places them in orphanages around the country. . . . Adoption by foreigners is not allowed by the government, officials say. 'We have hundreds of thousands of orphans,' said Aloisea Inyumbe, minister of women's affairs. 'Adoption to the outside means you are looting an entire population. The solution has to be from inside Rwanda'" (Lorch 1995).

This was true in Bosnia and Kosovo as well (Williams 2000; "Americans Offer" 2000). Orphanages in the Balkans were overwhelmed by requests from foreign couples who wanted to adopt war orphans and children born of the mass rapes. Interestingly, requests from Serbian citizens were given preference before foreigners of Yugoslav descent or other foreigners were allowed to adopt. The same policy was in place in Croatia. "'We have a centuries-old culture here, and we can manage to bring up these children. . . . We are not savages,' said the director of a charity managing an orphanage" ("Children of Rape" 1993).

By contrast, the three hundred children estimated to be born of rape in Kuwait after the Gulf War are taken care of financially by the government, although their identity is considered in question.

> The Kuwaiti government pays the equivalent of $90 US a month into a bank account in the child's name until it is 21 years old. This financial nest egg enables the orphans to finance their own dowries, which are traditionally high in the emirate. Education, clothes, and even presents on feast days are also paid for by the state. "I challenge anyone to say we are not looking after these children," said Mohammed Razooki of the social affairs ministry. "We will never forget what the Iraqis did, but we must heal the wounds." Some have also been lucky enough to be adopted by well-off Kuwaiti families. The uncertain area is their nationality and name. The orphanage official, Mrs. Ghareeb, explained that usually they make up names for the children like Abdul Lateif Mohammed, but no family name is added. "We can't give them family names because that is against Islamic law," she said. Citizenship is still a hazy matter, however, for the Kuwaiti government stopped granting even limited nationality to orphans in 1983. In Kuwait, citizenship is jealously guarded for the privileges and financial benefits it brings. (Evans 1993)

The assumptions that underpin sexual violence that takes place in warfare culminate in policies for treating the resulting pregnancies and births. When mixed-race pregnancies are forbidden and undesirable, abortion is permitted. More often in contemporary times, however, in cases where civil war has decimated a population, governments may seek to retain the babies in order to repopulate the country. Despite the desire on the part of governments to ensure the war babies stay in their respective countries, the cloud of shame that follows these children throughout their lives does not dissipate. They are nearly always considered second-class citizens and serve as a physical reminder of divisive conflict that devastated their nation states.

# Conclusion

This chapter has argued that identity is contingent and socially constructed as evidenced by state rape policy as well as redress for victims. Further, it has demonstrated that language matters; the way in which the atrocities are framed reproduces the identity narratives and make rape and discrimination against children born of war possible. Above all, this chapter illuminates the ways in which assumptions about gender, biology, and ethnicity promote dangerous policies that dehumanize women and the offspring they bear against their will during wartime.

Although more research is necessary to draw out the issues embedded in questions of war and identity, it is possible to assert that the discourse surrounding both have a profound effect on the lives of many. As Bruce Lincoln has written, "Together, discourse and force are the chief means whereby social borders, hierarchies, institutional formations, and habituated patterns of behavior are both maintained and modified" (Lincoln 1989, 3). We need to continue to winnow out the ways in which these two factors, discourse and force, affect gender relationships, the relationships among individuals identified with different social groups, and ultimately, the perception of mixed heritage children, the legacies of war.

Despite progress in scholarly and policymaking spheres regarding broadened notions of the war experience, rape, and gender violence in warfare, the discourse surrounding these issues suggests that we still have a long way to go before we achieve a complete understanding of them. The representations of rape, forced impregnation, and forced maternity in wartime continue to perpetuate gender stereotypes about women's social and biological passivity and to institutionalize the marginalization of war orphans resulting from rape. In addition, government policies regarding rape and the resulting children promote and solidify certain beliefs about genetics, culture, gender, and identity.

The most salient characteristics of women who undergo the trauma of rape, forced impregnation, and/or forced maternity for the media and scholarship on the topic are the women's age, sexual history, appearance, political passivity, and nurturing skills. The assumptions embodied in this discourse further suggest that the ideas of the perpetrators are a part of mainstream thinking about maternity and identity; that is, it has less bearing on offspring identity than paternity does. There is no other way to understand broad-based acceptance of the idea that rape and forced maternity may be used for genocidal purposes during wartime.

The narratives constructed surrounding the children born during wartime have a tremendous impact on the ways in which these war babies are then treated (Cruz 2000). Consider the following, for example:

He was a healthy little boy and Mirveta had produced him. But birth, the fifth in her short lifetime, had not brought joy, only dread. As he was pulled from her loins, as the nurses at Kosovo's British-administered university hospital handed her the baby, as the young Albanian mother took the child, she prepared to do the deed. She cradled him to her chest, she looked into her boy's eyes, she stroked his face, and she snapped his neck. They say it was a fairly clear business. Mirveta had used her bare hands. . . . "Who knows? She may have looked into the baby's face and seen the eyes of the Serb who raped her." (Smith 2000)

This narrative suggests that because this baby was one of the "children of shame," his death was less tragic, more understandable, than it would be if his identity had been more directly connected to his mother.[13]

Governments differ in their approach to dealing with the practice of rape during wartime as well as their policies regarding the children who are born of these rapes. The practices in which governments engage reflect broader social assumptions about the sources and derivatives of identity. For Nazi Germany, the smallest drop of what was deemed impure blood tainted an individual, whose identity thus derived exclusively from that taint. For the Serbian government and militias, identity was paternally given; thus, impregnating Bosnian Muslim women and forcing them to bring those pregnancies to term would prevent these women from having children of their own ethnic background. In Kuwait, the state's responsibility for the war babies included financial compensation but not citizenship. The Bosnian and Rwandan governments, however, viewed their war babies as an important way to replace at least a small proportion of the population lost in their respective wars, reflecting still a different social reality, that of opting to understand at least part of the identity of these children as deriving from their mothers. The interconnections among the agents constructing identity undermine in important ways the human rights of children born of war.[14]

The state, society, and media all play important parts in framing the discourse surrounding the issues of biology, genetics, ethnicity, and identity. These discursive practices reflect assumptions that are tied, at least in part, to cultural and historical practices. In order to understand better the nature of identity and its relationship to war, we need to continue to unpack the language that surrounds the issues of rape, forced impregnation, and maternity during wartime. While important steps have been taken in recognizing these events as critical ones in war, the ways in which they are treated reveal that a tremendous amount of work still needs to be done. Even more important is the work we have ahead in tracing the fates of these children and understanding their experiences as a central part of the larger issues of identity and war.

## Notes

[1] This was true in Kosovo as well (see "Americans Offer" 2000).

[2] The state also plays an important role in the perception of the rape survivors. While in many countries, such as Rwanda and Bosnia, the women are frequently ostracized by their families, in other instances the countries in question try to compensate in some fashion. In 1943–44, Moroccan soldiers of the French army were given license to rape. The Italian government offered rape victims a pension, although I have not uncovered any information about offspring (see Walzer 1977, 134; Niarchos 1995, 666). Thousands of Bengali women were raped by West Pakistani soldiers; some of the women were held in military brothels. These women were subsequently rejected by their spouses and families, but the government tried to restore their positions by calling them national heroines (see Niarchos 1995, 667; Brownmiller 1975, 61–62). One Peruvian woman, who sought to identify the soldiers who raped her, and the father of her child, was ridiculed to such an extent by the army commander about her gestating pregnancy that she gave up (see Human Rights Watch 1995, 88).

[3] Similarly, widescale rape also occurred at the Croat Camp Dretelj for Serbs and Muslims. Women were told that they would not be released until they gave birth to an "ustaša" (Croatian fascist) (Nikolić-Ristanović 2000, 61).

[4] In the United States, Indiana passed sterilization laws in 1907; by the late 1920s, twenty-seven other American states had them as well (see Proctor 1988, 97–98).

[5] The Lebensborn project was the Nazi child-rearing program in which thousands of children were taken from their parent or parents and raised by state-approved couples (see Proctor 1988, 87; Grieg 2001, 27).

[6] To curb fertility was considered "racial treason" and prosecuted in the same way as someone "contributing to the racial degeneration of the German people through intermarriage with members of the Jewish blood community" (Proctor 1988, 121).

[7] Human Rights Watch/FIDH interview, member, Association des Femmes Chefs de Familles, Kigali, March 28, 1996 (as quoted in Human Rights Watch 1996). See also Human Rights Watch 2004.

[8] See R. Charli Carpenter's discussion of the use of the terminology *forced impregnation* versus *forced maternity* in Carpenter 2000. I agree with her analysis and try to adopt her terminology here.

[9] Genocidal rape is conceptualized in three ways: (1) as a tool to drive ethnic undesirables out of an area, never to return; (2) when women are raped at concentration camps and then killed; (3) as rape occurring at rape camps where women are systematically raped for long periods of time by Serbs. In other words, women are either driven out of an area, killed, or impregnated (see Allen 1996, 62–63; Salzman 1998, 360–61; Carpenter 2000, 453).

[10] This is not to say that sexual relations did not occur; indeed, numerous acts of rape and sexual enslavement took place during the war. My point here is merely that it was not official policy sanctioned by the state.

[11] My thanks to Amy Bernath for pointing this out to me.

[12] By contrast, the German women who conceived from the wide-scale rapes by the Soviet army in World War II at the end of the war used the racial hygiene discursive practices of the Nazi government to petition the government for abortions (see Grossmann 1997, 47).

[13] R. Charli Carpenter points out the outrageousness of this perspective in quoting Beverly Allen's remark that many women "attempt to kill their babies at birth in a reaction that, speaking strictly in terms of the mother's psychological well-being, might even be considered healthy" (Allen 1996, 99, quoted in Carpenter 2000, 458).

[14] For more on the human rights of and justice for war babies, see chapters 8 and 9 herein.

# References

Allen, Beverly. 1996. *Rape Warfare: The Hidden Genocide in Bosnia-Herzegovina and Croatia*. Minneapolis: University of Minnesota Press.

"Americans Offer to Adopt War Child Born of Rape: A Home Must be Sought in Kosovo First." 2000. *The Ottawa Citizen*, May 11.

Bauman, Zygmunt. 1989. *Modernity and the Holocaust*. Ithaca, NY: Cornell University Press.

Branson, Louise. 1993. "A Generation of Children of Hate: The Unwanted Children Conceived in the Rapes of Some 20,000 Women May Be the Most Lasting Scar Left by Yugoslavia's Bitter Civil War." *The Toronto Star*, January 29.

Brownmiller, Susan. 1975. *Against Our Will*. New York: Simon and Schuster.

Carpenter, R. Charli. 2000. "Surfacing Children: Limitations of Genocidal Rape Discourse." *Human Rights Quarterly* 22, no. 2: 428–77.

"Children of Rape: The (Balkan) War Produces a New Generation of Victims." 1993. *Maclean's* (Toronto edition), May 24.

Coser, Lewis A. 1968. *Functions of Social Conflict*. London: Routledge and Kegan Paul.

Cruz, Consuelo. 2000. "Identity and Persuasion: How Nations Remember Their Pasts and Make Their Futures." *World Politics* 52, no. 3: 275–312.

Danziger, Nick. 2002. "Caught in the Crossfire," *The Times*, October 12.

Evans, Kathy. 1993. "Legacy of War: Kuwait's Littlest Victims." *Calgary Herald*, July 29.

Fearon, James D., and David D. Laitin. 2000. "Violence and the Social Construction of Ethnic Identity." *International Organization* 54, no. 4: 845–77.

Fisk, Robert. 1993. "Rape Victims Say Serb Troops 'Wanted Babies.'" *The Toronto Star*, February 8.

Grayzel, Susan R. 1997. "The Mothers of Our Soldiers' Children: Motherhood, Immortality, and the War Baby Scandal, 1914–1918." In *Maternal Instincts: Visions of Motherhood and Sexuality in Britain. 1875–1925*, edited by Claudia Nelson and Sumner Holmes, 122–40. London: Macmillan.

———. 1999. *Women's Identities at War*. Chapel Hill: University of North Carolina Press.

Grieg, Kai. 2001. "The War Children of the World." Bergen: War and Children Identity Project.

Grossmann, Atina. 1997. "A Question of Silence: The Rape of German Women by Occupation Soldiers." In *West Germany under Construction: Politics, Society, and Culture in the Adenauer Era*, edited by Robert G. Moeller. Ann Arbor: University of Michigan Press.

Gutman, Roy. 1993. *A Witness to Genocide*. New York: Macmillan.

Harris, Ruth. 1993. "The 'Child of the Barbarian': Rape, Race and Nationalism in France during the First World War." *Past and Present* 141: 170–206.

Human Rights Watch. 1995. *Global Report on Women's Human Rights*. New York: Human Rights Watch.

———. 1996. *Shattered Lives: Sexual Violence during the Rwandan Genocide and Its Aftermath*. New York: Human Rights Watch.

———. 2004. *Struggling to Survive: Barriers to Justice for Rape Victims in Rwanda*. New York: Human Rights Watch.

Lincoln, Bruce. 1989. *Discourse and the Construction of Society*. New York: Oxford University Press.

Lorch, Donatella. 1995. "Rwanda: Rape, Used as Weapon, Creates 'Genocide Orphans.'" *The Ottawa Citizen*, May 20.

MacKenzie, Hilary. 1999. "One Family's Agony: After Rape and Butchery, How Do You Rebuild a Shattered Life?" *The Ottawa Citizen*, August 22.

"Mass Rape in Bosnia Took Place on Orders From Above." 1996. Hamburg: Deutsche Press-Agentur. July 2.

McKelvey, Robert S. 1999. *The Dust of Life: America's Children Abandoned in Vietnam*. Seattle: University of Washington Press.

McKinley, James C., Jr. 1996. "Legacy of Rwanda Violence: The Thousands Born of Rape." *New York Times*, September 25.

Niarchos, Catherine N. 1995. "Women, War, and Rape: Challenges Facing the International Tribunal for the Former Yugoslavia." *Human Rights Quarterly* 17, no. 4.

Nikolić-Ristanović, Vesna, ed. 2000. *Women, Violence, and War: Wartime Victimization of Refugees in the Balkans*. Budapest: Central European University Press.

"'Perfect Gentleman' on Trial." 2002. *Irish Times*, February 16.

Polgreen, Lydia. 2005. "Darfur's Babies of Rape Are on Trial from Birth." *New York Times*, February 11.

Proctor, Robert. 1988. *Racial Hygiene: Medicine under the Nazis*. Cambridge: Harvard University Press.

Rodrigue, George. 1992. "Women: The Targets of Terror; Serbs Accused of Systematically Raping Muslims in Bosnia." *The Gazette* (Montreal), November 23.

Salzman, Todd. 1998. "Rape Camps as a Means of Ethnic Cleansing: Religious, Cultural, and Ethical Responses to Rape Victims in the Former Yugoslavia." *Human Rights Quarterly* 20, no. 2: 348–78.

Sarup, Madan. 1996. *Identity, Culture, and the Postmodern World*. Athens: University of Georgia Press.

Smith, Helena. 2000. "'Rape Victims' Babies Pay the Price of War." *The Observer*, April 16.

Socolovsky, Jerome. 2000. "Landmark Rape Case Opens Today at Tribunal on Balkan War Crimes." *St. Louis Post-Dispatch*, March 20.

Tierney Goldstein, Anne. 1993. *Recognizing Forced Impregnation as a War Crime under International Law*. New York: Center for Reproductive Law and Policy.

UN (United Nations). 1994. *Final Report of the Commission of Experts Established Pursuant to Security Council Resolution 780 (1992)*. UN Doc S/1994/674.

Walzer, Michael. 1977. *Just and Unjust Wars*. New York: Basic Books.

Wax, Emily. 2004. "Rwandans Are Struggling to Love Children of Hate." *Washington Post*, March 28.

Weindling, Paul. 1989. *Health, Race, and German Politics between National Unification and Nazism, 1870–1945*. Cambridge: Cambridge University Press.

Williams, Carol J. 1993. "Bosnia's Orphans of Rape: Innocent Legacy of Hatred." *Los Angeles Times*, July 24.

———. 2000. "Americans Offer to Adopt War Child Born of Rape: A Home Must Be Sought in Kosovo First." *The Ottawa Citizen*, May 11.

# 8

# Theorizing Justice
# for Children Born of War

## DEBRA DELAET

Only recently have scholars begun to draw attention to the issue of children born of war in war-torn societies. The label *children born of war* has been used to describe babies born due to rape and sexual exploitation during wartime. Systematic data on such children is nonexistent. Nevertheless, anecdotal evidence suggests that the category encompasses a wide variety of children who experience differing degrees of victimization. Although some women impregnated by wartime rape have abortions, many women who become pregnant as a result of wartime rape and sexual exploitation carry their pregnancies to term, either by choice, as a result of coercion, or due to their lack of access to abortion services. Some women who experience forced pregnancies kill their babies at birth or later in infancy. Surviving children born of war are vulnerable to being orphaned, to rejection by their parents, to stigmatization by the communities of both parents, and to discrimination in general (Grieg 2001; McKay and Mazurana 2004; Niarchos 1995; Nowrojee 1996; Salzman 1998; Stiglmayer 1994). Others are accepted by their communities while they continue to be a reminder of the wartime violence that produced them. In yet other communities, such children are accepted without any stigma attached (McKay and Mazurana 2004).

The primary purpose of this chapter is to theorize justice for children born of war in societies emerging from violent conflict. To this end the chapter begins with a brief discussion of the unique obstacles to pursuing justice for children born of war. Then the chapter provides an overview of punitive and restorative models of justice, the two dominant approaches to pursuing justice in war-torn societies, and considers the potential strengths and weaknesses of these models as they apply to the issue of children born of war.[1] Finally, the chapter includes an exploration of alternative approaches to justice for children born of war. Because of a lack of extensive empirical data to date, the findings and recommendations of this chapter are necessarily preliminary and tentative. Nevertheless, a basic theme emerges in this preliminary attempt to theorize justice for children born of war: the predominant mechanisms for pursuing justice in war-torn societies are not currently designed in a manner that promotes justice for these particular children; indeed, in some cases, existing models of justice are altogether inappropriate. In their place, alternative approaches will be necessary for bringing justice to children born of war.

## Obstacles to Justice for Children Born of War

The issue of children born of war represents a potentially thorny and multilayered obstacle to the pursuit of justice in war-torn societies. As discussed above, the label *children born of war* can be applied to a wide variety of victims of wartime sexual violence, and the status of these children as victims can be contested. Does it make sense to characterize children born of war as victims, since the birth of these children is the very source of their existence (Carpenter 2000)? One of the underlying factors that complicate any consideration of justice for children born of war is that this category involves not one but two general categories of possible victims who have been harmed in different ways: children born of war and their mothers.

As discussed above, children born of war are harmed in a variety of ways. Some children born of war are victims of infanticide. Surviving children born of war are subject to a variety of harms, including abandonment, abuse, stigmatization, and discrimination. These categories are complicated by the fact that the division between these two groups of victims is not simply a matter of age. Rather, the mothers of children born of war might themselves be children (McKay and Mazurana 2004, 33–40). At the same time, the label *children born of war* can be applied to adults who were born of wartime rape.

The mothers of such children are victims in many ways. Initially, they are victims of wartime sexual violence or coercion. In cases where these mothers have not voluntarily chosen to give birth, they can be considered victims of enforced pregnancy. When mothers are forced to marry their rapists, they also become victims of forced marriage. They can be victims of social stigma and discrimination in societies where women are blamed for rapes perpetrated against them. Indeed, choosing to parent a child born of war is an inherently dangerous choice for women in some societies, because men in these societies have often killed women who return with children born of rape, clear evidence that their "sexual purity" has been violated (Meintjes, Pillay, and Turshen 2001, 12). When it does not lead to outright violence against them, the stigmatization of women who have been raped hinders the capability of these women to provide for their basic economic needs (Goldblatt and Meintjes 1998, 32, 53). Moreover, it should be noted that women who abandon children born of rape are sometimes forced to do so. In such cases the mothers as well as the abandoned children are victims of the social stigma attached to babies born of wartime rape.

Despite the importance of this issue, children born of war remain virtually invisible in international political and legal discourse. The international community and nongovernmental bodies involved in humanitarian relief, peacebuilding, and post-conflict justice efforts have neglected this issue to date. A striking example of the invisibility of children born of war is provided by a UNICEF report outlining a series of recommendations for addressing the involvement of children in the Truth and Reconciliation Commission for Sierra Leone (UNICEF 2001). According to the report, one of the key purposes of the Truth and Reconciliation Commission for Sierra Leone is to create an authoritative historical record documenting what happened to children during the armed conflict in Sierra Leone. The commission's mandate also involves promoting the reintegration and reconciliation of children, a goal that is directed primarily at child soldiers. UNICEF's report was designed to provide recommendations and guidelines for achieving these goals. However, despite the report's emphasis on children, nowhere does it mention the issue of children born of war. Given the social isolation and ostracism apparently faced by many children born of war, this is a conspicuous omission in a report intended to aid a truth commission in fostering reconciliation and reintegration of children in a war-torn society.

In the same way that the international community has neglected children born of war to date, scholarship on peacebuilding, post-conflict justice, and reconciliation has not yet explored this issue in detail. Just as this volume seeks to render children born of war visible, this chapter represents a preliminary effort to bring children born of war to the center of analyses of efforts to pursue justice in war-torn societies. This effort involves exploring several important questions. What would justice for children born of war look like? Are existing models for pursuing justice in war-torn societies appropriate for children born of war? What are the limitations of existing models in terms of addressing the problems of children born of war? Do children born of war require altogether new mechanisms for pursuing justice in war-torn societies?

These questions are especially important because many children born of war are not yet at the age of majority, particularly in the case of more recent wars. Thus, children born of war often are not in a position to demand justice for themselves or to articulate a vision of justice, especially in the immediate aftermath of war, when they may still be very young. (Upon reaching adulthood, children born of war may, in fact, become outspoken proponents of justice for themselves, other children born of war, or even their mothers and other women victimized by wartime sexual violence).[2] Complicating matters, when children born of war are socially ostracized and isolated within their communities, they do not have vigorous advocates to demand justice on their behalf. This suggests that human rights advocates and the international community will need to play an especially prominent role in bringing attention to the needs of such children in war-torn societies.

With this background in mind, the following sections of the chapter presents brief overviews of punitive and restorative approaches to justice. These sections examine the logic of punitive and restorative approaches to justice and identify their strengths and weaknesses. This framework then serves as the basis for the examination of the appropriateness of existing mechanisms in seeking justice for children born of war.

## Punitive Justice for Children Born of War?

One of the two prevailing approaches to justice in war-torn societies, the punitive model of justice emphasizes the punishment of perpetrators of war crimes and human rights abuses (DeLaet 2005b, 159–62). Punitive justice is fundamentally concerned with questions of guilt and accountability. A punitive model prioritizes the punishment of perpetrators of war crimes and human rights abuses as the central component of justice in war-torn societies. As a general rule, punitive justice calls for the punishment of *specific* individuals guilty of perpetrating war crimes and human rights abuses and seeks to avoid ascribing collective guilt to groups that have been involved in violent conflict. Although in some cases punitive justice may involve a punishment imposed on a society at large (for example, taxpayers whose government funds reparations to a victimized group), the primary focus of a punitive model of justice is on individual perpetrators of war crimes and human rights abuses. Accordingly, the identification of "the guilty" is one of the essential elements of a punitive approach to pursuing justice in the aftermath of human rights abuses and war crimes.

Because of its emphasis on identifying and punishing guilty parties, the primary mechanism for pursuing justice within the punitive model has been judicial trials (Mendez 2005). However, it should be noted at the outset that punitive justice is not limited to trials. Other mechanisms that fall under a punitive model of justice include retributive killings,

purges, and reparations imposed on guilty parties. However, trials, ranging from national trials, to ad hoc tribunals created specifically for postwar contexts, and now the International Criminal Court, have been the
most visible and prominent punitive approach to pursuing justice in war-
torn societies. Accordingly, the discussion in this section focuses on the
appropriateness of trials as a mechanism for pursuing justice for children born of war.

Proponents of trials identify a number of strengths of judicial efforts
to punish war crimes and human rights abuses. One of the strongest
arguments for trials as a path to justice in war-torn societies is that they
represent a legalist response to wartime violence. Judicial mechanisms
are intended to be "neutral" legal institutions that mitigate against the
impulse for vengeance as a path to justice in war-torn societies. For understandable reasons, emotionalism and hostility typically characterize
interactions among groups in conflict, and such conditions are not likely
to produce a careful parsing of the "innocent" and the "guilty." Unlike
retributive killings without trial or purges of members of "enemy" groups
and their collaborators, which express the impulse for vengeance, trials
are intended to inject fairness and due process into efforts to seek justice
(DeLaet 2005b, 181–84; Minow 1998, 25–51). Thus, effective trials are
supposed to identify and punish fairly the guilty while protecting innocent parties (Mendez 1997, 277). In doing so, trials ideally will help to
break a cycle of violence by helping to reduce the ascribing of collective
guilt to groups in conflict and convincing victims that they can seek justice through neutral institutions rather than through violent counter-
measures.

Although trials have many potential strengths, critics also have identified several weaknesses that limit the effectiveness of trials as a mechanism for pursuing justice in war-torn societies. In general, trials, by
emphasizing individualized guilt, may inappropriately remove the burden of guilt from collective groups (Fletcher and Weinstein 2002, 601).
Trials are also limited in their effectiveness by a number of political and
structural barriers. National trials commonly face significant obstacles
due to the absence of a rule of law tradition and the lack of financial or
social resources in many war-torn societies, as the case of Rwanda clearly
demonstrates (Neuffer 2000). Ad hoc tribunals, which have been created by the international community to fill the gap when national trials
have not been a realistic option, also have a number of weaknesses. The
Nuremberg and Tokyo tribunals have been widely criticized on the
grounds that they imposed "victor's justice," were based on an
ex post facto application of the law, and blurred the lines between individual and collective guilt. The tribunals created by the United Nations
for the former Yugoslavia and Rwanda can be said to have avoided the
problem of the ex post facto application of the law (due to the extensive

codification of international human rights and humanitarian law after World War II) and, to the extent that the UN is not viewed as a partisan in these conflicts, with victor's justice. Nevertheless, a lack of resources has led to the prosecution of relatively small numbers of individuals in each case. Moreover, critics note that these tribunals have been created in only very limited cases and do not begin to scratch the surface in terms of addressing violations of the laws of war and international humanitarian law in war-torn societies. The International Criminal Court, created by the Rome Treaty in 1998, is intended to address these weaknesses of both national trials and ad hoc tribunals. It is designed to be a neutral legal institution with universal jurisdiction over crimes that violate the laws of war and humanitarian law. Nevertheless, with powerful states like the United States still refusing to join, the International Criminal Court does not have universal participation or support. Thus, it remains to be seen whether or not it will become an effective punitive mechanism for pursuing justice for the victims of violence in war-torn societies.

As this brief overview has shown, trials represent an imperfect mechanism for pursuing punitive justice in war-torn societies. Even without these fundamental limitations, it is not clear that trials would be particularly well suited to promoting justice for children born of war. Indeed, a punitive model, especially in the form of trials, poses particular difficulties for the pursuit of justice for children born of war. As discussed above, trials prioritize the punishment of perpetrators and stress an individualized conception of guilt.

Applying this model to children born of war begs the question: who are the perpetrators? On one level, the answer to this question is easy. The perpetrators are the men who raped and forcibly impregnated the mothers of children born of war. Working at this level, pursuing justice for children born of war would not require a dramatic overhaul of international human rights law. Rape is now clearly recognized as a grave breach of international law, as evidenced by the 1998 ruling by the International Criminal Tribunal for Rwanda that wartime rape during internal armed conflict constitutes genocide and as codified in Article 7 of the Statute of the International Criminal Court. Thus, one could argue that justice for children born of war merely requires broadening international human rights law to recognize children born of war as another category of victims of wartime rape.

However, this response is not as straightforward as it might first appear. Indeed, a variety of problems are inherent in a punitive, judicial approach to justice for children born of war. One can identify the rapists as the primary perpetrators responsible for children born of war as victims of human rights abuses. Nevertheless, the categorization of perpetrators remains problematic. In some cases wartime rape has been perpetrated by men who are forced to rape their victims. In such cases, when pregnancies result, albeit presumably small in number, these men can be considered victims rather than perpetrators. Moreover, wartime rapists are not the only perpetrators. Some opponents of abortion would argue that women who get abortions, even those who are victims of sexual violence, perpetrate violence against unborn fetuses. The mothers of these children, themselves victims of rape or sexual coercion, are perpetrators when they kill children born of war in infancy. Mothers of children born of war are often also responsible for the political, social, and economic vulnerability of children born of war when they reject and abandon them. Similarly, members of the community who ostracize, isolate, and discriminate against children born of war can be seen as perpetrators who deprive children born of war of fundamental human rights. Even those members of the community who simply embrace the cultural norms that create the pressures that result in the marginalization of children born of war have some culpability for the vulnerable status of these children.

Of course, the argument here is *not* that the mothers of children born of war, or the communities in which they live, should be prosecuted in trials. Rather, the point of discussing these examples is precisely the opposite—to underscore the limitations of a punitive approach to justice in the case of children born of war in which the lines between perpetrators and victims can become blurred in fundamental ways.

Despite the fact that they may have some culpability, it is simply not realistic to imagine that entire communities will be put on trial for contributing to an atmosphere in which children born of war are marginalized. A punitive approach toward the mothers of children born of war would be especially problematic in that it creates a potential tension between women and children born of war as victims. It is unlikely that the international community would embrace, or that national societies would accept, an approach to justice that punished women whose basic human rights have been violated in such a stark and devastating way. Indeed, such an approach likely would exacerbate the hostility directed toward children born of war and risk increasing their social isolation. Finally, treating children born of war as victims in jurisprudence raises another thorny issue. As discussed in the introduction to this chapter, the category of children born of war can be problematic in that it suggests at some level that their very birth makes them victims. Since the birth of these children is the source of their existence, does it really make sense to identify their birth as a harm requiring legal redress?

Even if a punitive approach toward the mothers of children born of war were desirable or realistic, it would risk exacerbating the problem of silence about wartime sexual violence and forced pregnancy. Any effort to render children born of war visible as a category of victims of wartime violence faces a formidable obstacle in the cross-cultural pattern of silence about sexual violence during wartime (Copelon 1998; Meintjes, Pillay, and Turshen 2001). Already constrained by conservative social and gender norms, women who have been raped and forcibly impregnated will be even more reluctant to acknowledge the sexual violence that has been committed against them if they are characterized as perpetrators rather than victims. If women who have been victimized by wartime sexual violence do not acknowledge the sexual violence that has been perpetrated against them, then neither they nor the communities in which they live can openly address the issue of the children born of war living in their midst. Such an approach might also reinforce the tendency of some women to reject children born of war as representative of the "enemy" rather than perceiving their needs as interconnected. In other words, a punitive approach that treats women who have been victims of sexual violence as perpetrators risks marginalizing children born of war further.

A related problem with a punitive, judicial approach to justice for children born of war is that the victims of wartime violence in this case are not in a position to bring charges. In other words, questions about who the complainants in any judicial process will be mirror the questions about who should be punished as perpetrators. Many such children literally are not in a position to comprehend that they have been deprived of basic human rights or to recognize, let alone bring charges against, perpetrators, at least until they reach adulthood, when trials may not be an option for responding to historical violence. To the extent that children born of war have been rejected by their mothers and their communities, who can be expected to press charges on their behalf and to seek redress within the judicial system? Of course, human rights advocacy groups could bring charges on behalf of children born of war. However, in light of the complications outlined above, trials as a response to the problem of children born of war ultimately seem to be counterproductive.

The limitations of a punitive model of justice apply not only to the case of children born of war but also to justice in war-torn societies in general. An emphasis on punishment and individualized justice does not always sufficiently take into account the social nature of violence and the structural context in which human rights abuses occur. Recognition of this point does not discount the justice contributions of trials when they are feasible and appropriate. For instance, in the case of children born of war, trials for rapists that treat children born of war as secondary victims of rape may be appropriate. In general, as discussed in the previous section, trials offer many advantages in terms of pursuing justice for individual perpetrators of war crimes and human rights abuses. However, the bottom line is that punitive models of justice simply may not be appropriate when the lines between victims and perpetrators are so blurred, as in the case of children born of war, where the violence and discrimination practiced by many mothers and their communities is understandable, if not justifiable.

## Restorative Justice for Children Born of War?

Unlike the punitive model of justice, a restorative model of justice suggests that genuine justice is more likely to be produced by processes that seek to repair social relationships among groups that have been in conflict than by processes emphasizing the punishment of the "guilty" (Llewellyn 2005). In addition to stressing the potential of restorative mechanisms to contribute to social repair, proponents of restorative justice also argue that these mechanisms may, in fact, do a better job than punitive mechanisms of assessing the guilt of perpetrators and responding appropriately. Unlike trials, which seek to ascertain individual guilt, restorative mechanisms encourage communities at large to wrestle with their collective guilt.

Truth commissions represent the most prominent restorative approach to justice in war-torn societies. Other restorative mechanisms include public apologies, public memorials, and social rituals intended to promote reconciliation among groups in conflict. Reparations, which are punitive in the sense that they impose a penalty on guilty parties, also have restorative dimensions to the extent that they are intended to encourage social repair among parties to conflict. Because the international community has most strongly emphasized truth commissions in its efforts to promote justice in war-torn societies, the discussion in this section focuses largely on truth commissions and considers the extent to which they are appropriate for promoting justice for children born of war.

Proponents of restorative justice often embrace truth commissions as the most appropriate method for pursuing justice in war-torn societies. Truth commissions offer a number of potential strengths as a path to justice in war-torn societies. First and foremost, advocates of truth commissions contend that they play an essential role in creating an authoritative record of past atrocities that will help to prevent the recurrence of violence (Rotberg 2000, 3). Moreover, rather than focusing on individual guilt and accountability, truth commissions emphasize a collective sense of guilty and accountability. Whereas critics of truth commissions view this emphasis on collective guilt as a flaw of restorative mechanisms (Mendez 2005), proponents of truth commissions argue that a collective conception of justice acknowledges the reality that there is not a clear line dividing victims and perpetrators in most war-torn societies (Fletcher

and Weinstein 2002). In recognition of the complexity of guilt and victimization during war, truth commissions stress social repair and peace
as higher priorities than punishment in the pursuit of justice. In this way
truth commissions, according to proponents of restorative justice, are
more likely than trials to break entrenched cycles of violence.

Although truth commissions have many potential strengths, they, like
trials, are imperfect mechanisms for pursuing justice in war-torn societies. In practice, the effectiveness of truth commissions as a path to justice
has been limited by narrow mandates, insufficient resources, and time
constraints that hinder the extent to which the full truth can be explored
and disclosed (Hayner 2001). Despite claims to the contrary, truth commissions are not necessarily better than trials at contributing to reconciliation or social repair. As Juan E. Mendez has pointed out, truth without
punishment for perpetrators may lead to lasting bitterness in the heart
of victims of atrocities that, in turn, may serve to perpetuate cycles of
violence rather than foster social repair (Mendez 1997, 255–82). Mendez
also has argued that truth commissions are not necessarily better than
trials, where testimony is subject to cross-examination and the testing of
evidence, at producing an authoritative record of the violence that has
occurred in war-torn societies (Mendez 1997, 277). In short, Mendez
and other critics of truth commissions reject the assumption implicit in
the restorative model of justice that an emphasis on collective guilt and
accountability is preferable to the prioritization of individual guilt. According to critics, even though restorative models do not call for the
punishment of the guilty, a collective conception of guilt risks condemn-
ing the innocent along with the guilty and, in this way, will not serve the
goals of social repair.

A restorative model of justice seems more promising than a punitive
approach in many respects, but significant obstacles remain. Because they
represent the most prominent approach to restorative justice in war-
torn societies, an exploration of the ways in which truth commissions
might contribute to justice for children born of war is illustrative. As
discussed previously, one of the basic objectives of truth commissions is
to contribute to an authoritative record of past atrocities in war-torn
societies. In doing so, truth commissions are intended to prevent a denial of historic violence. The logic of truth commissions, in part, is that
an acknowledgment of the violence and abuses that victims have experienced is one form of justice for these victims. In turn, creating a record
of "the truth" ideally will help to prevent the recurrence of violence.
Applying this model to the problem of children born of war simply requires rendering them visible and adding children born of war to the
mandates of truth commissions. In this regard the "truth" produced by a
truth commission is incomplete if it does not document the extent to
which children born of war exist as a category of victims of wartime

violence as well as the subsequent violence and discrimination that they experience at the cessation of violent hostilities. By adding children born of war to their mandates, truth commissions ideally would contribute to justice for children born of war by raising awareness about the violence and discrimination that they experience. In turn, the logic of truth commissions suggests that acknowledging the existence of children born of war and the human rights abuses they suffer is the first step toward preventing similar abuses in the future.

A more ambitious application of a restorative model of justice suggests that a focus on the issue of children born of war in truth commissions could present new possibilities for social repair. As Siobhán McEvoy-Levy has written, children born of war "might even offer a road-map for transformation involving radical social change" (chap. 9 herein). The very existence of children born of war symbolizes the violence and conflict between warring parties in war-torn societies. In fact, children born of war are a physical embodiment of the wartime violence that produced them. This reality is what makes the problem of children born of war so vexing. On the one hand, it explains precisely why children born of war are so often killed, ostracized, or rejected; to victims of wartime violence they represent the enemy and the violence that has been perpetrated against them. On the other hand, there is the *possibility* that communities recovering from wartime violence could choose to emphasize children born of war's connection to their birth mothers and their communities. Doing so might contribute to the blurring of rigid distinctions between enemy perpetrators and victims. In short, if communities can recognize the humanity of children born of war despite the violent circumstances leading to their births and the apparent inhumanity of the rapists or sexually exploitive men who fathered them, then perhaps such recognition could be a tentative first step toward social repair among groups in conflict in war-torn societies.

In spite of their potential, truth commissions still face many obstacles in terms of providing justice for children born of war. A recognition of children born of war as a category of victims does not guarantee that truth commissions will produce justice for them. The way in which truth commissions have dealt with sexual violence toward women is instructive. To date, truth commissions have not seriously incorporated attention to gender and sexual violence (DeLaet 2005a). This lack of attention to sexual violence results, in part, from mandates that prioritize "politically motivated crimes" and an interpretation of these mandates that treats rape and other forms of sexual torture as nonpolitical crimes (Hayner 2001, 79–80). In this regard it should not be surprising that truth commissions have not treated children born of war as a category of victims of wartime violence.

Even if truth commissions prioritize sexual violence against women and human rights abuses against children born of war, there is no guarantee that truth commissions will elicit the truth about the prevalence of children born of war and the human rights abuses they face. Despite the fact that truth commissions, unlike trials, are based on a non-adversarial approach to justice, victims of sexual violence may remain reluctant to testify about sexual violence due to deeply entrenched norms that encourage silence on the part of victims of sexual violence (DeLaet 2005a; McKay and Mazurana 2004, 44–45). So long as victims remain reluctant to testify before truth commissions about sexual violence, children born of war will remain at the margins of justice processes in war-torn societies. If victims of wartime rape will not discuss their own victimization before truth commissions, then it is unlikely that they would testify about the victimization of children born of war to whom they have given birth, particularly in the cases of mothers who have abandoned or rejected such children.

In the case of infants or very young children, children born of war cannot, of course, be expected to testify on their own behalf. Older children or adults who grew up as children born of war could testify before truth commissions, and testifying before truth commissions might be empowering for these victims.[3] Nevertheless, important obstacles remain. In many cases truth commissions are instituted closer to the time of violent hostilities rather than after an extensive time period has lapsed (Hayner 2001, 291–97). In these cases many children born of war are still very young children, rarely older than teenagers, lessening the likelihood that truth commissions will be an option.[4] Even if children are old enough to testify before truth commissions, they might face emotional trauma that renders the process more harmful than beneficial. Many adults testifying before truth commissions argue that they have found the experience psychologically traumatizing, and critics have charged that truth commissions generally have not done enough to provide psychological support for victims (DeLaet 2005a).

Once again, we are left with a problem of agency—children born of war as victims often are not in a position to act as agents on their own behalf. Even if they are old enough, testifying before a truth commission could be a traumatic and ultimately counterproductive experience in terms of promoting justice for *individual* victims. Certainly, the goal of restorative justice should not sacrifice the psychological well-being of individual children born of war in an effort to promote social repair among groups in war-torn societies. As a result, even if justice mechanisms acknowledge children born of war as a category of victims, there is no guarantee that the problems of children born of war will truly be addressed by these mechanisms.

## Beyond Narrow Conceptions of Punishment and Restoration: Alternative Approaches to Justice for Children Born of War

Despite the fundamental differences between punitive and restorative models of justice, it is worth noting that they share one thing in common—to date, both the punitive and restorative mechanisms for pursuing justice in war-torn societies that have been promoted most widely by the international community have neglected the issue of children born of war. In large part this neglect simply mirrors the invisibility of children born of war in international legal and political discourse (Carpenter 2000). Proponents and practitioners of "transitional" or "post-conflict" justice have not intentionally dismissed or disregarded children born of war as a category of victims. Rather, they simply have not *seen* the children born of war living at the margins of societies in conflict.

In the end, the previous exploration of punitive and restorative justice as responses to the problems of children born of war suggests that existing mechanisms for pursuing justice in war-torn societies are limited in their applicability to children born of war. Putting individuals who have perpetrated wartime rape and forcibly impregnated women on trial may lead to a certain degree of justice for children born of war as victims. However, this approach does not in any way address the structural context that contributes to violence and discrimination against children born of war in the societies in which they live and the often blurred lines between victims and perpetrators.

Encouraging truth commissions to prioritize the issue of children born of war theoretically leads to a more comprehensive account of the truth about violence in war-torn societies and may even render children born of war symbolically important as an embodiment of the humanity that connects groups that have been involved in violent conflict. Nevertheless, drawing attention to the plight of children born of war as an abstract issue does not ensure that truth commissions will document the victimization of real children who fall into this category due to apparently global norms that encourage silence on the part of victims of sexual violence. Moreover, to the extent that restorative models, reflected most visibly in truth commissions, prioritize a vision of *collective* justice that stresses social repair among groups rather than justice for individual perpetrators and victims, they may not meet the needs of children born of war and, indeed, may be counterproductive. Ultimately, then, this analysis suggests the need for new mechanisms and approaches in any effort to bring justice to children born of war in war-torn societies.

The previous examination of punitive and restorative justice as possible responses to children born of war indicates that alternative approaches, or at the least modifications of dominant punitive and restorative mechanisms, need to be considered. Trauma therapy represents one possible approach for seeking to promote healing for children born of war. Admittedly, a focus on healing for individual victims falls outside the bounds of what is traditionally considered justice. Nonetheless, therapy at least puts individual victims at the center of the process, unlike trials, which emphasize the punishment of perpetrators, or truth commissions, which prioritize a collective conception of justice (DeLaet 2005a). Thus trauma therapy that seeks to promote healing for individual children born of war might be more likely to bring some sort of justice to these children than trials or truth commissions. However, trauma therapy also presents at best a limited approach to promoting justice for children born of war. While it might give children born of war psychological tools for dealing with the trauma they have faced, therapy does nothing to address the social context that sanctions ongoing violence and discrimination against such children.

Indeed, while it might be useful to consider therapy as an alternative approach to justice, individualized therapy will be an entirely inappropriate mechanism for pursuing justice for children born of war in many cultures. The inappropriateness of a therapeutic approach may be especially pronounced in non-Western cultures in which community-based as opposed to individualized approaches to justice will be more suitable. In these cultures specific social rituals, including the real or symbolic burying of the dead, storytelling, the use of art and drama, and ritual baths and meals, represent culturally sensitive methods for pursuing justice (Eppel 2005; Kelsall 2005; Nordstrom 1997). Community-based social rituals, the specifics of which will vary from culture to culture, may be more effective methods for bringing justice to children who have been victimized by wartime violence and for integrating them effectively into their communities (Errante 1999). As noted by McKay and Mazurana, "Rituals can facilitate the process of healing, reconnect the child to the community of both living and dead and facilitate social reintegration" (McKay and Mazurana 2004, 47). Social rituals, which may include storytelling, drama, dance, prayer, or other religious practices, allow victims of wartime violence to express sadness and grief in culturally appropriate ways and often mark a break with a traumatic past (McKay and Mazurana 2004, 46–48). Thus, culturally sensitive social rituals may serve as valuable mechanisms for promoting justice for children born of war. More generally, social rituals may foster reconciliation in war-torn societies.[5] In this latter regard these types of social rituals can, in fact, be characterized not as an alternative approach to justice for children born of war but as a form of restorative justice. However, whereas restorative justice emphasizes social repair among groups, the emphasis here is on the potential for these social rituals to contribute to healing and justice for *individual* victims of wartime violence. In this way it is appropriate to consider such social rituals as an alternative to mainstream restorative justice approaches for children born of war.

Another alternative approach toward justice for children born of war would be to seek reparations for the victims of wartime sexual violence, including both children born of wartime rape and their mothers. Such an approach would treat both mothers and children born of war as victims with shared needs and interests. Reparations as an approach toward justice would be based on a recognition of the structural context in which violence occurs. A pursuit of justice for children born of war that also recognizes this structural context might serve to alleviate the economic inequalities that drive violence in general and that contribute to the deprivations faced by children born of war and their mothers in particular. Because economic inequality significantly contributes to the vulnerability of women who have been victimized by wartime sexual violence and, in turn, to the vulnerable status of children born of war, an approach that seeks to provide economic support to women and children born of war merits serious consideration. In this regard it is important to note that programs that provide economic and social resources based on needs rather than the classification of individuals as victims of wartime violence may be more effective. For example, programs addressing child protection, maternal and child health, or child care could be designed to serve the community in general rather than singling out children born of war. Such programs may meet the needs of these children and their mothers without focusing on them as a marginalized and vulnerable group (McKay and Mazurana 2004, 38–40). In this way programs based on *needs* rather than *identities* may promote justice for the children born of war without perpetuating any stigma that attaches to their identity.

Scholars and practitioners of justice in war-torn societies also need to consider seriously international adoption as a response to children born of war. Despite skepticism among human rights organizations and governments in war-torn societies (Carpenter 2000; Williamson 1993), international adoption as one possible solution to the plight of children born of war in war-torn societies needs to be given serious consideration. Critics resist international adoption for a variety of reasons, including the argument that it represents a form of cultural imperialism (see chap. 7 herein). Opponents of international adoption also raise concerns about the exploitation involved in child trafficking. Furthermore, opponents of adoption also argue that international adoption works against the need to repopulate countries whose populations have been decimated by violence (Stanley 1999). Moreover, as discussed in the previous section, the symbolic importance of children born of war positions them to serve as an impetus to social repair in war-torn societies as representations of the humanity of enemy communities. Obviously, if children born of war are removed from war-torn societies, they cannot play this symbolic role. However, the fundamental rights of *real* children born of war should never be sacrificed to the *possible* contributions they might make to demographic rejuvenation or collective reconciliation in war-torn societies. Accordingly, international adoption should be treated as an appropriate response if it can be shown that children born of war are more likely to gain access to fundamental human rights in the process.

Ultimately, the ideal solution for bringing justice to children born of war will require a dramatic transformation of socially constructed norms governing gender and ethnic identities that currently encourage communities to ostracize children born of war as representations of "the enemy." Gender norms that construct ethnic identity as stemming strictly from the father play a key role in the marginalization of children born of war. Thus, efforts to deconstruct these norms might play an essential role in creating recognition of the humanity of children born of war. Of course, the reality that both gender and ethnic norms are typically deeply entrenched suggests that any effort to deconstruct them will face significant obstacles. Nevertheless, the fact that some mothers of children born of war and their families embrace babies born of rape suggests that this goal is possible (chap. 1 herein). The task for future scholars and practitioners will be to delve more deeply into whether, when, and how such dramatic reconstruction of gender and ethnic norms is appropriate and, when it is inappropriate, what alternatives remain.

Similarly, justice for children born of war also is likely to require challenging entrenched gender norms that encourage silence on the part of victims of sexual violence. Because silence as a response to sexual violence has resulted in the marginalization of women as victims of wartime violence, most feminist analyses of sexual violence during war suggest that breaking the silence about sexual violence during wartime is an essential step toward achieving justice for its victims. However, it is not absolutely clear that breaking the silence about sexual violence during wartime is the most appropriate method for bringing justice to children born of war. In fact, one reason that humanitarian agencies have *not* drawn attention to the plight of children born of war is that they have assumed that silence may be an important device for protecting these children (chap. 1 herein). If it is unlikely that children born of war will be welcomed into a community devastated by wartime violence, then perhaps silence about their status is a more appropriate approach toward encouraging their acceptance and integration than drawing public attention to and scrutiny of the circumstances of their birth.

Although the logic underlying justifications for silence on the issue of children born of war is persuasive in certain respects, there are compelling reasons for nonetheless ending this silence and rendering children born of war visible as a category of victims of wartime rape and sexual violence (Carpenter 2000), along with the women who have been raped, sexually exploited, and who have either chosen or been forced to carry and bear children produced by sexual violence. As long as children born of war remain invisible, they will be denied access to fundamental human rights to which they should be entitled under international law. Indeed, the failure to recognize children born of war as victims of human rights violations demonstrates the limitations of international human rights law as a framework for advancing children's rights as human rights (Carpenter 2000). If the idea of human rights as *universal* rights applying to all people is to have meaning, then the existing gaps in international human rights law that fail to address the basic rights of children, including children born of war, must be closed.

At the same time, this analysis of the relationship between gender norms and silence in the face of sexual violence suggests that any effort by humanitarian actors and scholars to render children born of war visible should be sensitive to the role that gender norms play in encouraging silence on the part of victims of sexual violence. Any effort to bring justice to children born of war will be counterproductive if it does not reflect sensitivity to the constraints faced by women who have been victimized by wartime sexual violence. In short, efforts to pursue justice for children born of war must be based on a careful consideration of how to balance the needs of different categories of victims, including both children born of war and women.[6]

## Conclusion

The invisibility of children born of war in existing international efforts to pursue justice in war-torn societies reflects the reality that international actors involved in efforts to pursue justice in war-torn societies have wrongly assumed that the effects of war are gender neutral and, accordingly, have not paid attention to the gendered nature of violence (DeLaet 2005a). As a result, they have not sought to scratch beneath the surface of conflict to identify categories of war crimes and victims that are not immediately apparent. The historic failure on the part of the international community to examine and identify carefully the gendered nature of violence has been especially evident in the case of sexual violence. The fact that international organizations, NGOs, and scholars are increasingly paying attention to gender issues provides some hope that this pattern is changing, though the historic inattention to these issues has reinforced silence as a response to sexual violence and, in doing so, has perpetuated the invisibility of children born of war.

Although the invisibility of children born of war is a large part of the problem, the difficulties involved in the pursuit of justice for children born of war are more complicated than that. To modify a common criticism of the contributions of liberal feminism to the study of international relations, it will not be enough to "add children born of war and stir." On the one hand, recognizing children born of war as a category of victim of wartime violence and designing justice mechanisms accordingly represent an important first step. War-torn societies simply will not be able to pursue justice for children born of war if they do not acknowledge and address their existence. On the other hand, rendering children born of war visible in and of itself will not be enough to bring them justice. Existing justice mechanisms are limited in their applicability to the problems posed by children born of war. Although in some cases existing mechanisms may be useful for bringing justice to children born of war, in other cases they are at best unhelpful and at worst counterproductive. In place of traditional punitive and restorative justice mechanisms, alternative approaches, including therapy, social rituals focused on healing and justice for individuals, international adoption, and reparations for children born of war and their mothers, need to be considered. In the long run the international community will need to challenge entrenched gender norms that lead to violence and discrimination against both children born of war and their mothers.

This exploration of possible paths toward justice for children born of war is necessarily tentative and incomplete. Not only have scholars to date largely neglected the issue of children born of war, but the invisibility of children born of war also has been replicated in global efforts to pursue justice in war-torn societies. As a result, this is not a critique of existing institutional practices toward children born of war because the problem simply has not been widely addressed by the international community. Rather, this chapter represents an effort to preemptively shape global efforts to bring justice to children born of war. If this volume is successful in its goals, children born of war will be rendered increasingly visible as victims of violent conflict. It is to be hoped that international organizations, states, and international humanitarian agencies working to bring justice to war-torn societies will put children born of war on their agenda. When that time comes, it will be essential for policymakers and activists to have a thoughtful understanding of the potential obstacles to justice for children born of war and the inevitably gendered framework in which children born of war exist.

# Notes

[1] The terminology used by practitioners and scholars on this subject varies. Often, scholars refer to *transitional justice*, which technically deals with cases involving a transition from an authoritarian to a democratic government. The term *post-conflict justice* also is widely used and refers to cases where violent conflicts ostensibly have ended. Because violent conflicts are typically more fluid and do not abruptly come to an end, the term *post-conflict justice* is problematic. Additionally, the term *transitional justice* may be too narrow, because it seems to apply only to societies actively in the transition from authoritarianism to democracy. Therefore, I have chosen simply to refer to *justice in war-torn societies* in this chapter.

[2] See the story of Ryan in the film *War Babies*, directed by Raymond Provencher (Montreal, Quebec: Macumba Productions, 2001).

[3] There is no consensus regarding the minimum age at which children should be able to speak on their own behalf.

[4] An examination of Priscilla Hayner's list of twenty-one truth commissions instituted since 1974 shows that six of these truth commissions (Bolivia, Chile, Ecuador, El Salvador, Sri Lanka, and Chile) covered a time period in which at least some teenage war babies would have been able to testify if this category of victims had been covered. Six additional truth commissions (Germany, Guatemala, Nepal, Nigeria, South Africa, and Uganda) covered a time period that would have enabled war babies who had reached adulthood to testify had war babies been included in their mandates (Hayner 2001, 290–97). Whether teenage or adult war babies are able to testify is a function not only of when a truth commission is created but also the duration of the violent conflict.

[5] As McKay and Mazurana note, some social rituals, including genital mutilation, reinforce gender discrimination and sexual mutilation (McKay and Mazurana 2004, 50). Thus, scholars and practitioners of justice for children born of war need not embrace all social rituals as appropriate for fostering justice for children born of war.

[6] It is important to note that men also are victims of sexual violence during war (DeLaet 2005a; Sivakumaran 2005; Zarkov 2001). However, war babies are the product of sexual violence against women. It should be noted that men who have been forced to rape women might be implicated in the problem of war babies when such forced rapes result in pregnancies. Consideration of this issue is beyond the scope of this chapter.

# References

Carpenter, R. Charli. 2000. "Surfacing Children: Limitations of Genocidal Rape Discourse." *Human Rights Quarterly* 22, no. 2: 428–77.

Copelon, Rhonda. 1998. "Surfacing Gender: Reconceptualizing Crimes against Women in Time of War." In *The Women and War Reader*, edited by Lois Ann Lorentzen and Jennifer Turpin, 63–79. New York: New York University Press.

DeLaet, Debra L. 2005a. "Gender Justice: A Gendered Assessment of Truth-telling Mechanisms." In *Telling the Truths: Truth Telling and Peace Building in Post Conflict Societies*, edited by Tristan A. Borer, 151–79. Notre Dame, IN: University of Notre Dame Press.

——. 2005b. *The Global Struggle for Human Rights: Universal Principles in World Politics*. Belmont, CA: Wadsworth Publishers.

Eppel, Shari. 2005. "Healing the Dead: Exhumation and Reburial as Truth-Telling and Peace-Building Activities in Rural Zimbabwe." In *Telling the Truths: Truth Telling and Peace Building in Post Conflict Societies*, edited by Tristan A. Borer, 259–88. Notre Dame, IN: University of Notre Dame Press.

Errante, Antoinette. 1999. "Peace Work as Grief Work in Mozambique and South Africa: Post-conflict Communities as Context for Child and Youth Socialization." *Peace and Conflict: Journal of Peace Psychology*, 5: 261–79.

Fletcher, Laurel E., and Harvey M. Weinstein. 2002. "Violence and Social Repair: Rethinking the Contribution of Justice to Reconciliation." *Human Rights Quarterly* 24: 573–639.

Goldblatt, Beth, and Sheila Meintjes. 1998. "South African Women Demand the Truth." In *What Women Do in Wartime: Gender and Conflict in Africa*, edited by Meredeth Turshen and Clotilde Twagiramariya, 27–61. London: Zed Books.

Grieg, Kai. 2001. *The War Children of the World: Report 1*. Bergen, Norway: War and Children Identity Project. Available on the warandchildren.org website.

Hayner, Priscilla B. 2001. *Unspeakable Truths: Confronting State Terror and Atrocity*. New York: Routledge.

Kelsall, Tim. 2005. "Truth, Lies, Ritual: Preliminary Reflections on the Truth and Reconciliation Commissions in Sierra Leone." *Human Rights Quarterly* 27, no. 2: 361–91.

Llewellyn, Jennifer. 2005. "Restorative Justice in Transitions and Beyond: The Justice Potential of Truth Commissions for Post-Peace-Accord Societies." In *Telling the Truths: Truth Telling and Peace Building in Post Conflict Societies*, edited by Tristan A. Borer, 83–113. Notre Dame, IN: University of Notre Dame Press.

McKay, Susan, and Dyan Mazurana. 2004. *Where Are the Girls? Girls in Fighting Forces in Northern Uganda, Sierra Leone, and Mozambique: Their Lives during and after War*. Montreal: International Centre for Human Rights and Democratic Development.

Meintjes, Sheila, Anu Pillay, and Meredeth Turshen. 2001. "There Is No Aftermath for Women." In *The Aftermath: Women in Post-Conflict Transformation*, edited by Sheila Meintjes, Anu Pillay, and Meredeth Turshen, 3–18. London: Zed Books.

Mendez, Juan E. 1997. "Accountability for Past Abuses." *Human Rights Quarterly* 19: 255–82.

——. 2005. "Truth-telling and Sustainable Peace: An Overview of Latin-American Experiences and Developments in International Human Rights Law." In *Telling the Truths: Truth Telling and Peace Building in Post Conflict Societies*, edited by Tristan A. Borer, 115–50. Notre Dame, IN: University of Notre Dame Press.

Minow, Martha. 1998. *Between Vengeance and Forgiveness: Facing History after Genocide and Mass Violence*. Boston: Beacon Press.

Neuffer, Elizabeth. 2000. "It Takes a Village." *The New Republic*, April 10: 18–20.

Niarchos, Catherine. 1995. "Women, War, and Rape: Challenges Facing the International Tribunal for The Former Yugoslavia." *Human Rights Quarterly* 17, no. 4: 649–90.

Nordstrom, Carolyn. 1997. *A Different Kind of War Story*. Philadelphia: University of Pennsylvania Press.

Nowrojee, Bianifer. 1996. *Shattered Lives: Sexual Violence during the Rwandan Genocide and Its Aftermath*. New York: Human Rights Watch.

Rotberg, Robert I. 2000. "Truth Commissions and the Provision of Truth, Justice, and Reconciliation." In *Truth v. Justice: The Morality of Truth Commissions*, edited by Robert I. Rotberg and Dennis Thompson, 3–21. Princeton, NJ: Princeton University Press.

Salzman, Paul. 1998. "Rape Camps as a Means of Ethnic Cleansing." *Human Rights Quarterly* 20, no. 2: 348–78.

Sivakumaran, Sandesh. 2005. "Male/Male Rape and the 'Taint' of Homosexuality." *Human Rights Quarterly* 27, no. 4: 1274–1306.

Stanley, Penny. 1999. "Reporting of Mass Rape in the Balkans: Plus Ca Change, Plus C'est Meme Chose? From Bosnia to Kosovo." *Civil Wars* 2, no. 2: 74–110.

Stiglmayer, Alexandra, ed. 1994. *Mass Rape: The War against Women in Bosnia-Herzegovina*. Lincoln: University of Nebraska Press.

UNICEF (United Nations Children's Fund). 2001. *Children and the Truth and Reconciliation Commission for Sierra Leone: Recommendations for Policies and Procedures for Addressing and Involving Children in the Truth and Reconciliation Commission*. UNICEF National Forum for Human Rights. Report based on a technical meeting on children and the TRC in Leister Peak, Freetown, June 4–6.

Williamson, Jan. 1993. *Bosnian Children of War: The Adoption Question*. New York: International Social Service.

Zarkov, Dubravka. 2001. "The Body of the Other Man: Sexual Violence and the Construction of Masculinity, Sexuality, and Ethnicity in Croatian Media." In *Victims, Perpetrators, or Actors? Gender, Armed Conflict, and Political Violence*, edited by Caroline O. N. Moser and Fiona Clark, 69–82. London: Zed Books.

# 9

# Human Rights Culture and Children Born of Wartime Rape

## SIOBHÁN MCEVOY-LEVY

One woman . . . made a sweeping movement with her hand in the direction of all the widows gathered around the exhumation site. She said, "All the women were raped. The soldiers raped us all. Some of us had babies from these rapes and some of us used remedies to stop the pregnancy." Sometimes, when I admired a baby or child, a woman would say, "Un soldado me lo regalo," a soldier gave him/her to me, meaning she was raped by a soldier or soldiers.[1]

Children born of wartime rape exist, and often die, on the margins of the already marginal. The exact figures are contested. But it is clear that in many war zones a significant population of children is born as a result of forced maternity or pregnancy incidental to rape. In Rwanda, for example, as many as ten thousand babies were born as a result of the rape campaigns of 1994, according to the Rwandan government (Wax 2004; Donovan 2002).[2] But as Charli Carpenter notes, they "have yet to penetrate legal discourses on the rights of civilians in war" (Carpenter 2000, 476). Indeed, children born of war are all but invisible too in the literature on war-affected children (Becirbasic and Secic 2002; McEvoy-Levy 2006). In studies of child soldiers and refugees they are implied but rarely identified as a distinct group. The babies born as a result of wartime rape slide into view only obliquely. They reside in the space between the lines recognizing rape as a weapon of war, a tool of genocide, and a gross violation of human rights.[3] In reality, many children conceived as a result of rape are aborted before birth, and others are killed in infancy (see chaps. 1 and 2 herein). The survivors are vulnerable to all the perils of other displaced, orphaned, and stigmatized children in regions of turmoil. They are more likely to become child soldiers, child laborers, and exploited sexual slaves as cycles of war and peace turn (McEvoy-Levy 2006; Machel 1996). Yet, as Victoria Sanford's conversations with the Mayan widows above suggest, in some situations children born of rape are integrated into communities and seemingly embraced. They embody hope for the future as well as being permanent reminders of the horrors of the past (see also Wax 2004).

When wars end, among the most frequently declared aspirations of internal and external actors is the development of a human rights culture.[4] A human rights culture, it is theorized, will prevent gross violations of human rights in the future. Sometimes it is suggested (or cautiously theorized) that a human rights culture will also help produce "a reconciled society" (Slye 2000, 182). The texts of truth commissions include recommendations to build human rights cultures.[5] Yet, the aspirations in these documents come up against an enormous challenge in the seemingly agency-less person of the child born of forced maternity. Hidden, denied, and at least temporarily voiceless, these children are configured out of the picture at precisely the moment in which they are most vulnerable.

The primary question addressed through this chapter is this: what does a focus on children born of war reveal about the challenges of developing human rights culture? The first section of the chapter surveys existing ideas of human rights culture. The second section examines dilemmas raised by children born of war. The chapter argues that a children-born-of-war lens reveals new dilemmas and asymmetrical conflicts over rights. Conflicts exist between the rights of children born of rape and ex-combatants and between the rights of children born of rape and their mothers. While these conflicts create barriers to the development of human rights culture, they also possess the capacity to "start something new" (Arendt 1970, 80). Competing rights can "transform each other in each complex strategic situation" (Wilson 1997, 18). But the risks to these children and to their mothers are great. Making them visible is not sufficient to secure their rights. It may even be counterproductive. Their special circumstances need to be analyzed and understood carefully.

The second argument of the chapter is that new constructions of the child that emerge in war zones must be integrated into discourses of human rights culture. Cynthia Enloe writes: "No person, no community, no national movement can be militarized without changing the ways in which femininity and masculinity are brought to bear on daily life" (Enloe 1995, 25). She argues that militarization changes what it means to be a man, which changes what it means to be a woman (Enloe 1995, 27). At what point does militarization change what it means to be a child?

Is childhood transformed when children witness violence, when they become child soldiers, when they are in the womb conceived as a result of rape? And how is the child changed? Conspicuously absent from theorizing and planning for human rights culture (and from the more general discourse of peace processes and peacebuilding) is any deep and critical rethinking of "childhood" as intersecting with war. But children born of war prod us to address the impact of militarization and patriarchy on children's social agency as well as their rights.

This investigation reveals yet more dilemmas, including tensions about the role of silence versus human rights storytelling in war zones and about post-conflict education as a means of building human rights culture. Out of the lived experience of children born of war, values supportive of human rights culture can be crafted and passed on, because children are carriers of memory and creators of culture. But the opposite can occur. Children born of war will pose an insurmountable barrier to human rights culture if their existence, rights, and agency are not recognized and valued.

As Carpenter suggests in the introduction to this volume, the local and global politics that shape the destinies of children born as a result of wartime rape need to be closely examined. Theorizing the relationship between human rights culture and children born of war contributes to such an investigation. Such children make us think differently about the perpetrators of rape, the meaning of infanticide and abortion, and the value and justice of including the subaltern in practices to foster human rights and peace. They make us think critically about the usefulness of the concept of human rights culture for humanitarian protection and human rights advocacy. Because they stimulate difficult questions, children born of war complicate rather than clarify the concept of human rights culture. But, potentially, the treatment of children born of war can act as a test of the depth and permanence of human rights culture in postwar societies. Their survival or death, their displacement or reintegration in societies undergoing transition, their marginalization or inclusion in the new national narrative and new institutions, and their economic and social fates will be important indicators of local progress toward human rights culture and of the international community's commitment to protecting war-affected civilians.

## What Is Human Rights Culture?

Scholars and practitioners writing about human rights culture tend to conceptualize it in three interlocking forms that involve both cultural and institutional (Gibson 2004) or individual and governmental (Howland 2004, 2) levels of activity. First, the development of human rights culture entails the creation of legal and political institutions that protect the population from human rights violations. Included in such a list of institutions would be an independent judiciary, reformed police and military, democratic political structures, human rights commissions, and inquiries and bodies to address specific issues such as land reform or victims' compensation.

Second, a human rights culture is theorized to require a transformation of culture and values. As James L. Gibson puts it, the aim is to "nurture" values in the populace that would make "gross violations of human rights" in the future impossible (Gibson 2004, 6). For Gibson, the relevant values are support for rule of law, political tolerance, rights consciousness, support for due process, commitment to individual freedom, and commitment to democratic institutions and processes. Gibson's definition of culture is useful here, too. He defines it as "the politically relevant beliefs, values, attitudes, and behaviors of ordinary citizens" (Gibson 2004, 9).

If this political-science definition of culture is combined with an anthropological definition, more of the challenge of creating human rights culture is revealed. Kim Hopper states that culture

> is not a tight, hypercoherent program for action and thought, but rather a "tool kit" of images, frames, skills and worldviews from which people assemble heuristic "strategies of action." Though these stores of motives and explanatory constructs, of reasons for doing and compulsion to do, have inertial force (tradition, received lore), they are also subject to editing and correction in the daily round of living. (Hopper 2003, 163–64)

Mahmood Mamdani has noted that anthropological culture, which is "face-to-face, intimate, local and *lived*," contrasts with what he calls "culture talk," which is "highly politicized and comes in large geo-packages" (Mamdani 2004, 17). All of these views of culture are important to the discussion of developing a human rights culture. Together they envision culture as a body of accepted but always changing values that influence people's behavior. These values emerge and are agreed upon in the convergence of lived experience at the grassroots with the functions of official institutions. Noting Mamdani's cautions against conflating cultural and political history, we are challenged to investigate human rights culture for how it is lived locally, how it is officially pursued and politicized, *and* for how these processes interact.

The cultural transformation aspect of the development of human rights culture is seen throughout the human rights literature to support the first aspect of institution building. Susan Dicklitch and Doreen Lwanga argue that the components of a "positive human rights culture" are "a rights-protective regime" and "a rights-respective society" (Dicklitch and Lwanga 2003, 484). This formulation creates the possibility for negative human rights culture[6] and demonstrates a link with the peace studies literature on positive and negative peace (Galtung 1969). Francesca Marotta describes the same linkage between the building of legal frameworks and institutions and a cultural underpinning in terms of "human rights awareness among the general population" (2000, 69).[7]

Education in human rights and practice in political participation are considered central to this initiative. As Todd Howland writes, a human rights culture exists where the populace has "a history of participation in political decisions affecting them" and practice in demanding their rights; in Angola, he argues, the problem is a lack of formal education (Howland 2004, 12). The education component has also been recommended in several truth commission reports. Priscilla Hayner records the following examples in her review of truth commission recommendations:

Argentina: Laws should be passed to make the teaching and diffusion of human rights obligatory in state educational establishments, including civilian, military, and police academies.

Uganda: Qualifications in human rights education should be a requirement for admission to all stages of education after primary education, for appointment to public offices, and for standing for elective office at local and national levels. . . . The people of Uganda should overcome their passive response to government abuses and develop a culture of solidarity to fend for their rights and protect those whose rights are violated.

South Africa: The truth commission report, as well as accompanying video and audio tapes, should be made widely available as a resource for human rights education. (Hayner 2001, 308–9)

The third component of a human rights culture identified in the literature links it with processes for dealing with the past and reconciliation.[8] Ronald C. Slye, for example, seems to view human rights culture as "a reconciled society" which he further defines as "one that strives to respect the dignity of all its members" (2000, 182). Julie Mertus writes that "instead of merely helping to *manage* conflict, human rights norms and institutions may actually perform a transformative role. . . . Human rights thus play a role in reconciliation by providing the means for transforming relationships through acknowledgment of the past, and by providing a shared vision for the future" (Mertus 2004, 336). While the literature on reconciliation is too large to review here, most discussions of human rights culture identify it as a mechanism for affecting national rather than individual reconciliation. Terence Duffy, in a discussion of Cambodia, links "creating national reconciliation and human rights culture" together in the following way:

> Cambodia must confront the worst of its past if it is to move from negatively apportioning blame for past wrongs to recognizing that a whole society has been victimized. The challenge now for Cambodia is to transmute itself so that it can find in its most tragic events the emotional stairway to national forgiveness and economic reconstruction. It is vital that societies like Cambodia find ways of confronting the physical legacies of their pasts so that they can extricate themselves from the weight of human suffering by finding in their human experience the potential for reconciliation. . . . Ultimately it is Cambodian society that must confront the task of nurturing and sustaining a human rights culture. (Duffy 1994, 82–83)

In pursuit of a human rights culture, the task of dealing with the past is envisioned broadly as a national, societal process of narrative building. But a human rights culture, Thomas Osborne states, also entails "a contract to the effect that *this cannot happen again*" (Osborne 2003, 528). Osborne calls this a "politico-ethical" agreement on the obligations and rights of the governing and the governed. He reaffirms the notion of human rights culture as an institutional arrangement rather than at the level of individual transformation.

So, in theory, human rights culture is political, ethical, psychological, and social in nature, and it involves the provision of concrete rights and protections and the fostering of more amorphous "reconciliation"—which is mostly conceived in national, rather than individual, terms. The theorized and desired outcomes are both short term and long term. The priority would seem to be a situation in which gross violations of human rights are no longer possible (Gibson 2004). This has come to be known in shorthand as the *Nunca Mas* (Never Again) principle, after the report of that title on the practice of mass kidnapping, torture, and murder by the Argentine military in the 1970s (Argentine National Commission on the Disappeared 1996). While priority is given to institutional transformation (Gibson 2004), in the long term it is expected and hoped that a "reconciled society" will emerge (Slye 2000, 182). Human rights culture is created, then, in the intersection of formal institutions and society at large. Harder to identify in the literature is how personal processes of dialogue, restitution, and healing are part of building a human rights culture. This is one underdeveloped aspect of the theory of human rights culture that a children-born-of-war lens may help to clarify.

A further problem that a children-born-of-war lens helps underline is the problem that rights discourse always involves privilege, whether local, global, or both (Mamdani 2004; Nhlapo 2000). Human rights culture, like other cultures, is not seen as a static endpoint but as part of a *process* of post-conflict peacebuilding. Scholars suggest that human rights culture can exist in stages and states.[9] But given the hierarchies of privilege in post-conflict situations, an acceptable level of human rights culture is likely to be one in which the powerless secure the fewest benefits. Can such a creation rightly be called human rights culture? If an emphasis is placed on legal and political institutions and participation, does the idea of a human rights culture adequately engage children as well as protect them? If not, can a human rights culture be sustainable? Other questions specific to children born of war emerge. How are children born of war to be educated for human rights culture? How may their existence and experience be employed to educate for human rights? Is human rights culture a useful concept for the humanitarian practitioner community concerned with securing the rights of children born of war? Can a children-born-of-war lens improve the theory and practice of building human rights culture?

So, while a considerable theoretical consensus seems to exist on the need for three interlocking pillars—the creation of legal and political institutions to guarantee human rights, cultural and values transformation, and a "human rights positive" reckoning with the past—many questions remain. Great value exists in looking at human rights through the lens of a most vulnerable social group. We can examine and refine assumptions about human rights culture through an analysis of a vulnerable group's experience. "Representations of violence whether political or structural, that are detached from the concrete and specific experiences of people, and in particular, from the complex consequences of suffering, have tended to reduce theorizing to an autonomous, disembodied activity" (Green 1999, 11). Few would dispute the suffering of war-rape victims, their children, and their communities. But how can that suffering be operative in building human rights culture? The next section of the chapter examines this problem using a children-born-of-war lens.

## Human Rights Culture and Children Born of Wartime Rape

This part of the chapter explores what children born of war teach us about human rights culture and to what extent children born of war can lead us toward an expanded and better understanding of human rights culture in theory and practice. A comprehensive exploration of the intersections between human rights culture and children born of war would take volumes. As a beginning, this chapter focuses on some of the most perplexing problems that a children-born-of-war lens exposes. First, such a lens reveals at least three sets of *conflicts* over rights: tensions between the rights of children born of war and former combatants; tensions between the rights of children born of war and their mothers; and tensions surrounding the recognition of the human rights of rapists. In addition, such a lens exposes three sets of *practical dilemmas* for practitioners engaged in building human rights culture: how to conceptualize children's agency; how to invoke their status in education initiatives; and the relative merits of breaking the silence regarding their existence.

### Conflicts over Rights

Theorists and practitioners seem to agree that the first aspect of human rights culture is the building of new legal and political institutions to protect human rights. New and reformed institutions are considered necessary to make a break with the past, stabilize society, create popular confidence, and most important, to ensure that gross violations of human rights do not recur. However, I argue below that a children-born-of-war lens exposes *conflicts* that are pertinent to this first dimension of building human rights culture. First, the process of bringing militants to a peaceful settlement and reintegrating them into new institutions may contribute to the vulnerability of children born of rape and their mothers and undermine human rights culture. Second, the rights of women who have been raped may not be easily reconciled with the rights of their children or of other children born of rape. In particular, the issues of infanticide, abortion, and how to provide legal redress for rape victims demonstrate this tension. Finally, while a children-born-of-war lens highlights the plight of victimized women and children, it also forces us to make an uncomfortable reckoning with the other side of rape: the perpetrator and his rights.

### Children Born of War and Ex-Combatants

Integration of former combatants into new armed forces and law and order institutions is a central proposal of many peace processes. It seems counter-intuitive that perpetrators of horrific acts of violence can become the practical cornerstones of a new human rights culture in this way. But both the prevailing international practice and a broad range of scholarly literature suggest that the integration of ex-combatants is desirable for both the success of negotiations and for sustainable peace (Brett and McCallin 1996; Darby 2001; Stedman, Rothchild, and Cousens

2002; Darby and McGinty 2003; Crocker, Hampson, and Aall 2004; Özerdem 2004).[10] However, this practice seems to produce a fundamental conflict in institutional efforts to build human rights culture.

Rape and children born of war are not mentioned in the texts of peace accords.[11] Wartime sexual violence (although often politically motivated) is not included in any official list of violent acts that would constitute a violation of a ceasefire agreement. These omissions reflect a widely accepted pragmatism in peace processes—that disarming militants is more important than addressing entrenched gender norms or even acknowledging certain crimes. This political pragmatism not only makes prosecutions for war rape less likely, but it also makes children born of war and their mothers invisible in official discourse, and it makes securing their rights more difficult in the future. A female combatant may seem poised to benefit from reintegration, but her gender creates special obstacles and funding for female soldiers' reintegration is often insufficient.[12]

Not all former combatants are war rapists, of course, and they are entitled to a new life, livelihood, and identity. However, it is a measure of the extent to which rape is used as a military strategy in contemporary warfare that removing war rapists from the streets is logistically impossible in postwar contexts. As a practicality, even where prosecutions of perpetrators of wartime atrocities are extended, they are of limited numbers (see chap. 8 herein). When truth commissions provide amnesty for disclosure and apology, they can deal with more—but still limited—numbers of offenders, and many perpetrators remain at large. Therefore, it is inevitable that some of these perpetrators will reappear after war in new police and military uniforms. How likely are these new police and military to protect the rights of children under their jurisdiction when these children may pose a reminder of their own past crimes of rape? In general, how likely are ex-combatant law enforcement personnel to recognize domestic and sexual violence as a problem[13] if gender-based violence has been ignored in a peace processes and in postwar training?[14] On the other hand, if pragmatic decisions about integrating militants are not made to smooth peace negotiations, then wars and atrocities against civilians will certainly continue. These problems reflect an even wider dynamic of peace settlements: male-centered, military negotiations set up new governance structures that tend to exclude women and that certainly exclude children. Rectifying that imbalance means transformation of the very values that a human rights culture is supposed to foster. But if hierarchies of privilege—ex-combatant over civilian, men over women—shape how the institutions of human rights cultures are established from the outset, how and when will this occur? Can a "rights-protective regime" that characterizes a human rights culture emerge from these dynamics? (Dicklitch and Lwanga 2003, 484).

So, the first aspect of building a human rights culture after war that emphasizes creating new political and legal institutions is a double-edged sword for children born of war and their mothers. To create a human rights culture inclusive of children born of war and their mothers would, minimally, require much better training for police and military in gender and human rights issues. A human rights culture would require that, at least, post-ceasefire crimes of gender-based violence by these entities be aggressively prosecuted. An early emphasis on postwar institutions that serve public health and educational needs would also be essential. The interests of children born of war and their mothers would need to be represented in peace processes and in new governance structures. The humanitarian community's advocacy in this regard is crucial. But, as noted by Carpenter in the introduction to this volume, there does not seem to be much space for children born of war on the global humanitarian agenda. Further exploration of conflicts over rights may help explain why.

### Children Born of War and Their Mothers

In seeking to secure the rights of children born of war and of rape survivors, the visibility of one may not serve the interests of the other. For example, rape and sexual violence are offenses under international humanitarian law,[15] and the prosecution of these crimes would provide a measure of justice for the women involved. But prosecutions for rape, or for "wrongful procreation" as proposed by Goodhart in this volume, may have the counter-effect of forcing children born of war even deeper underground or causing them to be harmed by perpetrators seeking to hide the "evidence" of their crimes. A problem of this kind has been documented as a barrier to the demobilization of child soldiers. Some armed groups have attempted to conceal their child soldiers during peace processes in order to avoid international condemnation (Sultan 2000).

The dilemmas and dangers involved do not mean that war rape and forced impregnation should be ignored or go unpunished. Lack of enforcement of laws against sexual violence and an absence of media coverage enable the continuation of war rape elsewhere, as it has done recently in the Congo (Goodwin 2004). But these dilemmas underline a great difficulty for the humanitarian and human rights community in extending protection and justice to children born of war without compromising the rights of victims of war rape, and vice versa.

The killing of children born of rape at birth by their mothers or other family members poses another related dilemma. Should women who kill their children be prosecuted as a punishment and deterrent to others? Are such prosecutions necessary to lay the basis for a "rights-respective society" (Dicklitch and Lwanga 2003, 484)? Or, would acknowledgment in a national narrative that these acts occurred be a necessary and suffi-cient foundation for a human rights culture? Which approach would best prevent future abuses of rights?

Infanticide is a violation of a child's survival rights under the Conven-tion on the Rights of the Child (1989). Yet, while rule of law is a founda-tional component of a human rights culture, retroactive prosecutions for infanticide would be unjust and unlikely. Still, a human rights culture would demand a national narrative acknowledging that these children born of rape did have a right to life and that their mothers' rights were also violated. It might be noted that infanticide is a classic form of double scapegoating that girds patriarchal power.[16] Women kill their children in trauma, or to take back power from men who have violated them, or to appease patriarchs who will shun them. Their murderous acts are wrong, but they occur because of war. Incorporated in this discourse could be Rimmer's innovative idea (chap. 4 herein) of treating mothers and children as war veterans. Certainly, ex-combatant status could be more easily applied to raped women who commit infanticide than to all women who have experienced forced maternity. A role exists for schol-ars and practitioners to explore more fully how the story of children born of wartime rape can be told to educate against the reproduction of militarism and patriarchy in postwar societies. As part of international human rights advocacy or truth commission reports such narratives would not have to identify individual women and children or entail risks to them. But these narratives might have the power to transform terrible acts into reconciling stories. In that sense they would be early preven-tion against future infanticide and even against wartime rape.

Inevitably, questions will emerge about whether fetuses produced as a result of rape have rights. A genuine human rights culture would pro-mote these and other discussions mediating the multiplicity of compet-ing rights claims that can be imagined. If, as Rimmer suggests, children born of rape were to be classified as veterans, some would argue that such status be extended to children *conceived* of war rape as well. Would such a move have a healing effect on their mothers and war-torn com-munities, or would women who had such abortions (or any abortions) be further stigmatized?

A genuine human rights culture cannot accommodate forced mater-nity; it cannot justify it, rationalize it, or attempt to make women the villains. Where abortion is the strategy of "choice" for raped women, the freedom from forced maternity it provides is an important right. Yet, the precarious economic and security situations in war zones mean that various indigenous methods of abortion are used with a variety of medi-cal complications for women that may then mean additional injury to reproductive capabilities, to physical and mental health,[17] or even death (see chap. 5 herein). Further complications exist in late-term abortions and the particular vulnerability of disabled children born as a result of failed abortion attempts (Hess 2004). These, in particular, may create a tension between the reproductive rights of women and the protection of children. The Western "choice" debate does not adequately encompass the moral, spiritual, political, and health issues at stake here.

A human rights culture would have to coexist with, not replace, other belief systems. It would have to take into consideration how abortion rights may affect the moral, spiritual, and communal cohesion of war-torn societies in the long term. This is very much dependent on how abortion is viewed within a local cultural and religious framework, not only related to beliefs on the beginnings of life but also to beliefs about the spiritual fate of dead children and their effects on communities. For example, are the spirits of aborted fetuses reborn in future children? Or, do they remain as angry spirits plaguing communities with ill health and bad luck?[18] Providing safe abortion services to raped women would be part of the rights dimension of human rights culture. But such policies might not address an important cultural dimension. Unwanted children, death, and motherhood, for example, are conceptualized and experienced differently in their local contexts. These particularities would also need to be well understood and accommodated in delivering reproductive health services to women in war zones.

Much of the impetus for mass rape in wartime on the part of the aggressor is to create new human beings that form living reminders of subjugation and humiliation and dilute culture. Abortion, then, may be seen as an active rejection of that attempt to subjugate. But it can be argued, too, that to destroy or to purge the "evil seed" or "evil gene" (Balorda 2004) is to give credibility to the aggressor's strategy, to repro-duce it, and to lose the potentially positive role of children born of rape in building human rights culture. Building on this point, the *agency* of children born of rape is important to explore. When we ask questions about children born of war, we create claims for power on their behalf. To what extent do children born of war exert their own claims for power? This will be explored below. First, though, we must examine another difficult issue exposed by the children-born-of-war lens.

### The Human Rights of Rapists

A children-born-of-war lens also humanizes and complicates the per-petrators of war rape, reminding us that rapists have human rights too. Nowhere is this recognition more important and more troubling to ac-commodate than in the real world of developing human rights culture. The tendency to highlight the mass rape campaigns in the Balkans may allow the heterogeneity of the rapist to be ignored. A major tension ex-ists between the literature on child soldiers, for example, and the human rights literature on war rape. Just as we have to read between the lines in official texts to find rape and rape victims and children born of war, we often have to read between the lines of the war rape literature to find any indication of who the rapists are, and that they have human characteristics, histories, and traceable pathways into armed conflict. But this is a tension that has to be bridged if a human rights culture that lives up to that name is to be possible in any situation where rape has been a weapon of war.

There are cases where the war rapist is also a child soldier—forcibly abducted into armed groups, drugged, and brutalized (including being raped) as prior steps to participation in rape campaigns (see Brett and McCallin 1996; UNIRIN 2004). They may be made to commit rape, including incest, on pain of death as a means of severing their links from their communities and accepted moral values. Men are also raped and sexually abused. Female soldiers have been recorded as rapists of both men and women.[19] If we accept, as the literature on child soldiers does, that the line between victim and perpetrator is blurred, we are left with another layer to the conundrum of how to serve justice to perpetrators and compensation to victims. This is one complication.

A second is that war rapists have human rights not just when they are children or child soldiers but throughout their lives, because of the nature of human rights, and those rights are not forfeited because of criminal acts, even the most violent. A third complication is that a strict prosecutorial sensibility doesn't accommodate the human capacity for remorse, contrition, and transformation.[20] This humanization of the perpetrator does not mean that perpetrators of war rape, particularly those who order such acts, should be immune from prosecution. On the contrary, confronting war rape as a male "choice" enhances accountability because it clarifies that "the perpetrators of war rape are not madmen or devils but ordinary men acting out of comprehensible motives" (Price 2001, 212). These motives will to some extent vary by war context. Explaining them, publicly, as part of a new national narrative perhaps, is an important part of preventing sexual violence by uncovering why it happened and by questioning the values and gender and power hierarchies that enabled it.

When the viewpoint is relocated from rapist to father, as effected by the children-born-of-war lens, the humanity of the rapist is recovered. Does not such a criminal also have a right to rehabilitation? Might he also have a responsibility to be part of a process of reconciliation? Difficult as it is to write, the possibility, indeed the guarantee, that the perpetrators of the most vicious acts of sexual torture, mutilation, and murder are also vulnerable human beings requires us to empathize with the perpetrators while remaining actively opposed to their acts and to the institutional reproduction of militarism and patriarchy. Measures to prevent war rape and to protect children born of rape will be improved, not hindered, by this recognition of the rapist's humanity and rights. And this insight into a requirement of human rights culture is helped along by the literal "new life" that sometimes emerges from the horror of war rape. In this sense children born of war really do challenge us to create what Arendt calls the politics by which we "start something new" (1970, 82).

## Conceptual and Practical Dilemmas: Agency, Education, and Silence

As discussed, the first aim of architects of human rights culture is to build legal and political institutions. But this aim is in tension with the second objective highlighted in this literature: transforming culture and values. Children are key sites of cultural reproduction and transformation. However, early in postwar reconstruction a discourse takes shape that sets children's issues as secondary and their roles as nonexistent. The role of women in cultural reproduction is well acknowledged and one of the main reasons they are targeted for rape in war.[21] Less well recognized, but critical to this discussion, are the roles children have in cultural reproduction.

Children have multiple roles in armed groups, in work forces, in the home (even as head of household), in schools, and in numerous other social and cultural institutions. And children also act as transmitters of knowledge and creators of meaning and culture as they interact (often simultaneously) in these spheres (McEvoy-Levy 2006). The children conceived and born as a result of systematic rape or sexual exploitation in wartime form a specific group within the category of war-affected children. They may have distinct potential and effects in terms of both cultural and conflict reproduction. But, so far, this has not been explored.

### The Social Agency of Children Born of War

Do children born of war have agency, and if so, how does that agency affect human rights? If one defines agency as the capacity to shape social outcomes, then children born of rape have a form of agency that is deeply significant for human rights culture. In the long term, surviving children born of rape will have many of the multidimensional social, economic, and political roles of other militarized children in post-conflict societies (McEvoy-Levy 2006). But the agency of children born of war is not postponed until a time when they are physically able to commit acts of violence, labor, vote, or work for peace. Even as infants, anecdotal evidence suggests that children born of war can foster microcultures of peace as well as traumatic memories. One mother of two children conceived as a result of war rape in Rwanda named each one Hope, noting: "Some people had different hearts. But the whole time I was feeling happy for the first time in so long. Here I was with my son, and another child inside me. We had walked all of that way together. My love really grew for them, and I just wanted to get back to Rwanda and be together" (Wax 2004, A01). This story suggests that values support- ive of human rights culture are inherent in the tolerance and trans- forming love that sometimes children born of rape inspire in their mothers. The knowledge these families have about forgiveness and tran- scending trauma needs to be incorporated into mechanisms of foster- ing human rights culture. Even children aborted or killed in infancy can have forms of agency because they too may remain as memories and symbols for their mothers, if for no one else. As noted earlier, human rights culture is usually conceptualized at the national level rather than at an individual level. But a human rights culture for chil- dren born of war would have to entail local and personal processes of dialogue, restitution, and healing.

Forced maternity can reconstruct the child in local contexts, making children born of rape into "little killers," "the children of bad memo- ries" (Wax 2004, A01), and carriers of "evil genes" (Balorda 2004), strip- ping them of their humanity and making them increasingly vulnerable. But children born of war may eventually be able to create bridges be- tween divided communities, because the other side to their invisibility and stigma may be the power of transformative hybridity. Because of their mixed origins, children born of war are not enemies or friends, but both. In this way they construct a new category of war-affected child: militarized bystander and, perhaps, mediator. The militarization of chil- dren born of war (they are the product of war rape), their innocence (they are bystanders, not victims or perpetrators of rape), and their mixed nationalities, races, or ethnicities make them complex participants in their own histories and in post-conflict reconstruction. Their hybridity leads to their greater insecurity, but it also holds the potential for them to shape new definitions of community, citizenship, and belonging that sup- port human rights culture. Admittedly, this may be an idealistic predic- tion given postwar situations where rival communities harden into distrustful coexistence (Bosnia) or strategies to erase ethnicity are intro- duced (Rwanda). But examples already exist of this kind of transforma- tion in action; for example, the questions some Bosnian teenagers are asking about their fathers stimulate a form of human rights storytelling about war rape (Jahn 2005). The Rwandan government, now recogniz- ing that many schools have students born as a result of war rape, is re- ported to be developing a national curriculum to explain the existence of children of rape (Wax 2004). In this case the agency of children born of war may exist in their capacity to affect educational policy.

It is possible that children born of war might even offer a road map for transformation involving more radical social change. Lynda E. Boose, writing about the Balkans, states that there was "a bitter irony inherent in the relationship among rape, patriarchy, and the vulnerability of a culture to the devastation of its identity: the more patriarchal the culture, the more vulnerable it becomes, because all the more likely are the women within it to become targets for enemy rape" (Boose 2002, 93–94). In a similar irony, attention to the plight of children who were fathered by war may help undermine both patriarchy and militarism—by pointing to the failure of both to protect women.

Yet there is even less acknowledgment of the agency of such children than there is of their rights. A children-born-of-war lens shows how a legal-political focus in terms of values transformation in support of human rights culture is related to a very narrow view of where and how cultures and values are formed and transformed. A children-born-of-war lens challenges us to think more complexly about infants, and all children, as human beings and social agents, creators of culture in general and of human rights culture. To attempt to identify and to foster the positive agency of children born of war in building human rights culture is to counter the intentions of the war rapists who perceived that children born of war would create cultural disintegration.

### Education for Human Rights Culture

In the context of a web of values that legitimizes rape and sexual violence and gender inequality—local and global patriarchy and local and global militarism—post-conflict education is faced with extensive challenges. Post-conflict education in support of human rights cultures has to address the practical impediments to children born of war and other children getting to school and being secure there, particularly girl children. Children born of war will face specific obstacles to gaining access to schooling because of difficulty proving their nationality and registering their births and/or because of stigma. Securing their rights to an education is an essential task. But postwar communities as a whole contribute to securing the rights or to the stigmatization of children born of war. So it is necessary to think broadly and creatively about the sites of delivery of education for human rights culture. Placing gender and gender-based violence issues into the kinds of postwar rehabilitation programs for adults that emphasize skills-training and livelihood would be one approach. National education reform is another.

Would integrating children born of war as a topic into an education curriculum help promote human rights culture? The content of such a curriculum would be challenging. Would such content expose locally hidden children and violate the rights of mothers to protect their privacy?

Where would blame for children born of war be placed? How would questions of justice and reparations be treated? What kind of follow up and support would be provided for teachers, pupils, and their families? Existing findings on the effectiveness of trying to promote empathy and tolerance through peace education seem to recommend against literally exposing homegrown children born of war (Salomon 2004). These results suggest the benefit of indirect attention to contentious issues—a task that, in the case of children born of war, requires very careful maneuvering around culture, traditions, and gendered and war-based habits.

Yet, in the existing literature, education is described as central to the cultural change aspect of human rights culture. Theorists of human rights culture emphasize the need to undertake values development, particularly through education, to create a "rights-respective" society and a human rights positive way of "dealing with the past." Incorporating a deep understanding of the complex pathways of individuals and groups into horrific violence is a critical part of the construction of new national narratives after war. Such public education is necessary for real values transformation that will prevent human rights abuses in the future. A narrative that accommodates the humanity of rapists, and of mothers who kill their children conceived as a result of rape, is one essential component of human rights culture, as noted above. A narrative that also respects the stories, privacy, and dignity of women who kept their children born of war is another. Moreover, a narrative that recognizes the existing agency of children born of war and opens a possibility for these children to continue shaping the "human rights positive" values of society is another essential element. Post-conflict education may provide one of the best venues for both constructively addressing past horrors and dealing with new contentious issues as they arise. Curricula that present complex, inclusive, and critical dialogues about human rights would help sustain a human rights culture for the long term.

Yet, education is not a priority in peace processes. And although increasingly presented as an element of post-conflict reconstruction plans, the implementation of education reforms lags behind other forms of institution building. As a starting point, then, the development of a human rights culture requires the elevation of educational institutions at least on a par with legal and political ones, making them priorities in a postwar situation. Human rights culture also requires official policies of promoting "critical pluralism"[22] that work against the reproduction of patriarchy and militarism in schools. Truth commissions may be problematic for children born of war (see chap. 8 herein). But where a truth commission does recognize children born of rape, there could be a place, too, for incorporating these findings into education curricula. But a strong human rights culture would be one in which children born of war were themselves eventually brought into the dialogues that create curricula. Such involvement would teach values of inclusion and empower children born of rape by involving them in the processes of negotiating the telling of their own history. Certainly, no curriculum supportive of human rights culture could be established without emerging from the desires and collaboration of the women, children, and communities most directly affected.

Another approach would be to integrate the topic of children born of war into education in countries that are not directly affected but have important roles in global politics. In addition to existing global and social studies units on child labor and child soldiers, courses could include units on children born through rape and sexual exploitation, and as a result of other wartime design, such as the Nazi Lebensborn. The existence and experience of children born of war may be employed to educate for human rights among citizens in other countries and help build or reinforce human rights cultures there too. Or the issue could be developed in training materials for NGO and aid agencies. These activities would serve the long-term objective of raising global awareness of children born of war in donor countries and other powerful international bodies.

### Breaking the Silence?

However, initiatives that involve surfacing children born of war for education for human rights in directly affected countries must be able to justify breaking the strategic and positive silence that sometimes surrounds children born of rape. A children-born-of-war lens once again reveals a conflict, because it challenges our assumptions about the justice and practicality of including the voices of the subaltern. It challenges the notion that cultural transformation will occur if marginal groups are brought in from the margins, surfaced, and included. The (de)militarist logic of war to peace transitions, though perhaps the primary factor, is not the *only* factor responsible for the invisibility of children born of war. As a practicality, these children may not be the most immediate issue facing women (chap. 10 herein). Their invisibility may also be a product of the assumptions of humanitarian workers that "silence is an important protection mechanism for children born of wartime rape" (Carpenter, chap. 1 herein). As Eunice Apio notes in this volume, a very real fear of death may motivate mothers to hide their experiences as rape survivors and members of armed groups (chap. 6 herein).

Can silence be compatible with the development of human rights culture? A children-born-of-war lens shows that there is a difference between strategic or positive silence and imposed silence. The effects of each form of silence on the project of human rights education and protection are potentially very different. Grassroots silence can be seen as a form of resistance on the part of raped women and their communities. Perhaps they are refusing to be colonized by international legal and humanitarian norms and agencies that they do not perceive as serving their interests. In this case, at least, they can exert some control over the uses and abuses of their bodies. While "silencing is a powerful mechanism of control enforced through fear," it is also possible that "silence can operate as a survival strategy" (Green 1999, 69). Secrecy, Allen Feldman writes in relation to Northern Ireland, is "an assertion of identity and symbolic capital . . . as . . . subaltern groups construct their own margins as fragile insulations from the 'center'" (Feldman 1991, 11). While the chapter has noted that children born of war do have social agency, as infants they cannot actively construct such insulated positions for themselves. But when their mothers and communities do so for them, these wishes for privacy must be respected and supported. The self-determination of the individual, the right of a rape survivor to create her own reality, to protect her children by hiding their origins, for example, is an important element of human rights culture. Silence may offer protection and a means of resistance, a way of carving out a safe space within which to create new forms of family.

The notion of human rights culture seems inconsistent with the existence of refugee camps, poverty-stricken enclaves, and rape survivors living of the edge of subsistence. However, an exploration of what happens to the children born of war reveals that, even within these spaces, human rights cultures can exist. Communities terrorized and under siege often powerfully resist their subjugation by forming alternative societies characterized by cooperative principles and social and economic justice.[23] Not all children born of war are stigmatized; some have been silently integrated into communities throughout the history of warfare. The chapter has noted some powerful contemporary examples of this.

The values that create and sustain these communities may be partially reflected in ideas such as "political tolerance, rights consciousness, support for due process, respect for life, support for the rule of law, and . . . democratic institutions" (Gibson 2004, 8). But the values of human rights culture are more completely defined with the addition of family responsibility, participatory democracy, cooperative economies, and gender solidarity. The past is stored and shaped by social institutions, with family being key. These spaces are crucial to building the values that support and sustain human rights culture, for they are at the very center of conflict and cultural reproduction.

On the one hand, it may be deeply counterproductive for international agencies to intervene against the strategic silence that surrounds children born of war with well-intentioned moves that only serve to disrupt existing support systems and increase the vulnerability of children born of war and their mothers. However, the oxygen of militarized societies is militarism, a value that becomes intrinsic to personal survival and that transmutes itself into domestic forms after war's end. So forms of silence that seem to protect the children born of rape must also be viewed with suspicion. Where mass rape has occurred, the collective desire to forget and obscure such horrors may resist dialogue about gender-based violence. When silence is imposed because of trauma, or because of a mother's fear of further victimization of herself or her children, it is perhaps not the positive and empowering silence of communities in resistance. "Silence is not forgetting" (Amadiume and An-Na'im 2000, 14), and it can enable renewed atrocity and quiet subjugation.

Moreover, strategic local silence is not the same as international silence. As Carpenter has very effectively argued, "surfacing" the children born of wartime rape and sexual exploitation is essential if we are to see such children fully as bearers of human rights, victims of human rights violations and, thus, address "the inadequacy of existing legal and theoretical approaches" to children's human rights (Carpenter 2000, 477). The invisibility of war-rape children in international law almost preordains their marginality in local attempts to build postwar human rights culture. But any human rights culture, whether theoretical or practical in construction, cannot have credibility without an active protection of marginal children. So a children-born-of-war lens suggests that building human rights culture requires a subtle identification of where imposed silences, not strategic, positive silences, are operative. A more systematic approach to distinguishing between positive, protective silence and oppressive, victimizing silence is a challenge that, while difficult, ought to inform post-conflict peacebuilding policies.

## Conclusion: Starting Something New?

What makes a man a political being is his faculty of action; it enables him to get together with his peers, to act in concert, and to reach out for goals and enterprises that would never enter his mind, let alone the desires of his heart, had he not been given this gift—to embark on something new. Philosophically speaking, to act is the human answer to the condition of natality. Since we all come into the world by virtue of birth, as newcomers and beginnings, we are able to start something new; without the fact of birth we would not even know what novelty is, all "action" would be either mere behavior or preservation (Arendt 1970, 82).

Children born of war challenge us to "start something new," although perhaps not about inclusion, or intervention, or women's and children's rights as conventionally understood. The male actor central to Arendt's philosophy above is a reminder of how birth and maternity are ascribed a romanticized responsibility for transforming bad into good—saving mankind—a vision that ultimately subordinates mothers, again. At the same time, attention to children as political and social beings, as bearers of human rights *and* agents of cultural and conflict reproduction and social change, pushes us toward the notion that new life actually contains potential for peacebuilding. This paradox or complication is at the heart of what a human rights culture needs to address: how complexly constructed "children" might transform women's rights and also require new ways of looking at women, childhood, motherhood, family, men, gender relations, human rights, and peacebuilding.

The aim of this chapter has been to start a discussion about what children born of war can teach us about what a human rights culture could really mean. Existing theory identifies three aspects that are central to the development of human rights culture, and the children-born-of-war lens confirms their importance and their deep interconnectedness. However, the prioritizing of the first dimension—legal and political institutional change led by war elites—is a weakness, because it places women and particularly children out of power. From the perspective of fostering a human rights culture, this exclusionary status quo begs action to "start something new."

At the same time, enabling children born of war to emerge organically, as symbols of tolerance and reconciliation, and as active agents for sustaining human rights culture, will require, in the first instance, creating institutions to protect them. New legal and political institutions do have a vital role in protecting children born of rape from victimization and allowing them to develop to their fullest potential. But this only underlines the need to think critically about how well human rights institutions that emerge from male-dominated and military negotiations can fully accommodate the most vulnerable of society. Much more commitment to education mechanisms, to public health, and to addressing social and economic violence is necessary at the very beginning of peace negotiations or transition processes. Folding these concerns more deliberately into reconstruction plans at their earliest points would strengthen human rights culture.

Children born of war will be better recognized when post-conflict reconstruction means mainstreaming attention to gender relations in all reconstruction activities.[24] Knowledge of children born of war might be incorporated into efforts to develop human rights culture in postwar situations, without obliging local parties literally to expose their children born of war, and this could be achieved through truth-and-reconciliation or education processes. Children born of war will have better informed theories of human rights culture when a commitment to addressing militarism and patriarchy at the root of culture is made through education mechanisms in a variety of arenas: legal, military, and political institutions; schools; workplaces; religious institutions; and informal community settings.

Yet the meaning of children born of war in global politics will not have been understood until domestic and sexual violence by members of armed groups in a peace negotiation is considered a ceasefire violation and until children have active roles in processes of peace negotiation and post-conflict reconstruction. It is essential to recognize that the concept and the practice of building human rights culture are neither gender neutral nor age neutral.[25] But starting something new involves having access to sources of power and decision-making, and this heavily circumscribes the action of civilian women, children, *and* civilian men in war zones. It leaves out children born of war—seemingly agency-less infants—entirely. Children are rarely franchised in post-conflict societies, or globally, and have very little political voice through other means. Agency is also limited by trauma and the harsh everyday realities of survival. Yet, this chapter claims that children born of war do have social agency, and although their power is limited, this agency, whether it is recognized or not, will affect the quality and sustainability of human rights culture.

As Richard Wilson argues, "Human rights are not founded in eternal moral categories of social philosophy, but are the result of concrete social struggles. Rights are embedded in local normative orders and yet are caught within webs of power and meaning which extend beyond the local" (Wilson 1997, 23). The case of children born of war illustrates this only too well. The challenge to advocates for the rights and welfare of children born of war is to transform the questions about the rights of children born of war into concrete political struggles; to ask questions about rights that make claims for power on the behalf of children born of war, or that create the conditions for children born of war to do so for themselves in time.

A children-born-of-war lens underlines the urgency of building human rights cultures in which children are centrally respected and involved. To do so we would need to know what war has done to them—and not just in terms of the physical and psychological damage to children over generations, but the damage war has done to the space in which it is possible to imagine children at all. When two and three year olds are raped during war in the Congo and UN peacekeepers stand by out of fear for their own safety (Goodwin 2004), a remarkable inversion, subversion, and perversion of the "proper" roles of children and adults has taken place—one that makes patriarchy and militarism, and perhaps even the politics of "protection," finally irrelevant to solving violent conflict. Similarly, while the children born of wartime rape lead us down many competing and contradictory roads, they at least offer us assurance that "something new" is long overdue.

An image of the militarized child, particularly one conceived through sexual torture, is a powerful reminder of what is at stake when wars begin and leads to a final conclusion about human rights culture. The development of a sustainable human rights culture entails a demilitarization that is much more thorough than the demobilization and reintegration of combatants. It entails a demilitarization of culture and values and a transformation at the interface of gender and lived experience, where relationships between men and women are constructed, and where family and child-rearing practices and children's rights are located, that transforms attitudes and predilections to war. It also involves a transformation at the international level where so much lip-service is paid to children's rights, to participatory processes, and to gender lenses,[26] and where so much expenditure is made on wars and militarized solutions to war.

## Notes

[1] Anthropologist Victoria Sanford shared this recollection with the author in a personal communication on May 7, 2004. Sanford's research on Mayan women in Guatemala is published in her book *Buried Secrets* (2003).

[2] Paula Donovan (2002) provides figures of between two thousand and five thousand, and Emily Wax "more than 10,000" (2004, A01).

[3] It needs to be noted that these areas of inquiry—rape as a weapon of war and the special situation of children in war—are themselves fairly new. Feminists helped push war rape onto the international agenda while noting it as evidence of the gendered nature of war (Enloe 1990; Stiglmayer 1994; Brownmiller 1975; and Reardon 1985). Still, as Katrina Lee Koo notes in an article highlighting the continued "disciplinary [gender] blindness" of international politics, while "war rape is as old as war itself . . . traditional forms of theorising about international politics fails to identify or vocalize the violent insecurities of women in domestic and international space" (2002, 525).

[4] This is different from the idea of an international or transnational culture of human rights or global human rights regime, but not unrelated. Apart from the scope of each endeavor, a significant difference between the two exists in the role of "shame." As Andrew Hurrell argues, human rights regimes function through "the mobilization of shame" (1999, 283). In postwar, transitional, or violently divided societies the internal construction of a human rights culture seems often to require a different encounter with shame—one that either pragmatically bypasses it, or in the case of truth commissions, may make shame the penalty for societal forgiveness. At the same time the two (international or transnational human rights regimes and internal human rights culture) are "a

conscious and artificial construction designed to uphold human dignity and prevent human suffering in the face of persistent human bestiality" (Carlos Santiago
Nino, quoted in Hurrell 1999, 299). So, they share the same normative framework.

⁵ See, for example, the report of the Chilean Truth Commission, which notes:
"The legal and institutional reforms proposed in the previous section do not in
themselves offer sufficient assurance that either government officials or politically motivated private citizens will actually respect human rights. Such an assurance can only be achieved in a society whose culture is truly inspired by
unrestricted acknowledgement of the essential rights of the human being. Respect for such rights flows naturally out of such a culture as a part of everyday life
and is manifested throughout the whole range of the nation's activity, political
and otherwise" (Chilean Truth Commission 1993, pt. 4, chap. 2).

⁶ A negative human rights culture could be defined as one in which political
rights are emphasized and gross violations of human rights are prohibited and
vigorously guarded against by state authorities. A positive human rights culture
would be one in which, additionally, the provision of economic, social, and cultural rights are guaranteed and in which all of these rights are embraced as inherent to the dignity of human beings.

⁷ In full, Marotta's argument on this point is as follows: "In practical terms,
integrating human rights in post-conflict reconstruction efforts means assisting
war-torn countries in establishing a sound legal framework for the protection of
human rights, backed up by adequate institutions with a sustainable capacity to
ensure respect for those rights on a long-term basis. It also requires fostering
human rights awareness among the general population so as to increase the level
of accountability of government authorities and institutions" (Marotta 2000, 69–
70).

⁸ Reconciliation is a highly contested concept and there is not the space here
to discuss it in depth. But briefly, it is necessary to point to two different approaches—one focusing on individual reconciliation and the other on national
reconciliation. John Paul Lederach, for example, defines reconciliation as "the
redefinition and restoration of broken relationships" (1997, 84). Hizkias Assefa
defines reconciliation as a conflict handling process that leads to healing and
entails eight different core elements (Assefa 2001). Assefa locates healing as the
effect of reconciliation. Others, such as Alex Boraine, find healing to be more
integral to the steps of a reconciliation process as a national process (2000, 151–
52).

⁹ James L. Gibson (2004), for example, describes South Africa as having a
degree of human rights culture.

¹⁰ Legitimizing previously demonized armed actors as partners in peace is
seen to be a good in terms of promoting reconciliation (perhaps illustrating how
reconciliation is gendered). It is often seen to be justice, depending on one's view
of the legitimacy and morality of a particular struggle, or a practical necessity,
and a custom. When wars end, POWs are released, recruits return to the civilian
economy, and standing armies are recomposed. In practice, this often means the
protection of armed actors from prosecution or other penalties (such as social
exclusion or vigilante reprisals). Some scholars, peace practitioners, and human rights advocates argue that prosecutions for war criminals/gross violators

of human rights and lustration for political officials of the old regime have a vital place in transforming society and demonstrating a clear break with the past and its atrocities. Others argue that only reintegration of combatants, attending to economic, psychological, and social needs, and amnesty and truth-telling processes can truly heal a war-torn society and create not only stability but a sustainable peace. While this has been the basis for a significant tension between scholars and practitioners of human rights and those in the field of peacebuilding, most recently the literature has emphasized how truth and justice mechanisms, such as truth commissions and war crimes tribunals, are complementary (Borer 2005). Yet the difficulties of implementing such dual strategies in practice are underlined by the privilege extended to armed actors in peace processes. And what has not been investigated until now is how the viewpoint of a most vulnerable group, in this case children born of war, might inform the discussion.

[11] Forty Peace Accord texts were consulted on the United States Institute of Peace's Peace Agreements Digital Collection (usip.org website).

[12] Sekaggya (2004) has reported that some former girl soldiers, accompanied by their children born as a result of rape, had to choose between abandoning their children to a child soldier rehabilitation center or taking them to an uncertain future in the Ugandan bush. These girls could not enter the center themselves because, at nineteen years old, they were one year older than the upper age limit.

[13] Gender-based violence continues in peacetime and affects women and communities in complex and multiple ways, as shown in recent studies on sexual violence in the Former Yugoslavia (Copic 2004).

[14] Special professional training is essential, which is often a low priority. In Sierra Leone, for example, it is reported that only sixteen police officers received training in dealing with sexual and domestic violence since the Lome accord. This training is part of a developing nationwide system of family support units set up to deal with sexual and domestic violence and funded by the British Commonwealth Community Safety and Security Project (Human Rights Watch 2003a, section IX). This neglect is not exclusive to transitional societies. In the United States, for example, only 30 percent of army bases have a victims' advocate to deal with spousal abuse cases (Cloud et al. 2002). Impunity for perpetrators of domestic violence is also a problem in the US military (Lutz and Elliston 2002). Moreover, there is a strong predisposition for male authority figures to dispute accusations of rape and deny paternity. Military commanders in Burundi, for example, recently claimed that women cried rape only after having consensual sex in hope of money that was not forthcoming (Human Rights Watch 2003c).

[15] The International Criminal tribunals for the Former Yugoslavia and for Rwanda recognized rape and sexual violence as specific crimes and acts of genocide providing good legal basis for arguing that rape and sexual violence are crimes against humanity. Prior to this, rape was already prohibited under the Geneva Conventions (Mertus 2000, 79–81).

[16] For an illustration of this dynamic in Greek myth, see Girard 1993.

[17] Brownmiller reports numerous medical complications from indigenous abortions methods in Bangladesh, as well as suicide and infanticide attempts involving "rat poison and drowning" (1975, 84).

[18] As Nhlapo has argued, the attempted importation of international human rights norms may be counterproductive in many contexts if they are associated in people's minds with other Western thought and values (2000, 137).

[19] However, these occur in lesser numbers than male rape of women (Human Rights Watch 2003a; Brett and McCallin 1996).

[20] Constanza Ardila Galvis quotes a Colombian father who sexually abused his daughter and fathered a child with her. A political activist, his admission emerged from a process of collaborative reflection and in response to a woman's story of her own abuse at hands of men.

> 'Companeros' he said with a broken voice, without lifting his eyes. 'I have something to confess to you. I abused my daughter'. His sobs shook him and stopped him from speaking. . . . 'The truth is that two men live within me and one of them is very bad. I apologise, I only told a part of my story, the heroic side, but not how despicable I've been, a man who took advantage of his daughter's innocence. Now she has a son of mine and I am jealous because she lives with another man. I'm a miserable coward and a bad father. . . . I thought that my daughter wouldn't suffer, that by being her man, I would prevent her from being taken away by men like Jacinto. . . . She went to live with a man who humiliates and mistreats her because she allows him to. Listening to Antonia I realise how my daughter must suffer because of me. (2002, 201–2)

Admittedly, this father's conversation with women, which begins his transformation, is a conversation with campaneros—equals—who were on the same side in war, and the rape survivor is his daughter. Yet, the gender equality and storytelling dialogic that is at the heart of this exchange provides a thought-provoking model of a response to the multilayered crime of war rape. The father goes on to say: "I don't want to justify myself before you, but if someone had helped me, I wouldn't have continued" (202).

[21] Biological reproduction is one only element of that role, which extends into numerous social arenas. As Elizabeth Porter shows, women function as "biological reproducers of ethnic collectivities; as reproducers of the boundaries of ethnic and national groups; as actors in the ideological reproduction of the collectivity and as transmitters of its culture; as signifiers of ethnic and national difference; and as participants in national, economic, political and military struggles" (Porter 1998, 42).

[22] A useful summary of the differences among conservative, liberal, and critical pluralism is provided by Alan Smyth and Tony Vaux. In brief, conservative pluralism emphasizes similarities among people, liberal pluralism emphasizes differences/diversity, and critical pluralism also recognizes "differences in status, privilege and power relations between groups" (Smyth and Vaux 2003, 27).

[23] Carolyn Nordstrom has spent an academic lifetime demonstrating this phenomenon and recently does so in a provocative study of street children in Angola (2006). Victoria Sanford shows a similar process in her study of the Communities of Population in Resistance in Guatemala and Colombian Peace Communities (2006). Julie Mertus notes how in the Bosnian case "the whirlwind of war opened up a space for the creation of local women's groups that could tackle oppression and work for a more just society" (2000, 36–37). Susan Brownmiller

reports raped women in a clinic in postcolonial Congo whispering to one another about their rapes: "How many times for you?" (1975, 137). In doing so, they quietly created solidarity, support, and community.

[24] A gender approach should be understood not just as involving women's issues, as Sultan Barakat argues is currently the case in Afghanistan, but also "the relationships between women and men in family, community, work and education" (Barakat 2002, 810).

[25] As Debra L. DeLaet (2006) shows the concept of truth and the practice of truth-telling in transitional societies are not gender neutral either.

[26] The historic UN Resolution 1325 on gender mainstreaming and attention to gender-based violence has yet to be adequately implemented in programmatic ways, which requires political commitment and funding.

# References

Amadiume, Ifi, and Abdullahi An-Na'im. 2000. *The Politics of Memory: Truth, Healing and Social Justice.* London: Zed.

Arendt, Hannah. 1970. *On Violence.* New York: Harcourt Brace.

Argentine National Commission on the Disappeared. 1986. *Nunca Mas: The Report of the Argentine National Commission on the Disappeared.* New York: Farrar Straus Giroux.

Assefa, Hizkias. 2001. "Reconcilation." In *Peace-Building: A Field Guide*, edited by Luc Reycher and Thania Paffenholz, 366–42. Boulder, CO: Lynne Rienner.

Balorda, Jasna. 2004. "The Role of the United Nations in Protecting Bosnia's War Babies." Proceedings of the War Babies: Human Rights of Children Born of Wartime Rape and Sexual Exploitation Interdisciplinary Workshop, University of Pittsburgh. November 13.

Barakat, Sultan. 2002. "Setting the Scene for Afghanistan's Reconstruction: The Challenges and Critical Dilemmas." *Third World Quarterly* 23, no. 5: 801–16.

Becirbasic, Belma, and Dzenana Secic. 2002. *Invisible Casualties of War.* London: Institute of War and Peace Reporting. Available on the iwpr.gn.apc.org website.

Boose, Lynda E. 2002. "Crossing the River Drina: Bosnian Rape Camps, Turkish Impalement, and Serb Cultural Memory." *Signs: Journal of Women in Culture and Society* 28, no. 1: 71–96.

Boraine, Alex. 2000. "Truth and Reconciliation in South Africa: The Third Way." In *Truth V. Justice: The Morality of Truth Commissions*, edited by Robert I. Rotberg and Dennis Thompson, 141–57. Princeton, NJ: Princeton University Press.

Borer, Tristan Anne, ed. 2006. *Telling the Truths: Truth Telling and Peace Building in Post Conflict Societies.* Notre Dame, IN: University of Notre Dame Press.

Brett, Rachel, and Margaret McCallin. 1996. *Children: The Invisible Soldiers.* Vaxjo: Radda Barnen.

Brownmiller, Susan. 1975. *Against Our Will: Men, Women and Rape*. New York: Simon and Schuster.

Carpenter, R. Charli. 2000. "Surfacing Children: Limitations of Genocidal Rape Discourse." *Human Rights Quarterly* 22, no. 2: 428–77.

Chilean Truth Commission. 1993. *(Text of the) Chilean Truth Commission Report*. Washington DC: United States Institute of Peace Digital Collection. Available on the usip.org website.

Cloud, John, Mike Billips, Amanda Bower, Constance E. Richards, and Douglas Waller. 2002. "Blood on the Home Front." *Time* 160, no. 6 (August 5, 160), 45.

Copic, Sanja, 2004. "Wife Abuse in the Countries of the Former Yugoslavia." *Feminist Review* 76: 46–64.

Crocker, Chester A., Fen Osler Hampson, and Pamela Aall. 2004. *Taming Intractable Conflicts: Mediation in the Hardest Cases*. Washington DC: United States Institute of Peace Press.

Darby, John. 2001. *The Effects of Violence on Peace Processes*. Washington DC: United States Institute of Peace Press.

Darby, John, and Roger McGinty. 2003. *Contemporary Peace Making: Conflict, Violence, and Peace Processes*. New York: Palgrave Macmillan.

DeLaet, Debra, L. 2006. "Gender Justice: A Gendered Assessment of Truth Telling Mechanisms." In Borer 2006, 151–79.

Dicklitch, Susan, and Doreen Lwanga. 2003. "The Politics of Being Non-Political: Human Rights Organizations and the Creation of a Positive Human Rights Culture in Uganda." *Human Rights Quarterly* 25, no. 2: 482–509.

Donovan, Paula. 2002. "Rape and HIV/AIDS in Rwanda." *Lancet* 360, no. 9350, Supplement: 17–18.

Duffy, Terence. 1994. "Toward a Culture of Human Rights in Cambodia." *Human Rights Quarterly* 16, no. 1: 82–104.

Enloe, Cynthia. 1990. *Bananas, Beaches, and Bases: Making Feminist Sense of International Politics*. Berkeley and Los Angeles: University of California Press.

———. 1995. "Feminism, Nationalism, Militarism: Wariness without Paralysis?" In *Feminism, Nationalism, and Militarism*, edited by Constance R. Sutton, 13–32. Arlington, VA: American Anthropological Association.

Feldman, Allen. 1991. *Formations of Violence: The Narrative of the Body and Political Terror in Northern Ireland*. Chicago: University of Chicago Press.

Galtung, Johan. 1969. "Violence, Peace, and Peace Research." *Journal of Peace Research* 6, no. 3: 167–91.

Galvis, Constanza Ardila. 2002. *The Heart of War in Colombia*. London: Latin American Bureau.

Gibson, James L. 2004. "Truth, Reconciliation, and the Creation of a Human Rights Culture in South Africa." *Law and Society Review* 38, no. 1: 5–40.

Girard, Rene. 1993. *Violence and the Sacred*. 8th ed. Translated by Patrick Gregory. Baltimore: Johns Hopkins University Press.

Goodwin, Jan. 2004. "Silence=Rape." *The Nation*. March 8. Available on the thenation.com website.

Green, Linda. 1999. *Fear as a Way of Life: Mayan Widows in Rural Guatemala*. New York: Columbia University Press.

Hayner, Priscilla. 2001. *Unspeakable Truths: Confronting State Terror and Atrocity.* New York: Routledge.

Hess, Rachel. 2004. "Babies of Girl Soldiers." Paper presented at the War Babies: Theorizing the Human Rights of Children Born of Wartime Rape and Sexual Exploitation Interdisciplinary Workshop held in conjunction with the International Studies Association Annual Conference, Montreal, Quebec, March 16.

Hopper, Kim. 2003. *Reckoning with Homelessness.* Ithaca, NY: Cornell University Press.

Howland, Todd. 2004. "UN Field Presence as Proactive Instrument of Peace and Social Change: Lessons from Angola." *Human Rights Quarterly* 26, no. 1: 1–28.

Human Rights Watch. 2003a. *"We'll Kill You If You Cry": Sexual Violence in the Sierra Leone Conflict.* Human Rights Watch report 15:1(A). Available on the hrw.org website.

———. 2003b. *Struggling through Peace: Return and Resettlement in Angola.* Human Rights Watch Report No. 15:16(A). Available on the hrw.org website.

———. 2003c. *Everyday Victims: Civilians in the Burundi War.* Human Rights Watch report 15:20(A). Available on the hrw.org website.

Hurrell, Andrew. 1999. "Power, Principles, and Prudence: Protecting Human Rights in a Deeply Divided World." In *Human Rights in Global Politics,* ed. Tim Dunne and Nicholas J. Wheeler, 277–302. Cambridge: Cambridge University Press.

Jahn, George. 2005. "More than a Decade Later, Bosnian Children Born of War Rape Start Asking Questions." *The Associated Press,* May 20.

Koo, Katrina Lee. 2002. "Confronting a Disciplinary Blindness: Women, War, and Rape in the International Politics of Security." *Australian Journal of Political Science* 37, no. 3: 525–36.

Lederach, John Paul. 1997. *Building Peace: Sustainable Reconciliation in Divided Societies.* Washington DC: United States Institute of Peace Press.

Lutz, Catherine, and Jon Elliston. 2002. "Domestic Terror." *The Nation* 275 (October 14). Available on the hws.edu website.

Machel, Graca. 1996. A/51/306. *Impact of Armed Conflict on Children: Report of the Expert of the Secretary-General, Ms. Graca Machel.* New York: UNICEF. Available on the unicef.org website.

Mamdani, Mahmood. 2004. *Good Muslim, Bad Muslim: America, the Cold War, and the Roots of Terror.* New York: Pantheon.

Marotta, Francesca. 2000. "The Blue Flame and the Gold Shield: Methodology, Challenges, and Lessons Learned on Human Rights Training for Police." In *Peacebuilding and Police Reform,* edited by Tor Tanke Holm and Espen Barthe Eide, 69–92. London/Portland: Frank Cass.

McEvoy-Levy, Siobhán. 2006. "Introduction." In *Troublemakers and Peacemakers. Youth and Post-Accord Peacebuilding,* ed. Siobhán McEvoy-Levy. Notre Dame, IN: University of Notre Dame Press.

Mertus, Julie A. 2000. *War's Offensive on Women: The Humanitarian Challenge in Bosnia, Kosovo, and Afghanistan.* Bloomfield, CT: Kumarian Press.

———. 2004. "Improving International Peacebuilding Efforts: The Example of Human Rights Culture in Kosovo." *Global Governance* 10: 333–51.

Nhlapo, Thandabantu. 2000. "The African Customary Law of Marriage and the Rights Conundrum." In *Beyond Rights Talk and Culture Talk: Comparative Essays on the Politics of Rights and Culture,* edited by Mahmood Mamdani, 136–48. Cape Town, South Africa.

Nordstrom, Carolyn. 2006. "The Jagged Edge of Peace: The Creation of Culture and War Orphans in Angola." In *Troublemakers and Peacemakers: Youth and Post-Accord Peacebuilding,* edited by Siobhán McEvoy-Levy, 99–116. Notre Dame, IN: University of Notre Dame Press.

Osborne, Thomas. 2003. "What Is Neo-Enlightenment? Human Rights Culture and Juridicial Reason." *Journal of Human Rights* 2, no. 4: 523–30.

Özerdem, Alpaslan. 2004. "Disarmament, Demobilization, and Reintegration of Former Combatants in Afghanistan: Lessons Learned from a Cross Cultural Perspective." In *Reconstructing War-Torn Societies: Afghanistan,* edited by Sultan Barakat, 161–75. New York: Palgrave Macmillan.

Price, Lisa S. 2001. "Finding the Man in the Soldier-Rapist: Some Reflections on Comprehension and Accountability." *Women's Studies International Forum* 24, no. 2: 212–27.

Porter, Elizabeth. 1998. "Identity, Location, Plurality: Women, Nationalism, and Northern Ireland." In *Women, Ethnicity, and Nationalism: The Politics of Transition,* edited by Rick Wilford and Robert L. Miller, 36–61. London: Routledge.

Reardon, Betty. 1985. *Sexism and the War System.* New York: Teachers College Press.

Salomon, Gavriel. 2004. "Does Peace Education Make a Difference in the Context of an Intractable Conflict?" *Peace and Conflict: Journal of Peace Psychology* 10, no. 3: 257–74.

Sanford, Victoria. 2003. *Buried Secrets: Truth and Human Rights in Guatemala.* New York: Palgrave Macmillan.

———. 2006. "The Moral Imagination of Survival: Displacement and Child Soldiers in Guatemala and Colombia." In *Troublemakers and Peacemakers: Youth and Post-Accord Peacebuilding,* edited by Siobhán McEvoy-Levy, 49–80. Notre Dame, IN: University of Notre Dame Press.

Sekaggya, Liza. 2004. "Ugandan Children Born in Captivity and Their Human Rights," comment during presentation at War Babies: Human Rights of Children Born of Wartime Rape and Sexual Exploitation Interdisciplinary Workshop, University of Pittsburgh, November 13.

Slye, Ronald C. 2000. "Amnesty, Truth, and Reconciliation: Reflections on the South African Amnesty Process." In *Truth V. Justice: The Morality of Truth Commissions,* edited by Robert I. Rotberg and Dennis Thompson, 170–88. Princeton, NJ: Princeton University Press.

Smyth, Alan, and Tony Vaux. 2003. *Education, Conflict, and International Development.* London: United Kingdom Department for International Development.

Stedman, Stephen John, Donald Rothchild, and Elizabeth M. Cousens. 2002. *Ending Civil Wars: The Implementation of Peace Agreements.* Boulder, CO: Lynne Rienner.

Stiglmayer, Alexandra, ed. 1994. *Mass Rape: The War against Women in Bosnia-Herzegovina.* Lincoln: University of Nebraska Press.

Sultan, Abubacar. 2000. *Testimony to the First Hearings of the International Tribunal for Children's Rights, Colchester, UK.* Montreal: International Bureau for Children's Rights. Available on the ibcr.org website.

UNIRIN (United Nations Integrated Regional Information Networks). 2004. "Uganda: At Least 270 People, Mainly Children, Freed From Captivity in May." Available on the allafrica.com website.

Wax, Emily. 2004. "Rwandans Are Struggling to Love Children of Hate." *Washington Post*, March 28: A01.

Wilson, Richard A. 1997. *Human Rights, Culture and Context: Anthropological Perspectives*. London: Pluto Press.

# 10

# Key Ethical Inquiries for Future Research

## JULIE MERTUS

The preceding case studies and analysis in this collection have pointed to the need for future research on children born of wartime rape. As Giulia Baldi and Megan MacKenzie observe in their study on Sierra Leone, for example, more targeted studies are urgently needed to help inform the social and political responses to the issue and, if all goes well, to improve the lives of the children and families that are central to this query. Expanded analysis of existing data alone, although certainly needed, is not enough to advance significantly our understanding of this complex topic. To make compelling contributions to existing literature, researchers must press deeper into existing case studies and gather new information for further comparative analysis. Additional fieldwork is necessary, accompanied by a variety of research methodologies, such as focus groups, field observations, structured and unstructured interviews, surveys, and participatory research.

This chapter seeks to explore the key ethical issues that will continue to present themselves as such research proceeds. The chapter explores three criteria social scientists generally apply to research on human subjects:

1. The research should maximize possible benefits and minimize harm;
2. Informed consent should be given from potential research participants or, where appropriate, their proxies; and
3. Local participation in research design, application, and evaluation should be maximized whenever possible (see, e.g., Cassell and Jacob 1987).

For researchers studying children born of rape, the emergency nature of the research and the particular vulnerability of the research population shape how these three criteria may be addressed.

## Conducting Risk-Benefit Analyses with Vulnerable Populations

With children as research subjects, the first ethical question concerns the age at which one is no longer considered a child. This definition varies greatly among international conventions, researchers, aid agencies, communities, and children themselves. For the purpose of working with children born of wartime rape, researchers have a responsibility to inquire about the age of childhood (and age of capacity) in the country in which the child presently resides (where the status of *child* may substantially inform access to social services) and in the country of origin and/or any transit countries where harm occurred.

Once the legal status of children is determined, a risk/benefit analysis should be performed. For this analysis researchers should weigh any potential benefits of the new research against any potential costs. The range of potential benefits and possible harms associated with future research on children born of rape in conflict area differs from other studies on stable adult populations.

The contributors to this volume agree that the benefits of additional research on this topic could prove substantial for the particular children and communities under study as particular needs and concerns are identified. As Eunice Apio notes: "It is increasingly recognized that challenges associated with the assimilation of children born in armed conflict require more systematic study. . . . Little is known about these children and how they can integrate with their mothers back into their community" (chap. 6 herein). Given this lack of information, Susan Harris Rimmer similarly concludes, "The first imperative is to gain qualitative and quantitative data on the situation of these children and their mothers" (chap. 4 herein). Only then can the social reintegration process be improved. Work with children in structured research projects will also lead to a better understanding of the types of social services that best address their short-term and long-term needs. Other related benefits of future research may involve lowering the probability of harm for other children who have already been subjected to abuse and are at great risk of further harm.

Balanced against the significant benefits of working with children, however, are several possible harms. Whenever children are involved in any research endeavor, the physical, psychological, political, and legal consequences for research participants are potentially more dangerous than in most research involving adult subjects. Children are at a legal and social disadvantage compared with adults, who enjoy greater protections under law and respect under social norms, enabling them greater latitude in exercising their agency. Poverty and its consequences, Marie Consolée Mukangendo observes, also severely curtail adequate access to food, education, and health, thus compounding children's vulnerability. This is particularly true with children born of rape, as Mukangendo highlights in her study on Rwanda: "Stigmatized as both illegitimate and as enemy children, their difficult situation seems complicated. . . . Often, the decision to keep the child causes conflicts in the family, pitting those who reject the child against those who want to raise the child" (chap. 3 herein).

The malfunctioning of legal and social institutions in emergency and post-conflict scenarios also renders children more vulnerable, when their precarious state is often compounded by their status as refugees, migrants, and noncitizens. By definition, noncitizens enjoy fewer rights than citizens. Noncitizens who are not afforded refugee status or some other official legal status stand outside the protection of both domestic legislation and international standards. The international guidelines that provide guidance on research with human subjects have not addressed research involving refugee populations. In his study of the ethics of conducting research on vulnerable populations, Jason Lott reports, "Neither the Declaration of Helsinki nor the Council for International Organizations of Medical Sciences (CIOMS) research guidelines specifically mention refugee populations, and neither the Belmont report and Nuremberg Code address the issue" (Lott 2005, 40). Without credible ethical guidance, refugees and other noncitizens are subject to breaches of ethically acceptable research protocols. Because refugees and other noncitizens are often economically destitute, researchers can easily entice them to participate in research for limited financial awards.

Even researchers with the best intentions may contribute to their research subjects' ongoing psychological stress. For many reasons this may be especially true in the case of children born of rape. As many of the contributors to this volume underscore, the agency of children born of rape and their mothers should be respected. However, the psychological distress that they have suffered may cloud their judgment and perceptions, thus interfering with their ability to choose to enter into and to participate freely in a research project. The stress of participation may be overwhelming for many research subjects because it forces them to relive the trauma. Moreover, the experience of children in wartime and post-conflict situations is of interest to many interviewers, and the same children and mothers may be put through multiple interviews, possibly with untrained or inexpert interviewers. Less experienced interviewers may conduct interviews with families as groups, thus destroying any hope children and mothers have of telling their stories in a safe and confidential environment.

Ethical problems also arise when researchers attempt to collect and use physical artifacts created by children, such as poems and drawings. To take one illustration, when children's artwork is handled by multiple agencies and moved from researcher to researcher, this leads to the invasion of children's privacy and the possible loss or damage of data. Because researchers have an obligation to protect and secure their data archives, research should not be conducted if security cannot be assured, yet in the rush to publicize the plight of children born of rape, these precautions are frequently not undertaken. The ownership by the children of drawings, writings, and other artifacts should be respected; it is the child, and not just the researcher, who should benefit from the use of his or her artifacts in a research project.

In sum, the nature of research as an intervention necessitates that the researcher engage with ethical concerns beyond not causing harm; the researcher must also consider who benefits from the research process and output. The researcher is clearly benefiting when the research fulfills a professional requirement. Professional benefit is perfectly legitimate, but the local participants in the research process must also benefit from the research process. The researcher should consider the ways in which the research can add value to the community rather than being only a situation in which knowledge is extracted. Ultimately, in making a cost/benefit analysis for future research on children born of rape, researchers should take into account the complicated impact of the emergency setting and of the post-conflict scenarios. The particular vulnerability of the research subjects due to their age and legal status should be a major factor in determining when and how to proceed. Another important factor in making these assessments should be whether the research subjects give free and informed consent, an issue to which we now turn.

## Obtaining Informed Consent with Vulnerable Populations/Emergency Scenarios

Researchers seeking to conduct future studies on children born of wartime rape face considerable challenges in obtaining informed consent, due to the emergency context in which they work and the often vulnerable state of their research subjects. This is especially true when the research subjects are children. The agency of children to decide whether, when, and how to participate in research should be respected. The requirement of informed consent is designed to protect potentially vulnerable research subjects by providing them with the kind of

information they need to exercise their agency. Informed consent, however, demands the capacity for rational, informed decision-making, characteristics that young children arguably do not possess. When children
cannot give their consent, research may still proceed, but ethical codes
suggest that in such circumstances children should not be subjected to
interviews but only to surveillance.

Proxy consent may be an acceptable alternative for children who cannot give their own consent, but proxy consent may be extremely problematic as well. One question that arises concerns who is an appropriate
proxy. Parents are likely candidates, but sometimes their interests diverge from those of their children, and often in wartime and post-conflict scenarios parents are not available to give consent. But even if a
parent is an appropriate proxy, should proxy consent be permitted? The
conditions under which proxy consent may be permissible are hotly de-
bated. Medical researchers considering this question generally make a
distinction between therapeutic (situations where the research is of direct value to the participants) and non-therapeutic research (situations
where the research is not of direct value to the participants). Questions
of consent are generally dealt with in a more permissive manner and
proxy consent is more often accepted when the research is therapeutic.
If this medical model were to be extended to the case at hand, given that
research on children born of wartime rape is rarely therapeutic, proxy
consent would rarely be permitted. This reasoning reflects the widely
shared belief that proxy consent may not sufficiently protect children
from research agendas that lack any direct benefit to the children. In
such cases it appears that the researcher is taking advantage of children's
vulnerability for the researcher's gain.

Complicating the issue of informed consent for research is the inter-
play between the definition of research and the realities of emergency
situations and conflict scenarios. Researchers often seek to use reports
and other written artifacts created in emergency scenarios. Are these
considered "research"? And, if so, are there limits on how and when they
can be used by researchers? Similarly, many NGOs collect program data
that are meant to be internal but are later used by researchers. What
ethical constraints apply to the use of "found data"? In answering these
questions, researchers should consider whether the use of found data
would subject research subjects to exposure, coercion, or retribution. To
take a concrete example, researches may seek to analyze as part of their
work family-tracing databases for lost children. Yet these databases were
created for humanitarian program purposes, not for researchers studying children born of wartime rape. Who should have control over the
use of the data: the refugees who are the subject of the database or the
humanitarian agency that created it? And how should the data be used?
Child research subjects and their families have a strong argument for

restricting the use of such records when public disclosure would likely be harmful.

Some researchers argue that research should be limited in all phases of emergencies, where it is difficult or impossible to obtain informed consent. Others argue just the opposite, contending that the informed-consent model may be waived during the acute emergency phase for public data collection activities (surveillance, outbreak investigations), but only for a short period of time. For example, once a refugee camp is more established and refugee camps become more like institutions, the situation may be deemed changed and specific consent may be necessary. In any case, informed consent needs to be seen as an ongoing process, not just a one-time event. Local participation in the research design and application may help enable researchers to understand and adapt to this process.

## Encouraging Local Participation

Research interventions that do not take into consideration the capacities and existing coping mechanisms of people in the locality will be less effective and even harmful. In designing future projects for research on children born of wartime rape researchers can take steps to reduce the relative power imbalances between themselves and local parties by creating mutual obligations and giving beneficiaries control over some aspect of the process. The research technique most associated with valuing local expertise and enhancing local participation is known as participatory research.

A central tenant of participatory research is that control and ownership of the research process (or the creation of knowledge) should be shared among all participants rather than having a research process imposed (Nelson et al. 1998). Outsider-conceived projects require, at the very least, endorsement and agreement (Reason and Bradbury 2001). In this reciprocal research relationship the researcher and the participant are dependent on each other, and each brings a particular set of skills and competencies to the endeavor. The researcher's skill and contribution is the intellectual framework and knowledge of process, while the "problem owner" brings knowledge of the context. The contributions of each are valued and considered essential to conducting research. Especially as research involves an element of problem solving, participatory research recognizes the value of engaging stakeholders, especially oppressed people, in informing research interventions.

Participatory research suggests that setting the research agenda should be a two-way process. The involvement of problem owners in setting the research agenda, defining the most important problems, and determining

an action strategy has two major results. The first is to break up dominant ways of producing knowledge and to contribute in an effective manner to the literature. The second is that by having the research process
be conducted in an organic way, with significant input from local actors,
the potential for participating individuals to be empowered in defining
their role is greater. Both of these goals are present in the case of babies
born of wartime rape.

Although not following all the tenets of participatory research, Eunice
Apio's work illustrates a keen understanding of the importance of researchers working in partnership with local populations. The inhabitants of the municipality under study in her case initially were suspicious
of her research. She describes them as "too resignedly traumatized to
contribute significantly and easily to change" (chap. 6 herein). Apio attempted to counteract these problems by cultivating a good working
relationship with NGOs and the affected population and making it known
that the research was purely academic, not aimed at affecting the political situation.

Similarly, Apio realized that direct interviews with the children and
their formerly abducted mothers also presented the risk that singling
them out would contribute to their marginalization. By working closely
with local NGOs, she learned that this risk was primarily salient outside
the reception centers. In contrast, direct interviews at reception centers
were much easier and less ethically problematic, as the interviewees easily identified themselves with all in the center community. Accordingly,
by working in partnership with the local community and drawing on its
ideas, Apio was able to gather interviews with children and their mothers primarily inside the centers. These interviews contributed greatly to
Apio's analysis and formation of general recommendations.

The work of Giulia Baldi and Megan MacKenzie similarly benefited
from a series of interviews informed by the needs and conditions of the
local population. Over a three-month period Baldi and MacKenzie conducted semi-structured interviews with humanitarian practitioners in the
region, which in turn led to open-ended, first-person interviews with
former women and girl soldiers conducted in Sierra Leone. The manner
in which they found their sample interview population and the way in
which they structured their questioning were informed by their understanding of who and what would be considered appropriate to the local
population. Thus, although they were not able to interview children,
they were able to reach a good number of former female combatants
who had been impregnated in circumstances of violence and exploitation.

There were limitations to their approach, Baldi and MacKenzie acknowledged. The "perspectives of the mothers are not the same as the
perspectives of the children themselves" and "former female soldiers are

only one group of women that experienced sexual violence and gave birth to children as a result" (chap. 5 herein). However, they found that the range of circumstances surrounding the birth of their children sheds light on some of the overlapping experiences and child-protection issues for the broader population of children born of violence during war. These interviews led them to the very interesting conclusion that "the stigma of 'rebel baby' is linked to both the act of rape and to the paternity of the child" and that the "boundaries between who is stigmatized as a 'rebel baby' and who is not" are often "fluid" in Sierra Leone (ibid.).

These examples illustrate how greater partnership with local communities may benefit future research on children born of wartime rape. Future researchers are encouraged to adopt a similarly conscientious approach. By adding new perspectives to the design, implementation, and evaluation of projects, participatory research may lead to more creative outcomes and interdisciplinary work with practitioners of all sorts. Through this method, major organizational changes may be possible which otherwise would not.

## Conclusion

This chapter provided an overview of the ethical considerations of researching children born of rape. The process of thinking through these issues can be difficult, especially if one has not been immersed in the reality of the field. However, many difficulties may be anticipated and prevented if the potential for negative impacts of research interventions are considered. Furthermore, increased attention to the researcher and community relationship will allow more research to be framed in a way that is not only academically appropriate and rigorous but also serves to foster capacity building and empowerment within the community.

## References

Cassell, Joan, and Sue-Ellen Jacob, eds. 1987. *Handbook on Ethical Issues in Anthropology* 23. Washington DC: American Anthropological Association.

Lott, Jason P. 2005. "Module Three: Vulnerable/Special Participant Populations." *Developing World* 5, no. 1: 40.

Nelson, Gregory, Joanna Ochacka, Kara Griffin, and John Lord. 1998. "Nothing about Me, without Me: Participatory Action Research with Self-help/ Mutual Aid Organizations for Psychiatric Consumer/Survivors." *American Journal of Community Psychology* 26, no. 6: 881–912.

Reason, Peter, and Hilary Bradbury, eds. 2001. *Handbook of Action Research*. London: Sage Publications.

# 11

# Children Born of War and Human Rights

## *Philosophical Reflections*

### Michael Goodhart

Systematic mass rape, forced impregnation, enforced pregnancy, and forced maternity shockingly demonstrate that we human beings possess a seemingly limitless capacity to devise ever more terrible forms of cruelty and misery for our fellows. To heap woe upon injustice, the children born of wartime rape and other forms of sexual exploitation are tragically often neglected, rejected, or simply ignored; we possess a prodigious capacity for cruelty toward unfortunates as well. When I agreed to contribute some philosophical reflections on the human rights of these children to this important volume, I envisioned something much like the essay that follows: a series of interconnected ruminations on various puzzles that arise concerning the identity and human rights of these children and on the normative and political implications of those puzzles. I failed to anticipate the profound sadness that would envelop me as I read and reflected on the chapters; academics are, after all, supposed to remain neutral and objective as we pursue our research.

Yet the urgency of the questions posed in this volume cannot be grasped without a deep appreciation of the injustice underlying them. Fortunately, we also possess tremendous capacities to hope, to empathize, and to effect social change, capacities displayed by the many mothers and communities who embrace their "children born of war" as they work to rebuild their societies and create better futures. One role of socially engaged research is to marshal empirical evidence in providing analytic and normative guidance that can inform such efforts; the chapters in this volume, and the reflections offered here, should be read in this spirit.

This chapter works through some issues raised in the foregoing chapters or in the interstices among them. For the most part, rather than engage directly with the individual chapters I step back from them to consider broad questions concerning identity, justice, and human rights, and the normative and political challenges they present. At times I discuss children born of war in the broad sense; at others I focus specifically on children born of wartime rape.

## Children Born of War and the Politics of Identity

As several contributors to this volume make clear, questions about identity figure importantly in the discourse surrounding children born of war. Among the rights of the child recognized by the UN's Convention on the Rights of the Child (CRC) are the rights to a name and a nationality and to know and be cared for, so far as is possible, by one's parents (Article 7). Children also have the right to the preservation of their identities (Article 8), a right originating in the Argentine experience of "enforced or involuntary" disappearances of children during the Dirty War (Freeman 1997, 66). While name, family, and nationality are obviously important dimensions of identity, these important rights must not be mistaken for a right to a specific identity, in the sense of membership of a particular social, cultural, or religious group. There is no right recognized in international law that guarantees an individual membership of any particular group. Insisting on this distinction clarifies what is at stake in the politics of identity in which children born of war become embroiled.

It does so by differentiating what we might call a *civic* identity, to which all children and indeed all human beings have a right, from a fuller sense of identity as membership of and belonging in a community that shapes one's values, outlook, and opportunities and provides a cultural frame of reference and way of being in the world. We might, as a shorthand, call this *deep identity*; it is the type of identity frequently associated with communitarian thinking, multiculturalism, and the politics of recognition (e.g., Sandel 1998; Kymlicka 1995; Taylor 1994). Deep identity is a characteristic of groups as well as of individuals; any group member's identity is in a sense negotiated within the framework of meaning that defines (and is defined by) the group. Group membership and identity are neither fully affective nor fully ascriptive; one cannot join just any community because one wants to, and one is never part of any community solely because one possesses (some of) its requisite traits or characteristics—values, language, religion, physiognomy, and so forth. Group identity is maintained in part through control over membership; groups define the criteria of membership and decide who qualifies as a member.

Transmission of membership to children usually has a biological or genetic component: the child of two group members typically qualifies as a group member, though even this generalization might not hold in cases where the circumstances of the child's conception are held to be "illegitimate" on the dominant understanding of group identity or where holding certain values or beliefs is crucial to membership (as in a religious community). None of this is to suggest that membership is uncontested or uncontestable within groups. Questions surrounding the definition and negotiation of identity and membership are, however, suffused with power; they are inherently political.

This distinction between a right to a civic identity—a right binding upon states and entailing nondiscriminatory application of standards for citizenship[1]—and a right to what I am calling a deep identity seems frequently to get lost in the discussion of the identities of children born of war. Several contributors to this volume write about these children's deep identities as if the children had a *right* to them and as if the facts of their parentage *proved* something about their claim to membership in their mothers' communities (I shall call this a claim of matrilineal membership). Such arguments are common in condemnations of patriarchal conceptions of identity that construct these children as children of the enemy, children of hate—in short, as inheritors exclusively of their fathers' identities. Claims of matrilineal membership make a category mistake, however; they confuse genetics with identity and membership.

This confusion is apparent in Weitsman's generally excellent discussion of identity politics (chap. 7 herein), in which she rejects the myth of genetic determination apparent in the patriarchal logic of rapists and communities who view children solely as inheriting the father's identity. This rejection follows from her (in my view correct) background assumption that identity is socially constructed. The tension arises because Weitsman appeals to the fact that children of war rape are "half the mother's genetic heritage" in countering claims about identity and membership that follow from this patriarchal logic. But as her own claim about the social construction of identity shows, genetic heritage and identity and membership are very different things. To suggest that biologically children "belong" to both parents' groups merely replicates the myth of genetic determination in a different form. No one disputes that the children are (biologically) their mothers' children, but a child's "genetic heritage" does not translate directly into group membership: it is one marker of identity whose significance must be apprehended within the broader cultural context and politics of group membership. The Nazis, whose view Weitsman discusses in comparing various constructions of identity, did not share the Serb view that paternity determines identity. Genetically the Nazi view is more correct, though the resulting view of group membership and its social and political implications were no less odious. Some sources cite matrilineal descent within Judaism as having proved useful and humane in the context of rapes attending the frequent pogroms suffered by European Jews;[2] this norm, while less correct biologically, helped to mitigate the trauma surrounding the identities of children born from the rapes. As these examples show, the point about social construction is that it is not the genetic or biological link but rather the *socially constructed significance of that link* that matters for the politics of identity.

The tough ethical and political questions concern whether groups whose constructions of identity exclude children born of war should be forced to accept them as members because of their mothers' identities. It might seem cruel or unreasonable to exclude these blameless children from matrilineal membership. Precisely because identity is socially constructed, however, conceptions of identity and membership cannot be easily criticized from the outside—or rather, the ethical status of such criticisms is uncertain. Because control over membership and definitions of identity are crucial to group survival (Walzer 1983, 32ff.), insisting on a strict biological "50 percent" rule for membership for a group that understands its identity differently is ethically problematic, especially if we take group identity and survival as prima facie goods to be preserved.

The underlying tension here is between groups' rights to define and control membership and individuals' need for the social and psychological goods that group membership and deep identity convey. To the extent that we treat group survival as a valuable and desirable end—as discussions framed by considerations of genocide and "ethnic cleansing" encourage us to do—we must recognize that a right to a deep identity of an individual's own choosing (or an obligation on the part of groups to recognize as members individuals who meet certain externally set criteria) could have profoundly negative effects on the groups to which it might be applied. Forcibly altering a community's membership through the imposition of requirements to admit individuals who the group would otherwise exclude would be tantamount to taking away the group's self-determination. It could even plausibly be constructed as genocidal under Sections (b) and (c) of Article II of the Convention on the Prevention and Punishment of the Crime of Genocide (Genocide Convention), which prohibits "causing serious . . . mental harm to members of the group" and "deliberately inflicting on the group conditions of life calculated to bring about its physical destruction," respectively. Counterintuitively, from the group's point of view a requirement to admit "nonmembers" could be both psychologically traumatic and reasonably construed as an infliction of conditions of life that would result in the group's (eventual) physical destruction.[3] Such a position seems to me both extreme and unwarranted, but it nonetheless highlights the very real tension we are considering here.

Whether discrimination by groups against putative or would-be members constitutes a human rights violation, or for that matter should even be considered discrimination, is a vexing question, one to which I shall return later on in a slightly more advantageous context. Here I want to emphasize that for groups, unlike states, formal membership requirements are not really the main issue. Belonging is primarily a social and psychological phenomenon; mandating acceptance of a member the group would otherwise not recognize seems unlikely to work. My point is not to prejudice the case in favor of group rights—about which I have certain reservations[4]—but rather to emphasize that concern with designing policies to help children born of war find places within the shattered societies that produce them does not obviate concern with the implications of those policies on the victimized communities.

These considerations raise an important question about the participatory method of research advocated by Mertus (chap. 10 herein). Participatory research, at least as imagined by Freire (1993), presumes a model in which clear, objective distinctions exist between members of the oppressing and oppressed groups (for Freire, these are class distinctions). Two aspects of this conceptualization seem inapposite to cases involving children born of war. First, the consciousness-raising aspect of participatory methodology seems explicitly designed to make members of the oppressed group aware of the oppressor, to help them liberate themselves from the internalization of oppression that characterizes the downtrodden as a group or class (see Freire 1993, 27ff.). In cases involving children born of war, the community in which research is conducted is frequently the oppressor (even though the oppression originates, as it were, in the violence perpetrated by outsiders). In this case it is not clear what exactly empowerment and ownership of the research process might mean for the children. Ending the oppression of children born of war requires a revaluation of the community's values, not the unmasking of an external ideology or the realization of an objective class situation. In such cases there is at least the real possibility that participatory research designs, instead of leading to liberation, might reinforce the community's rationale for rejecting the children and their mothers. In other words, empowering the community through research might reinforce rather than combat the oppression of children born of war.

A second and closely related challenge for participatory research in coming to grips with the social plight of these children concerns the complexities of the power hierarchies involved. The avowedly interventionist nature of participatory research, combined with this complexity, raises extraordinary ethical quandaries that deserve further attention. Where the lines between oppressor and oppressed are clear and relatively stable, it is easy enough for researchers to align themselves with the oppressed in such a way that the humanitarian values informing their work support the liberationist objectives of the participatory paradigm. Moreover, there is no obvious or necessary conflict in such cases between the researchers' values and agenda and those of the community. In cases involving children born of war, where oppression of children and mothers stems from oppression of the wider group to which the mothers belong, this felicitous alignment of values and interests can break down. There is potential tension between allowing the community to shape and direct the research and conducting research that gives voice to the oppressed children and mothers, a tension amplified in the case of mothers who internalize the community's attitudes and become oppressors of their own children. The problem is not just that researchers must be extra cautious in such cases, but rather that the easy harmony between their principled commitment to a certain research paradigm and their personal and humanitarian value commitments might slip into discord. In such cases, intervention risks slipping into advocacy, with implications not just for the researchers but also for the purported advantages and credibility of participatory research. Put bluntly, participatory research works best when the roles of victim and oppressor are clear; when those roles are blurred, ethical and methodological puzzles arise. In raising these concerns my point it not to criticize Mertus, with whose position on these questions I largely agree, but instead to point to an area of predictable tension where further normative and methodological reflection is warranted.

## Are Children Born of War Victims? Of What? By Whom?

Determining whether children born of war are victims of human rights violations is more complicated than the obvious wrongs committed in their conception and the disadvantages they often endure throughout their lives might suggest. The difficulties lie in determining what exactly they are victims of and who their victimizers are (see chap. 4 herein). In thinking about these issues it is essential to be clear about the nature of harm. In what follows I shall be concerned with what I shall call *wrongful harming*. Wrongful harming has two components: "it must lead to some kind of adverse effect, or create the danger of such an effect, on its victim's *interests*; and . . . it must be inflicted wrongfully in violation of the victim's *rights*" (Feinberg 1986, 145–46). One can be harmed without being wronged—by an accident, for example. Conceivably one can also be wronged without being harmed; Feinberg gives the example of a broken promise that, by some fluke, redounds to the advantage of the promisee (1986, 146). Wrongful harming, then, can be defined as "adversely affecting another party's interest in a way that wrongs him or, alternatively, wronging him in a way that adversely affects his interest" (ibid.). I shall define *interest* here as comprising those rights guaranteed to all children in the CRC and in other international human rights instruments. In the following discussion, when I write that a child has been wronged or harmed, I mean that the child's interest has been adversely affected, either as a result of the wrong action of another or in a way that wrongs the child.

Various scholars have identified four possible ways in which children born of war might be considered harmed in this sense: as victims of genocide, of war crimes, of infanticide, and of discrimination and stigmatization. In the first two instances the violator appears to be the rapist/father; in the third, usually the mother; in the fourth, the state and/or the child's maternal community. In three of these cases, however, things are much more complicated than they initially appear. Only in infanticide are the wrong, the victim, and the perpetrator all obvious; in such cases the child's status is clearly linked to the wrongful harm of murder. While this crime might be comprehensible to us in light of the circumstances preceding it (see chap. 9 herein), these circumstances do not obviate or excuse the crime (though they might reasonably serve as mitigating factors in deliberations about appropriate responses to it). These issues, while tragic, do not seem controversial to me, and I shall say nothing further about infanticide here, focusing instead on the other, more puzzling cases.

Let us consider first whether children born of war might be victims of genocide. This possibility must be distinguished from the claim that systematic rape and forced impregnation constitute genocide. This latter claim is obviously correct: systematic rape and forced impregnation (repeated rape carried out for the explicit purpose of initiating a pregnancy in the victim) qualify as genocide under Section (b) of Article II of the Genocide Convention, which prohibits "causing serious bodily or mental harm to members" of the target group. Some scholars and jurists have also argued that forced impregnation violates Sections (d) and (e) of the convention, which prohibit measures intended to prevent birth within the group and the forcible transfer of children out of the group to another group, respectively;[5] these claims are more problematic.

Carpenter (2000a, 224–27) argues that whether children born of wartime rape are victims of genocide depends upon how we understand their identity. It seems, however, that on any interpretation of the child's identity, the child cannot be a victim of genocide, at least not by virtue of his or her status as a child of genocidal rape. Consider first the patriarchal view of identity that seems to have informed the Serb campaign of forced impregnation of Bosnian Muslim women (see chap. 2 herein): the child's identity is the father's; the mother is merely a vessel for the nurture of the fetus. (This same view seems to inform the rejection by the children's maternal communities, in Bosnia and elsewhere, as "children of hate" or "children of the enemy.") In this view the child might be a tool of geno-cide but cannot be its victim because by stipulation the child belongs to the father's group; it cannot be a victim of genocidal acts either directly or indirectly (as a member of the target group). There is no transfer of the child out of the target group because, again by stipulation, the child never was a member of that group (cf. Carpenter 2000b, 464, 474).

Now suppose we take the opposite view, that the child's identity is its mother's (perhaps because it is typically born into the maternal commu-nity). The child's birth now represents an increase in the population of the maternal community; there is no transfer of the child out of the group. The child might plausibly be considered a victim of genocide qua member of the target group, but here it is crucial to note that *the child's status as a child of rape has no bearing whatsoever on this determination*; it is no more a victim of genocide by virtue of its status than any other child or adult in the group. We can see this by considering the nature of the harm such children suffer: they are wronged in a way that harms their interests as individual members of a target group; the wrongful acts in question consist in the genocidal acts committed against the group gen-erally. Note that I am not claiming that rape and forced impregnation fail to qualify as genocide; as stated above, they clearly do. I am con-cerned here only with whether children born of war are victims of geno-cide in any way that depends upon their peculiar circumstances of birth. I do not believe that they are.

Two types of confusion blur this point. One concerns identity; there is a temptation, as we have seen above, to consider the child as biologi-cally "half" a member of its mother's group (and half a member of the rapist/father's group). As I argued above, it is doubtful that such biologi-cal definitions have much traction against cultural understandings of iden-tity and uncertain how much traction they should have. Besides, I know of no international law that defines group identity and highly doubt whether biological "facts" could provide an uncontroversial basis for such a law. Second, arguments that interpret children born of war as victims of genocide because they involve the forcible transfer of children are incoherent because they assume *simultaneously* that the children bear ex-clusively their fathers' and their mothers' identities. The child can only be "transferred out" of the target group (the maternal community) if it is "in" that group, that is, if it carries its mother's identity. The purported transfer consists, however, in the birth of an "enemy" baby into the ma-ternal community. But according to this view the child possesses the rapist/father's identity, nullifying the claim of membership in the target group that is a legal and logical requisite of any "transfer."[6] If we regard the child as a "half" member of each group, it appears to be either a "half" victim of genocide or simultaneously a victim and a victimizer—absurdities we would do well to avoid. Only on interpretations that

construct the child's identity as its mother's is the child a victim of genocide, and only then in the same sense that any member of the target
group is also a victim.

Another argument views children born of war as victims of war crimes.
War crimes are typically defined as violations of the laws of war as set
forth in the Geneva and Hague conventions and the UN Charter. The
Fourth Geneva Convention defines "grave breaches" of those conventions as

> involving any of the following acts, if committed against persons
> or property protected by the present Convention: wilful killing,
> torture or inhuman treatment, including biological experiments,
> wilfully causing great suffering or serious injury to body or health,
> unlawful deportation or transfer or unlawful confinement of a pro-
> tected person, compelling a protected person to serve in the forces
> of a hostile Power, or wilfully depriving a protected person of the
> rights of fair and regular trial prescribed in the present Conven-
> tion, taking of hostages and extensive destruction and appropria-
> tion of property, not justified by military necessity and carried out
> unlawfully and wantonly.[7]

This list is representative rather than exhaustive of war crimes, but it
conveys a clear idea of what is imagined in international law.[8] Again, it is
eminently clear that women who suffer from rape, sexual exploitation,
and forced impregnation are victims of war crimes, including torture,
inhumane treatment, infliction of great suffering, and serious injury to
body and health.

Complex issues arise in assessing whether children born of war are
victims of war crimes. It is helpful to begin by specifying in what the
relevant harm consists. The most obvious candidate that would fall within
the definition of war crimes seems to be the willful "causing great suffering or serious injury to body or health." It is not completely clear, however, that such a crime exists in the case of children born of war rape.
Certainly they suffer higher than average rates of discrimination and
stigmatization in their maternal communities, and sometimes in their
states as well. Importantly, however, in neither of these cases is the rap-
ist/father the perpetrator of the direct wrong the child suffers. I shall
return to questions regarding how we should conceive ill treatment of
war-rape children by their maternal communities later on; here it suf-
fices to note that, however we conceive that treatment, it is not likely to
be as a war crime.

It is also unclear how far we can consider the rapist/father an indirect
agent of wrongful harm to his child(ren). The difficulty here lies in whether
it makes sense to talk about wronging someone through bringing him or

her into existence. In the case of children born of war rape, the act that links the rapist/father to the wrongful harms suffered by the child in his or her state or maternal community is the very same act that brings the child into existence (see Harman 2004).[9] Similarly, Carpenter maintains that "birth of a child can never be a crime against the child, for this is the event that brings about her status as . . . a rights-bearer" (2000b, 463). I am not certain this is correct, but I shall postpone that question for a moment to consider a logical problem with her proposed alternative, birth-by-forced-maternity. Unlike the conceptually muddled notions of "forced impregnation," "forced maternity," and "forced birthing," all of which conceptualize the wrong from the woman's perspective rather than the child's, birth-by-forced-maternity

> encompasses both forced impregnation and enforced pregnancy together (but not forced impregnation that results in an abortion). It is through forced maternity, not forced impregnation directly, that the child comes into being as a rights-bearer and has claims to make on the community. Yet it is the aspect of force in relation to the *conception* that matters. (Carpenter 2000b, 463)

The flaw in this conceptualization becomes evident when we consider the parenthetical note regarding forced impregnation that results in abortion. On this construction it is the combination of forced impregnation plus enforced pregnancy (no access to an abortion) and forced maternity that together constitute the crime of birth-by-forced-maternity. But imagine a case in which an abortion is available to a pregnant victim of forced impregnation who elects not to abort. The availability of an unutilized abortion eliminates the element of enforced pregnancy and thus of forced maternity, meaning that the resulting birth cannot, by definition, constitute birth-by-forced-maternity. Not only does this conclusion seem counter-intuitive, but, since abortion can in effect preempt or nullify this crime, it would seem to be morally obligatory when available, on this view. Now imagine two babies born on the same day, into the same community (their mothers are neighbors). Both women were raped and impregnated in the same camp; for reasons that need not concern us, one woman had the option of an abortion, which she declined, and the other was forced to bring her pregnancy to term. Both babies would be "children of the enemy," conceived in rape, and both would presumably be victims of the same discrimination and stigmatization in their maternal community. Yet, according to birth-by-forced-maternity, one would be a victim of a war crime and the other not; moreover, the reason the potentially aborted child would not be a victim has to do with the actions of its mother, not those of its rapist/father. This result seems to contradict Carpenter's assertion that it is "the aspect of force in relation to the *conception*" of the child in which the crime originates.

I think Carpenter's account moves us a good way toward a correct and revealing understanding of children born of war as victims of wrongful harms (human rights violations) perpetrated by their rapist/fathers. Specifically, I think she is right to focus on wrongs committed in the conception of these children; rape and forced impregnation by themselves are crimes against humanity, as recognized explicitly in the Rome Statute of the International Court (Part II, Article 7). Presumably these are crimes against the woman. The crime against the prospective child lies less in the force involved in conception than in the *calculation* regarding the wrongs the prospective child is likely to suffer. I would label this *wrongful procreation:* intentionally causing conception or pregnancy calculated to result in the birth of a child likely to suffer human rights violations.[10] Wrongful procreation violates what I call the right to have rights—the guarantee in Article 2 of the Universal Declaration of Human Rights that everyone has the right to enjoy all of the human rights. (Wrongful procreation is similar to what I take DeLaet to mean in arguing that rapist/fathers deny their children access to human rights.)

Wrongful procreation has distinct conceptual advantages as a way of thinking about the wrongs often endured by children of war rape. First, by locating the wrong in the intention of the rapist, it dissolves the philosophical confusion relating to acts that bring persons into existence by clarifying the sadistic and malicious nature of the act (cf. Feinberg 1986). While such motives might seem hard to establish, in many cases—like the camps described in these pages where systematic rape aimed to result in pregnancy occurred—there seems to be little difficulty. In addition, wrongful procreation clearly distinguishes the wrongs done to the children from the wrongs done to the mothers, opening space for the recognition and discussion of the former on their own terms. Moreover, because wrongful procreation does not suggest that the life of the child is inherently damaged or unworthy (the wrong lies in the act of the rapist/father, not in any fact about the life of the child), it does not further stigmatize the child. Finally, wrongful procreation lets us contemplate the maternal community's role and complicity in harming children born of war rape directly.[11]

This brings us to the fourth type of human rights violation frequently mentioned by scholars in connection with children born of war: discrimination and stigmatization within the children's maternal or birth communities. Even in this apparently clear-cut case, puzzles arise. There is no disputing that infanticide or other direct harms committed against children violate their rights. Less clear, however, is how far communities—as opposed to states—have affirmative obligations in connection with the human rights of children born of war. Part I, Article 2, Section 1 of the CRC clearly makes state discrimination on the basis of birth or status illegal. On the widest reading, discrimination in the extension or protection of any of the rights outlined in the convention would be included here, making any discrimination against or prejudicial treatment of children born of war a clear human rights violation by the state. The most common forms of discriminatory or prejudicial state action include the denial of citizenship or nationality; of health, education, or other social benefits; or of the necessary social minimum to the children.

Typically, many maternal communities take similar actions and make similar omissions, denying recognition, social benefits, and social support to the children and their mothers. Such social ostracism can at times have fatal consequences, as it is linked to women's and children's socioeconomic prospects (a point to which I return in the final section); cases exist of economically induced suicide and poverty-related morbidity resulting from such ostracism.[12] Whether stigmatization and discrimination in maternal communities constitute human rights violations, however, is unclear.

The CRC, like nearly all human rights law, is binding on *states*, and human rights violations have traditionally been understood as wrongs states commit against their citizens (see Donnelly 2003, 33–37). It is perfectly consistent, according to this state-centered view, for a state to fulfill all of its obligations with respect to human rights and for children and their mothers nonetheless to experience discrimination in their communities. To see this, consider the denial of deep identity to children born of war rape by their maternal communities. Let M be the maternal community of a "war baby," WB, born in state S. M might define itself on racial, ethnic, religious, or "cultural" grounds. Assume that M's definition of membership includes that for a child to be a member of M, both of its parents must be members. By stipulation, WB cannot be an M because its father is not an M. M therefore denies WB membership, excluding the child from religious and cultural rites and isolating WB socially. But M resides in S, a state which grants full citizenship to WB and guarantees WB the same social benefits as all other children. On traditional statist understandings of human rights, there is no obvious violation here. But suppose that S is poor and ravaged by internal warfare; it treats all its citizens equally, but that treatment still falls short of human rights standards. Suppose further that in S, communities like M traditionally see to the social and economic needs of their members as best they can. As a practical matter WB is denied enjoyment of its human rights by being excluded from M, yet on the traditional statist view the only violations occur in S's inability fully to meet its obligations under the CRC. While M's actions and inactions clearly affect WB's human rights, M insists that it is duty-bound to provide these benefits only to Ms.

WB's dilemma points to the shortcomings of existing human rights law and theory, which remain predominantly statist. While it might seem that a simple solution would be to hold groups and other non-state actors to the same human rights standards as states, lumping groups like M and other non-state actors into the statist framework misses that the point that it is not just whom to hold responsible for securing human rights but also how those rights themselves are conceived. Feminist critiques of human rights show that it is inadequate simply to "add women and stir," and the same intuition applies here (chap. 8 herein; Goodhart 2006). A thorough reconsideration of what rights mean and how they are constructed is necessary.

Applying the statist framework to groups would be detrimental and, in some cases, simply incoherent. Part I, Article 2 of the CRC, for instance, forbids discrimination on the basis of religion; application of such a requirement to all social groups would effectively destroy religion. The right to a nationality, discussed above, makes no sense if applied to groups, and there are good reasons to resist the apparent analogy between citizenship and group membership that application of this principle to groups would imply. Part I, Article 19 describes the appropriate legal, social, educational, and administrative measures and the social welfare programs states should utilize in guaranteeing rights to citizens. Should all groups be subjected to similar requirements? The point is neither that groups should be permitted to discriminate as they please nor that groups should be exempt from all human rights requirements in all instances. The point is rather that precisely how these various requirements should apply to which groups in what specific circumstances cannot be answered without a good deal of careful consideration.

Another puzzle that arises in cases like WB's concerns identity. Earlier I agreed with Weitsman concerning the social construction of identity and showed how such a view problematizes putative biological claims to membership. When we move from those abstract considerations to more realistic cases, like WB's, where stigmatization and discrimination have a dire and immediate impact on WB's welfare, things look somewhat different. To see this, consider a similar case in which K is an ethnic and linguistic minority within state T. K has for years suffered human rights violations from T (and committed some of its own against Ts). In particular, K has been subjected to a political and military campaign to stamp out its language and culture. Suppose that K provides benefits to its Ks that T cannot or will not provide to Ks. Suppose further that there are Ts living within the territory where K predominates, and that K does not provide these Ts with the same benefits it provides to Ks. We would be hesitant to call K's action or inaction a violation of the human rights of the Ts, I think, even if T is unwilling or unable to provide those Ts with comparable guarantees.[13]

The salient difference in our assessment of whether K is justified in withholding benefits to Ts and whether M is justified in withholding benefits to WB seems to be WB's claim to special consideration in virtue of a biological connection to M, a justification we rejected earlier along with the myth of genetic determination. Still, M's actions seem morally objectionable in a way that K's do not because of this claim and the special moral obligation it seems to create for M, raising anew the question of how much deference the human rights framework should grant to socially constructed norms of identity and membership. There are no easy answers here. Even if we think that groups deserve little latitude in denying benefits in such cases (a big if), we must recognize that coercing M to provide benefits to WB would likely have other negative effects on WB. Even if the tangible benefits can be mandated, the social and psychological benefits typically associated with membership would be unlikely to follow; indeed, resentment could well create new problems for WB and others like him or her. There is also the problem of encouraging states to make coercive interventions into the affairs of ethnic, religious, and cultural groups; the costs of such interventions must be weighed carefully against the anticipated benefits.

I cannot consider these complex issues further here; three provisional conclusions seem warranted, however, in light of this brief discussion. First, children born of war unquestionably suffer human rights violations whose sources are overdetermined; their rapist/fathers, the broad social and economic conditions in states like S, and the attitudes of groups like M all contribute to their plight. Second, the children's situation underscores the importance of *public* guarantees of all human rights, especially social and economic ones. Provision of such guarantees is especially important to the most vulnerable and marginalized members of society. Where states are incapable of providing such benefits, other generalized mechanisms of provision might be preferable to group-based provision. Obviously, state capacity-building should also be a high priority in such cases—a point to which I return below. Finally, whether or not groups like M are responsible for human rights violations in cases like that of WB, it seems clear they fall short of the high standards of human decency and compassion toward which human rights as a moral framework gestures. The only remedy for such deficiencies is a deeper social transformation and transvaluation of values—the creation of what McEvoy-Levy calls a human rights culture (chap. 9 herein). I shall return to this subject in the final section.

## Adequacy of Human Rights Discourse

This critique of the statist character of the traditional human rights framework raises the question posed by several contributors: whether the human rights discourse is adequate for addressing the myriad issues surrounding children born of war. Obviously I share these concerns. A focus on children born of war clarifies that one of the key failures of the CRC and many other human rights instruments is their tacit incorporation of assumptions about the "normal" situation of children. The CRC largely presumes that children live in stable families and grow up in the care of their parents; such presumptions limit the convention's relevance for children born of war and children in conflict zones. The situation of these children is doubly problematic in the context of failed states and war-torn states; not only are such states more likely to engender and sustain the kinds of conflicts in which systematic rape and forced impregnation occur, but they are also less capable of coping with the social needs arising from such conflicts. The CRC, with its optimistic assumptions about states parties' ability to provide a range of human rights guarantees ranging from security to health care, education, and social welfare support, clearly neither envisions the incapacity of failed and war-torn states nor the impact such incapacity might have on children.

These shortcomings reflect wider problems with the state-centered human rights framework, which makes it hard to conceive the role of non-state actors in violating as well as in protecting and promoting human rights, as we saw in the case of groups' discriminatory practices, and which provides little guidance about how human rights might be protected where states are unable or unwilling to do the job. Failed and war-torn states are in this respect just the tip of a much larger iceberg; repressive and recalcitrant states also fall outside what human rights law and institutions presently envision. It is this failure that entities like the permanent International Criminal Court are beginning to address—though we seem a long way from any kind of international agency that could guarantee, even in the last instance, social and economic security where states cannot do so. What an effective global human rights regime might look like and how we might get there are questions beyond my scope here (see Goodhart 2005, esp. chaps. 8 and 9); I raise them mainly to illustrate that the existing limits of human rights framework with respect to children born of war in failed and war-torn states are part of a wider problem involving the state-centric nature of the human rights regime and its optimism regarding the functioning of those states.

Sadly, however, in this respect the inattention to issues facing children born of war is hardly unique; consideration of the rights and needs of other vulnerable and marginalized classes of persons is similarly lacking. Just as taking women's rights seriously as human rights forced a complete reconceptualization of the human rights framework, so consideration of children born of war (of homosexuals, of stateless persons, . . . ) requires us again to rethink what human rights mean and how they can be realized.

I strongly disagree, however, that these failures of the human rights *framework*—the existing treaties and institutions through which human rights are protected and promoted—represent a failure of the human rights *discourse*. It seems to me rather a strength that human rights are both appealing enough and pliable enough to be adapted to the needs of real people across an amazing diversity of situations, some of which we can barely imagine today.[14] The theoretical resources exist within human rights discourse to reinvent human rights indefinitely, and such reinvention should be embraced as a requirement of the universality to which human rights aspire and a key to building the kind of human rights culture that McEvoy-Levy advocates.

## Justice for Children Born of War: Toward a Human Rights Culture?

Children born of war are so extraordinarily vulnerable in part for the obvious and easily overlooked reason that so many of them live in failed or war-torn states struggling to achieve peace or to consolidate fragile transitional regimes. This context means that they are also significantly affected by the measures taken (or not taken) in efforts to rebuild such states and to create a human rights culture. Each of these issues—the heightened incidence of human rights violations experienced by children born of war, failed states, and institution-building and reconciliation in conflict-ravaged societies—presents serious normative and political challenges for their human rights.

That children born of war and their mothers face a higher incidence of human rights violations reminds us of two central claims advanced by various authors in this volume: the plight of these children and their mothers cannot be separated, and it is primarily socioeconomic in nature. This inseparability stems from numerous factors, including the children's economic dependence on their mothers throughout infancy and childhood and the mother's corresponding responsibilities; the children's status as living evidence of rapes committed against their mothers, crimes for which the women, although victims, are frequently vilified and rejected; and, the grim fact that mothers are sometimes perpetrators of wrongs against their own children, whether through neglect, abuse, or, in extreme cases, reckless abandonment or infanticide.[15]

As several of the contributors argue, the socioeconomic challenges faced by children born of war and their mothers are paramount. To see why, consider that one of the most damaging effects of the discrimination and stigmatization directed toward the children and their mothers is their rejection by families and communities that would otherwise provide their primary social support networks. In failed, impoverished, and war-torn states, national social security systems are often wanting; more traditional arrangements for social support are likely to be primary in such cases. Given the limited economic opportunities for women working in the paid sector in many cultural contexts, discrimination and stigmatization can translate directly into poverty, which compounds the likelihood and severity of other violations the women and children suffer. The situation is only worsened by the failure of most peace accords, in their provisions for institution-building and political reconciliation, to attend to social and economic needs in general, and to the needs—indeed the existence—of the children in particular (see chaps. 4, 8, and 9 herein).

These observations indicate two broad challenges that must be overcome if efforts to ameliorate the situation of children born of war and their mothers are to succeed. The first concerns pervasive structural issues of patriarchy and sex and gender inequality. That many women depend for their (and their children's) well-being upon cultural institutions that construct and constrict their identities quite narrowly and in highly sexualized terms exacerbates the economic difficulties they face; such attitudes can exclude women from communal support and constrain their ability to support themselves outside of their communities. This observation underscores the need for long-term strategies to elevate the status of women.[16]

The second and closely related challenge concerns the immediate need for policies that provide economic security for women and their children. Calls and strategies for economic empowerment recur throughout the chapters, cited both as one of the clearly voiced needs of "war mothers" and as one of the possible tools for mitigating human rights violations experienced by these women and their children (see chaps. 5, 6, and 8 herein). In the long run, economic empowerment is complementary, indeed integral, to improving the status of women generally; feminists since Mary Wollstonecraft and Elizabeth Cady Stanton have clearly recognized the links among economic independence, political freedom, and moral development for women.

More immediately, schemes for economic empowerment of women must be supplemented with social welfare schemes to support them and their children. Such programs should include adequate funding for state institutions caring for orphans or children turned over by their mothers, measures to facilitate adoption of such children, and a guaranteed source of income for war mothers and other victims of wartime rape and sexual exploitation.[17] IN this volume Susan Harris Rimmer suggests treating women and children as veterans eligible for pensions and other social benefits, while Debra DeLaet suggests reparations as a mechanism for providing social support while recognizing the structural nature of the crimes and wrongs involved. Both of these measures and others should be seriously considered. What might work in one context might not work in another, depending on the nature of the past conflict and a variety of social and cultural factors. One of these factors is a state's (and the international community's) *willingness* to undertake measures to alleviate the wrongs experienced by the children and their mothers. Their performance with regard to the measures required to provide economic security is one indicator of such willingness. As noted earlier, most peace accords and transitional political arrangements avoid any mention of the problem, and most ignore the concerns of women and the society's economic, educational, and human welfare needs more generally. What Siobhán McEvoy-Levy has referred to as "patriarchal pragmatism" suffuses peace accords and transitional justice more generally.

Achieving justice for children born of war remains an elusive goal, in part because exactly what justice means and requires for these children is uncertain. In this volume Debra DeLaet analyzes the pros and cons of punitive and restorative approaches in achieving justice for them, and Siobhán McEvoy-Levy emphasizes the creation of a human rights culture, stressing reconciliation and understanding achieved in part through education as well as a more general restructuring of key social institutions. These are laudable and sensible aims. In making their arguments, however, both authors articulate what I view as a highly problematic notion of *agency* for children born of war. Both describe the potential role of the children as symbols of hope, reconciliation, and agents of social renewal.

Ascribing agency to individuals—by assumption, children—in this way strikes me as ethically problematic. To assert that a person, a child, has a particular social role to play or special social obligations and responsibilities owing to the circumstances of its conception strikes me as patronizing. It in effect *denies* agency to the person involved by suggesting that there is a role the person can and ought to play. Of course, many children born of war will, as adults, choose to play an active role in demanding rights and justice for themselves and similarly situated persons, and that role should be encouraged and supported. To suggest that certain persons have social duties by virtue of their birth or status, however, evokes a sort of feudal fatalism inconsistent with a human rights culture.

Creating a human rights culture that will achieve justice for children born of war requires, as I see it, two key changes. The first involves creating effective social institutions to guarantee economic rights and provide economic opportunities for women. I have already discussed the need and justification for these guarantees and will not rehash them here. The second change needed is a transformation of the social discourse surrounding children born of war. Such a change is integral to any effort to effect social reconstruction and reconciliation.

This effort is sometimes conceived as a need to break the silence surrounding these children. This view must be heavily qualified. First, as McEvoy-Levy rightly notes, there are two different kinds of silence concerning the children: strategic silences, which protect them and their mothers, and imposed silences, through which societies ignore or avoid the problem. I shall return to the former in just a moment; with respect to the latter, I am not sure that *silence* is the appropriate word. Recalling that actions sometimes speak louder than words, I submit that there exists in many of the societies examined in these page a deafening roar of callous contempt toward children born of war, one that constructs them and their mothers as objects of shame and humiliation, that facilitates their social exclusion, and that is often promoted by the media and by state agencies, as Weitsman argues (chap. 7 herein). This roar must be dulled, while at the same time a vocabulary and voice in which children and their mothers can express their legitimate claims must be developed.

It is true that international agencies have not succeeded in shaping the debate on this subject as they have on other issues. Again, however, this hardly seems due to silence. A scan of the references in this volume reveals reports and studies bearing the names of the IRC, UNICEF, Amnesty International, Physicians for Human Rights, and many other well-known human rights agencies and NGOs. Whatever the problem, finding a way to generate a discourse around children born of war that can help to overcome the neglect and indifference that frequently attend the issue is a significant priority.

With respect to strategic silences, it remains clear that a tension exists between creating a broader, more balanced discussion of these vulnerable children and protecting their safety, dignity, and privacy (see chap. 10 herein). In principle it should be possible to initiate and sustain a discourse that protects victims while also addressing their human rights constructively and effectively. One way to achieve this might be by building a discussion around the experience of communities elsewhere that have grappled with the problem and the myriad issues they raise within and among communities as a way of partially defusing the issue. Another might be to provide forums for anonymous testimony that could help to vivify the problem within a community while protecting individual victims—a variation on witness-protection programs. Institutionally, the current emphasis on police, military, and political institutions in post-conflict reconstruction should be supplemented by the creation of permanent institutions, like human rights ombudsmans' offices and democratic forums for deliberation and discussion of basic rights and freedoms that can address social wrongs in a sustained, political fashion.[18]

The challenge of creating a new human rights discourse reminds us that human rights play a dual role in contemporary politics. On the one hand, they provide urgent protection—or at least hold out the promise of such protection—in the face of monstrous evils and quotidian suffering alike; on the other, they point toward a world in which everyone might enjoy a free and dignified life. As we struggle to comprehend the injustices underlying the problems faced by children born of war and their mothers, we must keep both of these roles in mind. We must maintain unwavering faith in the possibility of a better world, one in which children born of war are rare and in which their human rights are secure. We must at the same time recognize that the violence from which they are born, which manages to shock even the twenty-first century moral conscience, can be overcome only through careful study, deep reflection, and effective, tireless action.

## Notes

[1] In practice, states have wide latitude in determining who qualifies for citizenship, so that nondiscriminatory application of the standards often turns out to be less important than the nature of the standards themselves; its actual terms are often prejudicial to immigrants and members of ethnic and religious minorities. What might constitute legitimate standards for citizenship is beyond my scope here.

[2] Of course, I do not mean to suggest that this fact in any way lessens the horror of these crimes.

[3] For a similar argument connecting the Convention on the Elimination of All Forms of Discrimination against Women to genocide, see Smolin 1995–96.

[4] For an excellent general discussion of group rights, see Jones 1999 (cf. Jones 1994).

[5] For a critical review of the literature, see Carpenter 2000b.

[6] On the patriarchal construction of identity one could argue (disingenuously, to be sure) that the birth of "Chetnik babies" to be raised in the Bosnian Muslim community represents a forcible transfer of Serbian children out of their group and constitutes genocide against Serbs! This interpretation, while clearly specious, would be consistent with the maternal community's rejection of the children as enemies.

[7] GC4, Article 147; this is the most comprehensive statement, comprising definitions in the previous conventions. For the full text, see the icrc.org website.

[8] Other war crimes concerning the *conduct* of battle (use of truce flags, for example) are omitted here.

[9] There is a great deal of philosophical debate about whether future persons have rights and whether it is possible to violate future persons' rights (see, e.g., Archard 2004; Feinberg 1986; Parfit 1984; Warren 1978). I have addressed these issues, insofar as they apply to children born of war rape, in Goodhart 2007.

[10] I borrow and adapt this term from Matthew Hanser (1990).

[11] For a more comprehensive treatment of wrongful procreation and related issues, see Goodhart 2007.

[12] I am grateful to Charli Carpenter for making this point clear to me and for helping me to grasp its implications for my argument in this and the following section.

[13] The case would be different if K were somehow preventing or interfering with provision of these benefits to Ts.

[14] I would wager that some readers of this volume will read an essay on the human rights of clones in their lifetimes.

[15] Women might responsibly give up their children to state agencies for care or ultimate adoption or entrust them to the care of willing relatives; unfortunately the term *abandonment* is sometimes used in describing such actions as well as actions like leaving children on the steps of hospitals and orphanages (or worse). The former set of actions seems qualitatively different from the latter, however, and I include the qualifier "reckless" in the text to indicate that I am referring the latter.

[16] Unfortunately I cannot discuss such strategies here. For an introduction and overview, see the United Nations Development Program's Human Development Report 1995, *Gender and Human Development*, available on the hdr.undp.org website.

[17] I cannot join the debate addressed by some of the authors regarding the merits and drawbacks of international adoption except to note that, like so much else connected with children born of war, much in that debate will turn on how the relevant actors construct the identity of these children.

[18] I have in mind here something like the Éspace d'interpollation démocratique in Mali (see Wing 2002).

# References

Archard, David. 2004. "Wrongful Life." *Philosophy* 79, no. 3: 403–20.

Carpenter, R. Charli. 2000a. "Forced Maternity, Children's Rights and the Genocide Convention: A Theoretical Analysis." *Journal of Genocide Research* 2, no. 2: 213–44.

———. 2000b. "Surfacing Children: Limitations of Genocidal Rape Discourse." *Human Rights Quarterly* 22, no. 2: 428–77.

Donnelly, Jack. 2003. *Universal Human Rights in Theory and Practice*. 2nd ed. Ithaca, NY: Cornell University Press.

Feinberg, Joel. 1986. "Wrongful Life and the Counterfactual Element in Harming." *Social Philosophy and Policy* 4 no. 1: 145–78.

Freeman, Michael. 1997. *The Moral Status of Children: Essays on the Rights of the Child.* The Hague: Martinus Nijhoff Publishers/Kluwer International.

Freire, Paolo. 1993. *Pedagogy of the Oppressed.* Rev. ed. Translated by M. B. Ramos. New York: Continuum.

Goodhart, Michael. 2005. *Democracy as Human Rights: Freedom and Equality in the Age of Globalization.* New York: Routledge.

———. 2006. "Human Rights and Non-State Actors: Theoretical Puzzles." In *Non-State Actors in the Human Rights Universive*, edited by G. J. Andreopoulos, Z. F. Arat, and P. B. Juviler. Bloomfield, CT: Kumarian Press.

———. 2007. "Sins of the Fathers: War Rape, Wrongful Procreation, and Children's Human Rights." *The Journal of Human Rights.*

Hanser, Matthew. 1990. "Harming Future People." *Philosophy and Public Affairs* 19, no. 1: 47–70.

Harman, Elizabeth. 2004. "Can We Harm and Benefit in Creating?" *Philosophical Perspectives* 18: 89–113.

Jones, Peter. 1994. *Rights.* Hampshire, UK: Macmillan.

———. 1999. "Human Rights, Group Rights, and People's Rights." *Human Rights Quarterly* 21, no. 1: 80–107.

Kymlicka, Will. 1995. *Multicultural Citizenship: A Liberal Theory of Minority Rights.* Oxford: Clarendon Press.

Parfit, Derek. 1984. *Reasons and Persons.* Oxford: Oxford University Press.

Sandel, Michael J. 1998. *Liberalism and the Limits of Justice.* 2nd ed. Cambridge: Cambridge University Press.

Smolin, David M. 1995–96. "Will International Human Rights Be Used as a Tool of Cultural Genocide? The Interaction of Human Rights Norms, Religion, Culture, and Gender." *Journal of Law and Religion* 12, no. 1: 143–71.

Taylor, Charles. 1994. *Multiculturalism: Examining the Politics of Recognition.* Edited by A. Gutmann. Princeton, NJ: Princeton University Press.

Walzer, Michael. 1983. *Spheres of Justice: A Defense of Pluralism and Equality.* New York: Basic Books.

Warren, Mary. 1978. "Do Potential People Have Moral Rights?" In *Obligations to Future Generations*, edited by R. I. Sikora and B. Barry. Philadelphia: Temple University Press.

Wing, Susanna. 2002. "Questioning the State: Constitutionalism and the Malian *Espace d'interpellation démocratique*." *Democratization* 9, no. 2: 121–47.

# Conclusion

# Protecting Children Born of War

## R. Charli Carpenter

In the spring of 2005 specialists from gender-based violence and child protection units of leading human rights and humanitarian organizations came together at University of Pittsburgh, Columbia University, and the University of Geneva to discuss strategies for protecting children born of rape and exploitation in conflict zones. The aim of these focus groups, funded as part of the same National Science Foundation grant that supported this book project, was to gauge existing knowledge and practice among humanitarians regarding these children.

Participants in these consultations stressed how little is known about children born of war beyond the anecdotal and how helpful concrete research to inform programming on this population would be. They pointed to such children's vulnerability to social exclusion and stigma from the societies into which they are born. This underlying risk factor was described as being connected to other sets of vulnerabilities: physical and psychosocial health; access to resources; risk of separation, abuse or neglect by caretakers; and early childhood mortality, including as a result of infanticide (Carpenter et al. 2005). They also struggled conceptually with a subject that has not been well articulated in their communities of practice and articulated several perceived dilemmas with respect to singling out children born of war for a policy response.

The case studies in this volume aggregate country reporting on this issue and paint a picture that in many respects confirms practitioners' fears about the vulnerabilities of these children. The chapters on Bosnia, East Timor, Rwanda, Uganda, and Sierra Leone demonstrate the complex ways in which conception as a result of wartime rape or sexual slavery affects children born as a result. Although the specific nature of these impacts varies across and within cases according to several factors, the overall pattern is one of structural and sometimes overt discrimination.

And the chapters on state and media framing, post-conflict justice mechanisms, and human rights discourse confirm practitioners' sense that very little specific attention has been paid to this category of child in the human rights and humanitarian communities.

Yet the substantive information presented in the case studies also challenges some of the assumptions articulated by practitioners in this area. For example, some had expressed the belief that silence about the issue can be an effective protection mechanism in itself; that such children's protection needs are adequately dealt with already in the context of broader child-rights programming; and that any additional efforts should be folded into gender-based violence work rather than child protection per se. But the analyses here suggest a different story: that failing to identify these children as a particularly vulnerable population has resulted in their marginalization and reinforced social taboos against them; that their needs are not necessarily met in the context of broader programming and may require some kind of targeted approach; and that dealing with them through a gender-based violence frame rather than a child-protection frame may reinforce the idea that they are primarily consequences of rights violations rather than human beings themselves with rights that also require protection. In this closing essay I draw together some of the insights of the previous chapters in order to outline an agenda for future research and policy attention to this population.

## Creating a Protective Environment for Children Born of War

Overall, the chapters demonstrate that although children born of war, in theory, are protected to the same extent as other children against violations of their human rights, specific barriers exist to securing these rights. These include (though they are not limited to) intransigence of national governments; the difficulties of legislating or altering cultural attitudes; the general taboos surrounding sexual violence and exploitation themselves; the general lack of resources and infrastructure devoted to child protection in post-conflict societies; conflicts of rights between these children and others; and the political and operational challenges to accessing, evaluating, and meeting these children's needs in practice.

Throughout, the chapters articulate, though not always explicitly and not always in concert, a multifaceted protection agenda for children born of war. This agenda includes recognizing them as a particularly vulnerable group; gathering data on their specific needs; developing appropriate programming for them in conflict settings; and advocating at the global level and with governments to develop accountability mechanisms and make decisions in the best interests of these children. I discuss each of these in turn below.

### Children Born of War: A Particularly Vulnerable Group

Few who consider the human rights of children born of war deny that they are a group in need of particular protection. A recent UNICEF document argues: "As with all children affected by armed conflict, children born as a result of rape may be vulnerable to violence, abuse and exploitation. . . . These children may also face increased vulnerability because they are children of survivors of violence and often children of single mothers" (UNICEF 2006, 1). At the same time, some practitioners working in the area of human rights and humanitarian action have at times been hesitant to label these children as a particularly vulnerable category specifically.

It is argued by some that these vulnerabilities are a matter of degree, not scope, and that many children in conflict zones are at risk of deprivation or social exclusion for a variety of reasons. On the other hand, without a means of articulating what is distinctive about the vulnerabilities of this particular group it can be—and has been—difficult to gather accurate data or to develop appropriate programming. Attempting to meet the needs of children born of war without thinking of them as a particular group results in systematic inattention to whether their needs are actually met, as has been documented by McEvoy-Levy, and feeds into the desire of governments to treat their particular needs as a non-issue, as chapters by Daniel and Weitsman show. As one focus-group participant put it, "If you don't classify, if you don't identify, if you don't know, then how do you plan the policy and the programs and how do you do the advocacy? So for advocacy, policy and program purposes you need to know. How much do you need to know, how do you want to break down the knowledge—that's the question" (in Carpenter et al. 2005, 11).

In making this determination child-protection experts need to pay close attention to conceptual issues. Considerable ambiguity and disagreement remains over precisely *which* children should be encompassed by such a category; as Weitsman points out in her chapter, "language matters." The labels and advocacy tropes assigned to particular groups of concern structure our thinking about international issues and, as Rimmer describes, can activate or occlude different ways of thinking about rights claims. It makes a great deal of difference, for example, whether one focuses attention primarily on children born of genocidal forced-pregnancy campaigns or on all wartime sexual violence; on marital as well as non-marital rape; on peacetime as well as wartime rape; on children born of sexual exploitation by peacekeepers as well as enemy soldiers.[1] To give one example of the implications of these distinctions,

Michael Goodhart's "wrongful birth" concept might be sensible for some of these children (those deliberately conceived through genocidal rape) but not for others, whose claims on their fathers (and fathers' states of origin) might be quite different.

The analyses in this book suggest the value of defining the population fluidly, in a manner that allows context-specific analysis. The emphasis should not be on the nature of the children's conception per se but on others' attitudes regarding their conception. Baldi and MacKenzie's case data tell us that the treatment of children born of war may in fact have little to do with the extent of their mother's actual victimization. Rather, it is a function of the social perceptions of the communities into which they are born, mitigated by cultural, social, and physical factors. It is these social perceptions of the children and the ways in which they do or do not function as signifiers of group identity that must be addressed in order to build an environment of protection around these and other children in conflict zones (Brysk 2004).

### Fact-Finding

As demonstrated by the case studies in this volume, the knowledge gaps surrounding children born of war are glaring. The first step to appropriate solutions is to move beyond the anecdotal record and produce some systematic facts about this population. Nearly every chapter in this volume laments the lack of better primary research on these children and their histories to flesh out and perhaps challenge some of the apparent patterns gleaned from existing reports.

One of the reasons for the lack of research on children born of war is the lack of information gathered by governments and humanitarian actors in conflict and post-conflict situations. Postwar governments have typically chosen not to collect statistics on the number of these children, their destinies, or their status. In addition to impeding independent research on the human rights of these children, such lack of data gathering prevents follow-up assessments of their well-being and allows governments to claim that their human rights are a non-issue.

The international community as well has been slow to collect relevant data on this issue. Asking questions about Sierra Leone's children born to abducted girls, Giulia Baldi and Megan MacKenzie point to a lack of useful data in mainstream documents on gender, sexual violence, and public health in West Africa. Although mention is made of such children in a few international documents, questions aimed at assessing their vulnerabilities have not typically been incorporated into research tools for assessing the consequences of gender-based violence in conflict and post-conflict settings (Ward 2002). We argue that humanitarian organizations not only should be incorporating such questions into their situation analyses but should be actively encouraging governments to monitor and maintain statistics on this category of war-affected child.

A useful first step would be for major humanitarian organizations (or their donors) to conduct or commission impact assessments of existing field guidelines regarding how to protect these children in conflict zones. As noted in the first chapter of this volume, UNFPA, ICRC, WHO, and UNHCR have issued recommendations regarding children born of rape, particularly the need to protect such children against stigma, but these documents provide no specific rules or initiatives for implementing such protection. Nor to this author's knowledge has there been an evaluation of the extent to which the recommendations have been carried out and with what degree of success. How have such guidelines informed assistance and protection operations in conflict areas since they were created? How have they affected the human rights situation of these children?

Participants in the Pittsburgh consultations echoed these concerns and put forth a variety of suggestions as to how future research on this subject might be crafted to be of most value to practitioners. These suggestions include longitudinal components to future studies; the children need to be monitored and tracked over several years in order to fully understand fully the variation in outcomes and to provide for appropriate follow up. Comparative analysis between types of conflict, cultures, and regions was also strongly encouraged. One pattern that emerges from the various case studies in this volume is the specificity of different contexts. Control groups of various kinds would also yield valuable insights about factors specific to the experience of children born of war. It might be useful for future research to compare outcomes for children born of sexual violence in conflict to those born of peacetime rape; or rape survivors raising children to other single mothers in a country context generally; or children born of rape to other infants born in displaced or conflict settings.

Yet any research on children born of war also involves methodological and ethical challenges. Many of the contributors to this volume treaded gently in conflict zones, avoiding families themselves and drawing data from secondhand sources. If human rights advocates are to take seriously the need to develop better measures for how these children are affected by war, they must go beyond this preliminary work. Nonetheless, as Mertus emphasizes, they must do so with great care.

As with other hidden populations and taboo topics (such as rape itself), it may be difficult to identify the population or to establish conclusively its scope. Researchers should also be concerned about the sensitivity and propaganda value of the issue for warring parties and conflict-affected populations. Numbers are important in generating donor and advocacy attention to marginalized groups, but quantifying this type of population is extremely difficult because so much of the data is anecdotal and cases can overlap. It is likely to be difficult, for example, to determine the number of rape-related infanticides, since many of these children are unlikely to appear on authorities' radar screens. Children who survive and are willing to speak out regarding the way that they have been affected by their social origins will be a self-selected sample and not wholly representative of the entire population. As with much human rights work, subjectivity of terms such as *best interests of the child* will need to be grappled with as researchers design appropriate tools for comparing the situation of these children to the child-protection standards found in international law.

Scholarly research and human rights fact-finding on this population also raises ethical concerns. The greatest of these involves the risk of exposing children or their families to greater stigma by singling them out for study. Perhaps the safest way to gather data on such children would be to study them in the context of a putatively larger group such as "single mothers" or "children born in camps." Measures to protect confidentiality would also be extremely important, particularly considering the real risk to girls, for example, who may have escaped captivity with their babies, as Apio highlights. A related ethical concern raised is the risk of re-traumatizing victims of rights violations by inquiring into painful issues. Rape survivors often prefer not to talk of the event; in the case of the children, many of whom may not be aware of their origins, it may actually cause psychosocial harm to ask them certain direct questions. Apio's discussion of children born in LRA captivity, however, demonstrates that some relevant data can be collected from even very small children by asking indirect questions designed to gauge a child's psychosocial health.

At the same time, as Mertus argues, participatory research is becoming the norm in conflict-affected settings. Many practitioners in the focus groups felt strongly that beneficiary populations on whom research is being conducted should be empowered to assist in designing, conducting, interpreting, and disseminating the research so that it serves the needs of the community itself. Without a participatory component, fact-finding can seem exploitative to these populations. Yet, as both Mertus and Goodhart point out, participatory research can pose specific problems when the subject population includes children, since it may be impossible to avoid allowing adults, whose interests may not coincide with those of children, to serve as gatekeepers. Although Baldi and MacKenzie's study of mothers' viewpoints provided insights into the needs and impacts on their children, this should not be considered a substitute for research on the children themselves.

Dialogue among scholars and practitioners about how best to approach this issue analytically will increase understanding and awareness, and contribute to the generation of best practices with respect to data collection.

Many of the lessons learned from gathering testimonies from rape survivors are applicable here. These include the need for researcher sensitivity, strict confidentiality measures, follow up and monitoring, and willingness to rely on illustrative cases rather than seeking vainly to create a "representative" sample (Andric-Ruzicic 2003; Sharatt and Kaschak 1999). The fact that there will be methodological and ethical tradeoffs, as in all research, should not preclude attempts to gather information but should instead generate particular care and sensitivity with respect to research design.

### Context-Specific Programming

Humanitarian organizations should also ensure that their assistance programming in conflict and post-conflict areas includes relevant psychosocial and economic support for these children as well as alternatives for mothers who choose not to raise their children. In the past decade the international humanitarian community and its donors have refined their emphasis on child protection and worked to mainstream a gender perspective into operations and funding priorities. These emerging gender-sensitive and child-rights approaches must be blended in initiatives aimed at protecting and assisting children born of war and their caretakers.

When asked, some humanitarian practitioners are skeptical that specific programming is necessary to protect children born of war. It is sometimes argued that while these children do have specific needs, these needs are already met by more general programming (Carpenter et al. 2005). Some contributors to this volume see this as a dilemma as well. Debra DeLaet argues that an alternative to programming for children born of war as a specific category would be to adopt a needs-based approach, looking at who the most vulnerable are in a conflict situation and then extrapolating the common factors from there. At issue here is the tradeoff between "marking" such children by identifying them according to biological origins and subsuming them into broader beneficiary populations and thus risking having their particular needs go unattended.

At a minimum, most of the authors conclude that the well-being of these particular children must be monitored, in order to determine whether they are in fact benefiting equally from more general programming; this in itself requires some programmatic innovations in order to identify them. Where gaps are found in the effectiveness of existing programs, appropriate solutions must be devised that do not exacerbate stigma against the children themselves. There is a well-founded concern that drawing attention to this population through advocacy would only reinforce stigma against them, and that specific programs targeted to children born of war in field settings would provoke a backlash from other members of the community.

In displaced and conflict-affected settings where sexual violence is prevalent, a solution could be simply to incorporate sensitivity to these children's needs into planning. This could mean training aid workers to identify neonates at risk of infanticide by their families; to take seriously the claims of new mothers that they do not want their children; and to provide psycho-therapeutic support to such women as well as opportunities to surrender their children if they choose. It can mean incorporating an understanding of food discrimination, abuse, and neglect of such children into vulnerability analyses. It can mean including efforts to combat stigma on the basis of illegitimacy or conception by rape into other tolerance programming under way in such settings. Such efforts need not identify specific families except in cases where they are already known to and stigmatized by the community. They must also take account of the specific situation and resources available in local contexts. For example, some of the case studies suggest that engaging religious authorities in these matters can be particularly helpful (Apio), although both Daniel and Rimmer suggest that this can be a double-edged sword if religious authorities adopt a conservative, gendered discourse in their own advocacy campaigns.

On balance, all of these suggestions imply that child-protection specialists in general must pay greater attention to gender issues in conflict zones rather than leaving this to practitioners specializing in women's issues. While there is some consensus among practitioners and the authors of this volume that special programs to address stigmatized groups can often do more harm than good, simply pretending the problem does not exist cannot be a solution either. More research is required to determine the conditions under which certain targeted programs are appropriate.

### Accountability Mechanisms

Several chapters in this book stress the importance of accountability to those who perpetrate both rape and abuses against the children who result. Generally, it is men in positions of coercive power who conceive these children, deliberately or incidentally, either through rape or through exploitation of impoverished and desperate women and girls in conflict situations.[2] Even when such men are not ordered to rape by their governments, they are generally under the command of either states or international institutions. These entities should be held accountable for preventing sexually exploitative or violent behavior and held responsible for the consequences of such behavior, including the upkeep of children born as a result. This would mean, for example, not only prosecutions for US prison guards responsible for raping Iraqi women but also compensation by the American government to those women and support for the children, if brought to term, that are now known to have been conceived as a result (Hardin 2004). Recent efforts by the United Nations to hold peacekeepers financially accountable for children fathered on mission are examples of steps in the right direction. However, this policy as currently constituted would apply only to children fathered in the future and does nothing to address international responsibility for the many such children already growing up in conflict zones.

In general, there is an enormous "accountability gap" when it comes to children born of war. While in a few cases government leaders have been tried and punished for organizing systematic rape campaigns, such punishment has rarely included compensation for the women victimized or the children conceived as a result. Moreover, while rape is condemned as a war crime, the international culture of militarized masculinity has tolerated and even promoted the "consensual" sexual use of local women by foreign soldiers and peacekeeping troops (Enloe 2000). The suggestion that Western powers should restrain their soldiers from sexual relations with women overseas or that soldiers (or Western governments) should be held liable for children fathered during tours of duty has been raised only very recently by the United Nations. State governments should provide mechanisms for protecting these children and providing support to their mothers, including child-support benefits and citizenship rights if desired, including the right to immigrate along with their mothers. Older war children seeking their fathers should be permitted to access identity records by relevant states. It has been suggested that campaigning for a multilateral treaty on dual citizenship for such children would be a step in the direction of closing some of the loopholes in state accountability for their protection. At a minimum, dealing with the consequences of violence and exploitation should be considered, along with prevention of abuse, in advocacy strategies for engaging international actors on gender issues.

### Global Advocacy

Given the nature of the international system, it is unlikely that any of the initiatives listed above will be undertaken spontaneously by powerful actors protecting their own interests and agendas. The necessary first step to initiating constructive change is therefore attention to the issue by the children's human rights network. Human rights actors play a key role in setting the international agenda by lobbying governments, organizing conferences on thematic issues, publicizing abuses, and gathering information relevant to the formulation of sound policy (Keck and Sikkink

1998). By the same token, human rights actors can exercise the power of omission by neglecting to highlight certain topics relevant to their mandate. If organizations concerned with war-affected children are silent on the needs of these children, the international community is unlikely to address them.

With this in mind, the authors in this volume concur that advocacy and awareness-raising at the global level must be part of any solution. However, this should *not* include identifying specific children as such in the local contexts; concerns have rightly been raised about the potential to sensationalize this issue or to exacerbate stigma by drawing attention to vulnerable individuals. Nonetheless, it is possible to find a balance between appropriate norms of confidentiality and the value of awareness-raising with powerful international actors. As McEvoy-Levy points out, "strategic local silence is not the same as international silence" (chap. 9 herein). One focus-group participant told us:

> "What we found [when we undertook a sexual violence study] is that women actually were surprisingly open about what had happened to them and the phrase we kept hearing was: tell people what you want but just don't tell my neighbors. Tell the people in the larger global context but don't tell the people I live with." (Carpenter et al. 2005, 14)

Thus *global advocacy* does not mean using specific children or their families as representatives for this population; drawing attention to their status in particular local contexts; or channeling donor contributions to programs that would set them apart from the rest of the recipient population. Rather, it means a willingness to acknowledge the situation facing such children, channelling attention to them into thematic concerns already prevalent within the human rights sector, and adopting a more gender-sensitive approach generally in child-rights programming.

Child-protection organizations can take simple steps in this direction. Currents in this area are emerging through the use of information technology, but these are nascent and must be strengthened by wider recognition among child-protection advocates. The War and Children Identity Project in Norway uses its website for activity in this area. Actors working in the field of war-affected children can make a small difference in awareness-raising by linking to this organization's website and supporting its work.

More important, the issue needs to be incorporated into the mainstream discourse of well-established organizations already working on war-affected children's issues. Children born of war can be discussed as a category of its own—alongside child soldiers, displaced children or girl children—and should appear as an agenda item on the websites and annual reports of organizations like the Office of the Special Representative, UNICEF, and Human Rights Watch. Alternatively, the existence of children born of war as a particular group might be mentioned under broader themes already on such organizations' web pages: discrimination, separation, statelessness, institutionalization, trafficking. The links between these broader issues and the social origins of children born of war should be explored and illuminated.

Beyond reframing the child-protection agenda to include children born of war as a means of raising awareness, human rights organizations are in a good position to conduct more systematic fact-finding work on the children themselves, an urgent necessity in order to craft specific policies. In 2000 the review document for the Graca Machel Report called for a study entitled *Where Are the Babies?* Any of the major child-rights organizations who engage in fact-finding as part of their mandate might reasonably be expected to commission such a study. Research initiatives should include efforts to estimate more systematically the scope of the problem; involve following up on specific children; analyzing the sources of different policies with respect to their rights and measuring these against international standards; and identifying and evaluating different programs aimed at addressing their needs and those of their mothers. The dissemination of empirical data on the children, their status, and potential best practices regarding their care would not only provide valuable data for programmatic purposes but would have an important awareness-raising effect.

### The Best Interests of the Child

Finally, the authors argue that fact-finding, advocacy, and programmatic attention to these children should include an explicit child-rights perspective distinct from the needs of their mothers, who themselves may be victims of armed conflict and who, even if children themselves, face a very different set of problems from those of their babies. Nor should the human rights of these children be folded into the rights of collective groups against whom forced pregnancy has been used as a tool of war.

Governments, for example, should be encouraged to make decisions about the placement and care of these children on the basis of the children's best interests rather than the interests of demographic or nationalist policies. In the past, postwar governments have often undertaken quite divergent policies affecting children born of war for symbolic reasons rather than with the child in mind. For example, Daniel describes the nationalist rationale behind a policy on raising Bosnian children in the country, some in institutions, rather than allowing them to be adopted by eager foreigners. Mukangendo describes a similar logic on the part of the Rwandan government, which emphasized repopulating the country as a primary motivation for keeping children born of genocidal rape in the country. Weitsman's analysis compares this practice to the Bengali government's policy that the children *must* be shipped abroad because of what they symbolized to the emerging nation, despite the fact that some Bengali birth mothers were desperate to keep their babies. In this example the question of whether an abandoned child's human rights can best be secured through domestic adoption, foreign adoption, or by supporting the child's birth mother should ideally be made through an assessment of the resources and possibility for a positive social environment available to the child in each case rather than for political reasons.

Governments should also take seriously the specific social difficulties these children may face when growing up and take steps to alleviate them. In the aftermath of conflict it is easy to underestimate the gravity of these children's situations, as most war-torn societies are facing many other problems of equal or greater scope and resources are often stretched. Nonetheless, from a child-rights perspective it is important to assess and address the various social factors underlying different children's particular vulnerabilities. For example, Mukangendo points out that in Rwanda the education ministry is designing an initiative to integrate awareness-raising regarding Rwanda's children born as a result of genocide-related sexual violence into the elementary school curriculum in an effort to offset peer discrimination in the school setting. There is a need for similar practices elsewhere.

However, the success of such initiatives also needs to be monitored so that best practices can be established. In some cases the establishment of a particular initiative may provide a sense of closure to the issue, precluding much needed additional programming. For example, a fatwa issued by the Islamic authorities in Bosnia stating that Bosnia's children born of rape should not be stigmatized is often cited by government authorities in Bosnia as "proof" that the children are integrated into society.[3] However, it is not clear how effective this proclamation has been in changing social attitudes, or whether, in the absence of other long-term economic, psychosocial, and sensitization programs, it was sufficient to address these children's needs.

An explicitly child-rights frame would also be a departure from the predominant approach among those few organizations paying specific attention to children born of war to date. An outcome document from a 2005 UNICEF meeting adopts the mother-centric approach, for example, arguing that the children's needs should be addressed in the context of programming for their mothers and that the subject of "children born of war" should be subsumed not under UNICEF's child-protection mandate but under its emerging work in the area of gender-based-violence:

"The most effective way to provide assistance and care to children born as a result of rape is by supporting their mothers—the girls and women targeted for violence—and supporting family and community-based recovery and healing" (UNICEF 2006, 3). Yet both the case studies and the theoretical chapters presented here suggest that the needs of these children are very different from those of their mothers and that, in fact, these needs are sometimes in tension. If so, a purely mother-focused approach to programming on their behalf is likely to be inadequate.

To be sure, effective responses to survivors of wartime sexual violence are vital and will do much to reduce the incidence of attachment difficulties these children may face with their birth mothers, as well as the incidence of stigma from the women's families and socioeconomic deprivation; such initiatives are of course worthwhile in their own right. However, programming aimed at birth mothers will not itself address the range of rights violations experienced by these children, such as the right of older "war children" to information about their identities. Nor will a "trickle-down" approach to meeting mothers' needs be likely to reach abandoned, adopted, or institutionalized children. Moreover, a mother-centered approach to protecting these babies' rights might forestall an effective response in cases where it is the traumatized mother who perpetrates abuse, neglect, or infanticide against the child, as Daniel reports, or contributes to the stigma against the child through discriminatory naming practices, as Apio documents. At any rate, without conceptualizing the children as a specific population in their own right, it will be impossible to assess how effectively the programming for mothers is actually addressing the babies' needs.

## Conclusion

The wide variety of suggestions put forth in this book, some contested among the authors here, suggests that there is no one right response to fill the gap in advocacy and programming for children born of war. At the least, such complicated issues will not be remedied overnight or through simplistic efforts but require a sustainable, multifaceted approach drawing in various stakeholders. As Michael Goodhart correctly notes, it is governments who are charged with the implementation of international standards with respect to the protection of children's rights; to prevent and ameliorate abuses against children born of wartime rape and exploitation, governments must ultimately take action. To the extent that international organizations are (a) complicit in the creation and perpetuation of abuses against the children and (b) pivotal in shaping government policies on human rights, international organizations must also pay closer attention to this issue. The academic and advocacy network around the protection of war-affected children could play a stronger role in encouraging such action on the part of both major international organizations and states.

Yet such proposals cannot be entered into blithely, given the sensitive, complex, and culturally specific nature of the issue at hand. In addition to a set of ideas for constructive change, authors in this volume also articulate and confront a set of dilemmas that must be considered and addressed in the process of building a protective environment around children born of war, particularly by researchers and fact-finders aiming to better conceptualize and understand the lives of these children.

In the past such conceptual, methodological, and ethical dilemmas have been posed as a rationale for avoiding careful consideration of how to address the particular needs of children born of rape and exploitation in conflict zones. By contrast, the approach taken by the authors of this volume is that such obstacles are problems to be solved rather than reasons for not going forward with investigations that could lead to better protective measures for these children. Indeed, they are no different from the dilemmas that obtain in much data collection and programming on sensitive human rights issues.

The chapters in this volume have aimed to provide a set of basic information resources and conceptual thinking space for pursuing this agenda, which we argue is of vital importance for those attempting to build a protective environment for all children in conflict zones. Though many open questions remain, these should not be used as excuses for failures to protect children born of war. Rather, the international community must rise to this challenge: filling knowledge gaps, identifying best practices, and challenging discourses of exclusion.

# Notes

[1] One focus group participant commented that it could be a conceptual mistake to link children born of genocidal forced pregnancy with those born to girls who were "wives" in rebel groups: "There's a lot of complexities to [forced marriage] and to define the children as being born out of that is in some ways denying the complexity of the relationship that that extended unit or however you want, has in terms of their [sic] connections to the origins of the child" (Carpenter et al. 2005, 11).

[2] However, at an interdisciplinary workshop on children of war held in Montreal, it was pointed out that in some cases female soldiers or aid workers may also engage in sexually exploitative behavior toward young boys in conflict situations.

[3] Personal interviews, Sarajevo, April 2004.

# References

Andric-Ruzicic, Duska. 2003. "War Rape and the Political Manipulation of Survivors." In *Feminists under Fire: Exchanges across War Zones*, edited by Wenona Giles et al. Toronto: Between the Lines Press.

Brysk, Alison. 2004. "Children across Borders: Patrimony, Property, or Persons?" In *People Out of Place: Globalization, Human Rights, and the Citizenship Gap*, edited by Alison Brysk and Gershon Shafir. New York: Routledge.

Carpenter, Charli, Kai Grieg, Donna Sharkey, and Giulia Baldi. 2005. *Protecting Children Born of Wartime Rape and Exploitation in Conflict Zones: Existing Practice and Knowledge Gaps*. Pittsburgh: University of Pittsburgh GSPIA/Ford Institute of Human Security.

Enloe, Cynthia. 2000. *Maneuvers: The International Politics of Militarizing Women's Lives*. Berkeley and Los Angeles: University of California Press.

Hardin, Luke. 2004. "The Other Prisoners." *London Guardian*, May 20.

Keck, Margaret, and Kathryn Sikkink. 1998. *Activists beyond Borders*. Ithaca, NY: Cornell University Press.

Sharatt, Sara, and Ellyn Kaschak. 1999. *Assault on the Soul*. New York: Haworth Press.

UNICEF. 2006. *Children Born of Sexual Violence in Conflict Zones: Considerations for UNICEF Response*. Outcome document of a meeting held November 23, 2005. On file with author.

Ward, Jeanne. 2002. *If Not Now, When? Addressing Gender-based Violence in Refugee, Internally Displaced, and Post-Conflict Settings*. New York: Reproductive Health for Refugees Consortium.

# About the Contributors

**Eunice Apio** holds a master's degree in human rights from Makerere University in Kampala and is currently executive director of Facilitation for Peace and Development (FAPAD), which champions a rights-based approach to development, operational in the rural districts of Northern Uganda, and works to prevent child-trafficking, child sexual abuse and exploitation, and child labor among conflict-affected populations.

**Giulia Baldi** is a candidate for the master's in public health at Columbia Mailman School of Public Health and is currently a program officer with the World Food Program in Peru. She previously served as a consultant within UNICEF Headquarters, Health Section; as program coordinator in the Center for Global Health and Economic Development at Columbia University; and on the research team for the report "Protecting Children of Rape and Sexual Exploitation in Conflict Zones: Findings from Consultations with Humanitarian Practitioners" (University of Pittsburgh).

**R. Charli Carpenter** is assistant professor of international affairs at the University of Pittsburgh's Graduate School of Public and International Affairs. She holds a PhD in political science from the University of Oregon, and an MA in government from New Mexico State University. She has published extensively on gender, children's rights, and humanitarian action in *Human Rights Quarterly, International Organization, International Studies Quarterly, Journal of Genocide Research, International Journal of Human Rights,* and *International Feminist Journal of Politics;* she is the author of *"Innocent Women and Children": Gender, Norms, and the Protection of Civilians* (Ashgate, 2006). Her research focuses on international norms and identities, transnational advocacy networks, and human security. She is currently writing a book on the social construction of children's human rights in Bosnia-Herzegovina. Dr. Carpenter spends the rest of her time raising two future members of the American electorate, surfing and snowboarding, and deconstructing science-fiction films.

**Joana Daniel-Wrabetz,** born in Coimbra, Portugal, has a license in literature and education from the University of Vila Real (UTAD), Portugal, and an MA from the European Masters Programme in Human Rights and Democratisation. She has taught in Portugal, Sao Tome e Principe, and the United States and has worked on various research projects and publications with particular emphasis on children's rights, birth registration, and democratization processes. She worked for the Portuguese Permanent Mission to the OSCE in Vienna as an adviser and at the UNICEF research center in Florence. She has undertaken several research missions to Bosnia and Herzegovina with UNICEF, inter alia, on the human rights situation of children born of wartime rape and forced impregnation.

**Debra DeLaet** is associate professor of politics and international relations at Drake University. She received her BA in political science from Miami University (Ohio) in 1990. She received the PhD in government and international studies from the University of Notre Dame in 1995, with major fields in international relations and comparative politics. Her primary research interests are in the areas of international human rights, gender and world politics, and international migration. She teaches courses on human rights, peacebuilding and justice, international law, the United Nations, gender and world politics, ethics in a globalizing world, and the introductory course on world politics at Drake University.

**Michael Goodhart** is assistant professor of political science and women's studies at the University of Pittsburgh. His research focuses on democratic theory and human rights, especially in the context of globalization. His recent publications include "Sins of the Fathers: War Rape, Wrongful Procreation, and Children's Human Rights," in the *Journal of Human Rights;* "Civil Society and the Problem of Global Democracy," in *Democratization;* "Origins and Universality in the Human Rights Debates: Cultural Essentialism and the Challenge of Globalization," in *Human Rights Quarterly;* and his first book, *Democracy as Human Rights: Freedom and Equality in the Age of Globalization* (Routledge, 2005). He is review editor for *Polity: The Journal of the Northeastern Political Science Association* and is a past president of the American Political Science Association's organized section on human rights.

**Megan MacKenzie** is a PhD candidate at the University of Alberta. Her research interests include gender and post-conflict reconstruction; NGOs and accountability; the construction of women post-conflict; the relationship among academics, aid agencies, and citizens in developing countries; and the link between particular discourses and the race for aid agency funding. More general areas of interest include gender and international relations and development studies. She has conducted extensive field research in Sierra Leone, including interviews with over fifty female former soldiers. One of her passions is investigating ways to alleviate the disconnect between experiences in the field and renderings in academic texts. McKenzie is the author of the following working papers: "Redefining Casualty and Weapon: Using the Human Security Framework to Identify the Effect of High HIV Infection Rates in Militant Groups," "Human Security: The Key to Unifying the Fragmented Literature on Children and War," and "The 'War Babies' of Sierra Leone."

**Siobhán McEvoy-Levy** received her master's and PhD degrees from the University of Cambridge (UK) and a BA honors degree from the Queen's University, Belfast. She is associate professor of political science at Butler University in Indianapolis, Indiana, where she teaches courses on peace and conflict studies, US foreign policy, political communication, and children and youth. She is the author of *American Exceptionalism and US Foreign Policy: Public Diplomacy at the End of the Cold War* (Palgrave, 2001). Since 2001 McEvoy-Levy has been researching, writing, and conducting workshops on children and youth in war and post-conflict peacebuilding. She has written a number of related articles and book chapters and is the editor of and a contributor to *Troublemakers or Peacemakers? Youth and Post-Accord Peacebuilding* (University of Notre Dame Press, 2006) and co-author (with Tristan Anne Borer and John Darby) of *Peacebuilding after Peace Accords: Violence, Truth and Youth* (University of Notre Dame Press, 2007). McEvoy-Levy's current research focuses on education in conflict zones, children and youth in international conflict and peace processes, and the role of the arts, narrative, and symbolic expression in conflict and peacebuilding.

**Julie Mertus** is an associate professor and co-director of the MA program in ethics, peace, and global affairs at American University. A graduate of Yale Law School, Mertus has twenty years of experience working for a wide range of nongovernmental and governmental human rights organizations. Her prior appointments include senior fellow, US Institute of Peace; human rights fellow, Harvard Law School; writing fellow, MacArthur Foundation; Fulbright fellow (Romania 1995; Denmark 2006); and counsel, Human Rights Watch. Her book *Bait and Switch: Human Rights and U.S. Foreign Policy* (Routledge, 2004) was named "human rights book of the year" by the American Political Science Association Human Rights Section. Her other books include *Human Rights and*

*Conflict* (editor, with Jeffrey Helsing; US Institute of Peace, 2006); *The United Nations and Human Rights* (Routledge, 2005); *Kosovo: How Myths and Truths Started a War* (University of California Press, 1999), and *The Suitcase: Refugees' Voices from Bosnia and Croatia* (University of California Press, 1997). Mertus has won several awards for her innovative curriculum design and teaching.

**Marie Consolée Mukangendo** joined UNICEF as a staff member in 2003 and is currently posted at the UNICEF Angola office, in the monitoring and evaluation section, having transferred from her position as assistant programme officer at the UNICEF Innocenti Research Centre in Florence, Italy. At the UNICEF Angola office she is providing technical support to the Government of Angola and, more specifically, the National Institute for Children in the elaboration of the WFFC +5 and Convention on the Rights of the Child reports for Angola. She also provides support for research development and monitoring of social data. Of Rwandese origin, she is a specialist in the fields of children's rights, in particular the Convention on the Rights of the Child; policy analysis; monitoring and evaluation; child-trafficking; children in armed conflict; juvenile justice; and a range of other "protection" concerns. She holds a university degree in international relations from the University of Buenos Aires in Argentina, a diploma in International Policy Cooperation and Development from Scuola Di Politica Internazionale per la Cooperazioneallo Svilluppo, Rome, Italy, and has a master's degree in social economy (MES) from the University of Barcelona, Spain.

**Susan Harris Rimmer** grew up in the small town of Coonabarabran, in the state of New South Wales, Australia. She received her BA(Hons)/ LLB (Hons) in international relations and English literature from the University of Queensland and received the University Medal. She is now an SJD candidate in international law at the Australian National University. She has worked for UNHCR and Australian NGOs and is currently a legal adviser specializing in human rights law for the Library of the Australian Parliament in Canberra.

**Patricia Weitsman** is professor of political science at Ohio University. She received her PhD from Columbia University and has been a fellow at the Graduate Institute of International Studies in Geneva, Switzerland, as well as the Hoover Institution at Stanford University. She is co-author of *The Politics of Policy Making in Defense and Foreign Affairs* (1993), and co-editor of both *Towards a New Europe* (Praeger/Greenwood, 1995) and *Enforcing Cooperation* (1997). Her most recent book is *Dangerous Alliances: Proponents of Peace, Weapons of War* (Stanford University Press, 2004). She is also the author of numerous articles and book chapters published in prominent books and journals in the field of international relations. She is currently working on a short monograph on coalition warfare, as well as a larger project on war and identity.

# Index

post-conflict reconstruction and, 169, 175n24
UN Resolution 1325 on, 175n26
gender-based violence, 144–45, 157, 173n13. *See also* sexual violence
child protection under, 211, 221–22
international law on, 41
legal incorporation of, 72
transitional justice and, 61
Geneva Convention
forced impregnation in, 36
rape prohibition under, 173n15
Rwandan ratification of, 41
war-affected children under, 7
genocide
forced impregnation as, 17n4, 23, 64
identity and, 115–16
rape as, 124n9, 133, 173n15
state legislation for, 62
survivors' assistance fund, 45
Genocide Convention, 7–8
Geri, Smiljan, 24
Gibson, James L., 152, 172n9
global advocacy, 218–19
Godinho-Adams, Natércia, 73
Goldstein, Anne Tierney, 117–18
Goljak Centre for Children with Special Needs, 25
Goodhart, Michael, 16
future person's rights, 208
on government responsibility, 222
on participatory research, 15, 215
on social exclusion, 6, 8
wrongful birth concept of, 14, 158, 213
Graca Machel Report, 11, 220
Guasmo, Kirsty Sword, 57
Gulu Support the Children Organisation (GUSCO), 103–4
GUSCO. *See* Gulu Support the Children Organisation
Gusmão, Emilia Baptista, 58
Gusmão, Xanana, 71
Guterres, Beatriz, 56

Hague Convention on Protection of Children and Cooperation in Respect of Intercountry Adoption (1993), 33–34
Hayner, Priscilla, 153
health, 84
Hercegovac, Advija, 25
HIV/AIDS
testing for, 88
treatment for, 44–46
Hopper, Kim, 152
Howard, Rhoda, 6, 31
Howland, Todd, 153
humanitarian organizations
context-specific programming of, 216
role of, 213–14
human rights, 4, 7, 45, 61, 144
international norms of, 174n18
organizations for, 218–19, 220
human rights culture
abortion in, 159–60
alternative societies and, 167, 174n23
child advocacy in, 170
development of, 152, 171
education in, 153, 164–66
ex-combatant integration in, 156–57
individual level of, 161, 163
infanticide and, 159
McEvoy-Levy on, 11, 201, 203, 205
national reconciliation and, 153–54
negative, 172n6
postwar institutions and, 158, 172n7
protective institutions in, 169, 172n5
questions about, 155
rights conflicts and, 156
role of silence in, 151, 166–68
shame in, 171n4
in South Africa, 172n9
transformational aim of, 162
truth commissions and, 150

# Also from Kumarian Press...

*Human Rights and Conflict Resolution:*

**A World Turned Upside Down:** Social Ecological Approaches to Children in War Zones
Edited by Neil Boothby, Alison Strang and Michael Wessells

**War's Offensive on Women:** The Humanitarian Challenge in Bosnia, Kosovo and Afghanistan
Julie Mertus

**Zones of Peace**
Edited by Landon Hancock and Christopher Mitchell

**The Economic Life of Refugees**
Karen Jacobsen

*New and Forthcoming:*

**Complex Political Victims**
Erica Bouris

**Twinning Faith and Development:** Catholic Parish Partnering in the US and Haiti
Tara Hefferan

**Everywhere/Nowhere:** Gender Mainstreaming in Development Agencies
Rebecca Tiessen

Visit Kumarian Press at **www.kpbooks.com** or
call **toll-free 800.289.2664** for a complete catalog.

*Kumarian Press, located in Bloomfield, Connecticut, is a forward-looking, scholarly press that promotes active international engagement and an awareness of global connectedness.*